What in the Word?

Origins of Words Dealing with People and Places

David Muschell

McGuinn & McGuire
PUBLISHING, INC.
Bradenton, Florida

Contents

Foreword

I've been fascinated by words for as far back as I can remember. It seems amazing that the odd sounds we make and the funny scribbles we write can communicate so much, inspiring nations to war, sealing men and women in marriage, causing a range of emotions that keeps us turning pages far into the night. When my fourth grade teacher, Mrs. Yeager, told us she had once been a torch singer, my nine-year-old imagination saw her on a lonely stage, a burning stick her only spotlight. When I learned much later that torch songs were about unreturned love, I found how well this blended with my first images, how nicely words can fit, moving our hearts and minds. Studying the history of the English language in college led me to realize how wild and sometimes accidental this language was, countering my eighth grade teacher, Mrs. Parrot, who had us diagramming sentences as if our forms of expression were a kind of orderly geometry. The tale of our tongue's journey – from invading Germanic tribes who conquered Britain some four hundred years after the death of Christ to domineering Norman French nobles, imposing their language on the English six hundred years later, to the booming British Empire, gathering in words from its colonies – is a story of change, growth, adjustment, and assimilation.

For the past fourteen years, I've considered myself a miner in the ore of words, looking for those glittering nuggets that have made me scratch my head in wonder, laugh, or pause in surprise. When I found that the leotard owes its naming to a French tightrope walker or that the cantaloupe's name grew out of the residence of a pope, I had that sense of the delight of the prospector hitting the motherlode. I've dug through dictionaries, encyclopedias, and etymologies in my shirt sleeves, gathering in my gold dust, and to the many great scholars who have dedicated their lives to this study I owe this book. I hope it will make you want to go into those hills, too, to discover the wealth that lies there. But as interesting as it is to know that there is a whole field of research at the base of this book (onomastics, the study of proper names and their uses) and a lot of terminology to describe the types of words here (eponyms, words from personal names [Section One]; toponyms, dealing with place-names [Sections Two and Four]; and anthroponyms, the meanings of personal names [Section Three]), that is not the real focus of *What in the Word?* Here I've concentrated more on the appreciation of the story of these labels, the enjoyment of the history, the telling of the tale. If this stimulates *you* to dig deeper or gives you more admiration for the complex background of our present-day usage, then *What in the Word?* has fulfilled its purpose. The best place for you to browse is the index of the book to learn about the "rebellious" Marys, "smelly" Chicago, or clever "maverick." I hope you have as much fun as I did.

SECTION ONE

Words from the Names of People
(Real or Imaginary)

A **academy** Our name for a first-class preparatory school has Greek origins. Many of our modern academies are private schools, and so was that earliest one from which we have taken the word. However, this Academy of ancient Greece didn't get its name from some root meaning scholarship or intellectual pursuit. When Socrates first began teaching his special students in Athens, he met them in the grove of Akademos, who was a Greek hero of the Trojan War. A citizen named Cimon owned the park at that time and added walks and fountains, making it a perfect place for young men to relax and let their minds explore. After the death of Socrates, his best student Plato kept the schooling going and continued to meet in the shade of this glade, discussing philosophy, science and religion. The name of the park was given to his school; and his students, including Aristotle, were called Academics. The writings on law, literature, mathematics and ethics that grew out of this Academy have been some of the most influential on the Western world, and its name has been used since then to describe schools of liberal arts and classical studies as opposed to technical, vocational training centers.

alabaster I can first remember seeing this word as a child learning the song "America, The Beautiful." One of the lines in the second verse reads "Thine alabaster cities gleam." Asking the teacher about it, I was told it was a color: a grayish white or yellowish gray. Later, I learned it was a kind of fine-grained gypsum used to make statues or fine pottery and sculpture. Most likely, it got its name from the Egyptian goddess Bast. This cat-headed woman was the deity of life, fruitfulness and the home, though later she got mixed up as a war goddess. Some of the first alabaster was found in the center of her worship, the town of Bubastis where special vessels were made in her honor, "'a la Bast," which translates as "a vessel of Bast." The Greeks took the word and applied it to the gypsum and forgot about the goddess.

Amish This stern but peace-loving sect of Mennonites took their name from Jakob Amman, a bishop of this Anabaptist group who came from Switzerland. These 17th-century Reformationists broke away from the main body of Mennonites because they wanted to keep the practice of "shunning," among other things. This term applied to the command of complete avoidance of one who has been excommunicated. Communities of Amish, believing in adult baptism, refusing to bear arms, and staying out of the affairs of state, still exist across North America, primarily in Pennsylvania, Ohio, Indiana, and Ontario. Interestingly, another sect broke off from this group when Moses Beachy led a move to allow his people to drive cars, establishing the Beachy Amish.

ammonia Yet another Egyptian deity is responsible for the name of this handy household substance. The Greek name for the Egyptian god of fertility was Ammon. When the stuff was found near the temple of Amen (the Egyptian version) in Libya, the name of the god got applied to the extract. Apparently, derivatives of ammonia were used for medicinal purposes as a stimulant and expectorant and could be found in gum form in the resin of a plant. A gaseous ammonia was made by the priests of the temple by heating the horns and hooves of animals. "Sal ammonicus," as the Romans called it, was also used as cement for porcelain. Physicians and alchemists of the Middle Ages also used the ancient method of preparing ammonia by distilling deer antlers. By the way, the Egyptian depiction of their fertility god was a man with a ram's head – not exactly Mr. Clean. The **"amen"** said at the end of prayers comes from the Hebrew for "so be it" or "let it be so."

ampere All right, maybe it's not too shocking that the father of electrodynamics gets a word named after him. We mainly see this in abbreviated form, and stereo buffs and electric guitarists can be heard talking about "amps." The Frenchman, André Marie Ampère, is just one of several electrical folks I'll talk about who probably got a charge out of having their names associated with measurements of that strange force, electricity. And, no, the **ampersand** has nothing to do with currents or wires. The "**&**" gets its name from a contraction of "and per se and," which basically means "the sign we make, '&,' stands for 'and'."

aphrodisiac   From oysters to powdered Rhino horn, men and women have sought substances that will add a little extra to their sexual pleasures. Though 99% of these stimulants are basically ineffective (except perhaps psychologically), the quest goes on; and we honor the Greek goddess of love and beauty, Aphrodite, by keeping this sexy word in our language. She was quite a lover also and could inflame the desires of gods and mortals alike. The strange and violent tale of her birth sees a Titan son, Chronos (Saturn in Rome), killing his father Uranus (god of the heavens), cutting off his genitals, and throwing them into the sea where they mingled with the foam ("aphros" is Greek for "foam") and gave birth to Aphrodite. One of her children, Eros, was named the god of love of a much more earthly, sexual kind. His name is Greek for "desire" and gives us all our **erotic** words. Now, the Romans seemed to turn things around just a bit as they called the goddess Venus. From her we get words like **venereal disease** and **venom**, which was originally a word used for love potions or aphrodisiacs. Some of these had poisonous results and the term gradually got a more harmful connotation. The Romans' version of Eros was our cute Cupid, from which we get our one greedy word, **cupidity**. "Desire" is the translation of this little fellow's Latin name and his famous aphrodisiac was his arrow.

August   Oh, boy, it's confusion-in-calendar time. This steamy month of our Northern Hemisphere's summer was originally named for the great Augustus Caesar, which became Gaius Julius Octavius' name about twenty-seven years before the birth of Christ. He ended up living about fourteen years after that birth, but didn't witness any of the changes that came about in his empire because of it. Translated, "Augustus" meant "imperial majesty" and was later used by many Roman emperors. The first Augustus, who presided over the golden age of Rome, had the month Sextilus renamed in his honor. Yes, at one time this had been the sixth month of the Roman calendar which had been composed of ten months named very nicely after numbers. Because this early measuring method, based on lunar cycles, didn't have enough days to encompass the whole cycle around the sun, early Romans wound up having different seasons in different months each

3

year. Around 700 B.C., one of the Roman leaders decided to add January and February to make it a twelve month year and keep the seasons and months consistent. There were still not enough days in the year, and by 46 B.C. things had once again gotten confused, until Julius Caesar straightened things out – temporarily. I'll talk about that later when I get to **July** which was named for Julius. And yes, that had been Quintilus, the fifth month, but was actually the seventh month because when the 700 B.C. addition was made, the names of the months weren't changed, just moved two places down on the calendar. That's why our **September, October, November** and **December** still have the Latin meanings, "seventh," "eighth," "ninth," and "tenth" even though they fall in the ninth, tenth, eleventh, and twelfth spots. Confused? Just wait. Back to Augustus and his month, Sextilus originally had twenty-nine days, then thirty when Julius made his calendar change and then thirty-one when the month was renamed for the new Caesar. Since July had thirty-one days, Augustus' month couldn't be short-changed and have one less; so he took a day away from poor February and added it to his month.

B | **beg** Here's a word that definitely has come through some changes in its seven hundred or so years of existence. A beggar today is usually someone to avoid; and begging has the connotation of weakness, poverty, or cowardice. Let's go back to the seed of this word's germination. It was 1170, and the Crusades were in full swing. Most of the young and old noblemen and their servants were gone, and their wives and sweethearts had time on their hands. With the religious fervor of these holy wars in the air, there were tasks that could be done at home. It seems that a priest at Liége, Netherlands, known as Lambert Le Bégue or Lambert the Stammerer, suggested that these good women form a kind of sisterhood. They wouldn't have to take vows of chastity or renounce property, but could help the Church care for the sick and poor. They called themselves Beguines and groups sprang up all over Holland, sort of Salvation Army/Goodwill groups. Inspired by these women who had Beguinages in almost every village by the end of the century, groups of men also decided to join in non-monastic groups to help others. Since most of the men from the upper classes were gone, these were usually tradesmen and laborers. They lived under one roof and shared expenses from one purse. They called themselves Beghards. As happens in this kind of communal existence, sometimes there are those who wish to do very little and sponge off of others who are attracted to these groups. Apparently, these men began to have a rather poor reputation for going out among the people and requesting their donations to the cause. By 1312, this peskiness, among other practices, led to the groups' suppression by the Pope. Later, they were reinstated into the Church's favor and a Beguinage still exists to this day; but the reputation of the "beghards" stayed with the word that transformed into "beggar" over time.

Now, the **beguine**, which is a dance that came from St. Lucia and Martinique and is famous in the song "Begin the Beguine," came from a kind of cap the women of the Beguinage wore. This cap became popular among young girls and somehow became associated with infatuation and flirtation. Wearing the cap in a jaunty way to impress a male, a girl was said "to have a beguine for him." Many a young woman has "set her cap" for a particular fellow.

begonia The television Laugh-In line, "Do the name Ruby Begonia ring a bell?" might ring a bell with non-plant-lovers, but those who prize the colorful leaves and flowers of the Begonia might find it interesting to know that a French governor of Haiti gave the plant his name. Michel Bègon was a patron of botany and took an interest in the lovely plant in the late 1600's while in Santo Domingo. You'll read about other plants and their discoverers in this section of the book.

biddy Call an old, gossipy woman a biddy and she'll not appreciate it very much, but she gets her derogatory nickname from a more interesting source than might be thought. This word doesn't come from the name for a chicken, which is thought to come from a common way of calling the birds by imitating their clucking. Neither is this name for a talkative woman a euphemistic way of saying "bitchy." No, the Irish fire goddess, **Bridget**, is the source of the old biddy's origins. I'll talk more about her later.

bloomers This word today is just a funny word for pants or underwear that is fast disappearing because of its old-fashioned quaintness. It was a new word in the language when magazine publisher Amelia Jenks Bloomer advocated these women's trousers in the 1850's. She got her idea after a visit from Elizabeth Cady Stanton, the famous suffragette, who had designed herself a pair of these loose-fitting, ankle-length pantaloons. It was the real beginning of the liberation of women from the indoors, tempered with the morality of the day. With these garments, a woman might ride a bicycle or perform in an athletic event without fear of showing a bit of leg. "Shocking fashion," thought most men and women of the day, but many of these costumes were purchased by the more modern-thinking women among them. And they were a great leap forward for active, competitive girls. Ms. Bloomer didn't see women get to vote, which she would have dearly loved, but she did get to see them on their bicycles built for one *or* two.

bobby The British slang for the police goes back to the founder of the London Metropolitan Police, Sir Robert Peel, who was Home Secretary when the gunless officers came into existence in 1828. For awhile they were also called "peelers." The **bobby socks** that have been around since the `40's probably got their name from that "bob" that we use to mean "shortened" – which we find in **bobby pins**, used first to hold bobbed hair, the **bobcat** and **bob-tailed** nag, so named because of their short tails, and the **bobsled**, which has shortened runners. The **bobwhite** and **bobolink** take their names from the sound of their calls. The British slang word for a shilling, a **bob**, has a hazy and uncertain origin . . . at least in my research.

bowdlerize I generally like the origins of words that we run across regularly, but this one is a bit less well-known. Still, when Thomas Bowdler decided to publish a version of Shakespeare in which all the "naughty" parts were cut out, he provided enough controversy to add a word to our language based on his bland censorship. Even people of the 1700's and 1800's had sense enough to know that you don't mess with Shakespeare, paint over Da Vinci's nudes, or strap a fig leaf on a Michaelangelo sculpture without a backlash somewhere down the line.

boycott Now here's a widely used term for protest by refusal. It's been an effective tool in opposing repression ever since it was coined in the late 1800's in Ireland. When Captain Charles C. Boycott retired from the military and became the land agent for the Earl of Erne in County Mayo, he kept raising the rents of the tenants of the land. He ignored their pleas, so the stubborn Irish banded together and decided not to harvest his crops or have any dealings with the man. He couldn't evict them all. He tried hiring outside labor, guarded by troops, to pick the crops; but eventually, he was forced out of a job by the little David's battling the Earl's Goliath. The use of his name to describe the protest spread across the world and gave an example for the oppressed everywhere.

boysenberry Not too many of our horticulturalists get the kind of recognition that a Burbank (see) or a Booker T. Washington get, but Rudolph Boysen will always be remembered. At least, his last name will have the attachment to the hybrid plant that put together the loganberry with the prickly blackberry and raspberry plants. After Boysen "invented" the new fruit in the 1920's in Napa, California, he turned it over to William Knott for marketing on a commercial basis.

Braille Blind from the age of three, the remarkable Louis Braille popularized a way of communication that opened doors to literature, mathematics, music, and the post office for the blind all over the planet. This three-dimensional, tactile Morse code was shown to the fifteen-year old Braille by a French army officer, Charles Barbier, who developed a very complex system of raised dots for soldiers who needed to send messages on a battlefield at night. Braille simplified the idea and pushed for its use, running up against strong opposition from sighted educators and eventually dying before the method was officially adopted. Speaking of Samuel F.B. **Morse**, I should mention that the American inventor, who was first an artist, pushed the telegraph into being, shrinking our world with electricity's help.

Brownie These junior Girl Scouts actually got their name from fairy folklore. The "wee brown man" would come at night and help clean around the house (don't you wish?) and maybe even cook up a batch of nutty little cakes. The legend of the Brownies led to the idea that these seven- and eight-year-old girls could be like the sprites and help Mom about the house. Today's more liberated world might fall into a brown study at the thought. Maybe a new legend should be that these are the creatures who cause brown outs.

C **Caesarean section** The early clans of Rome were the basis for the later empire. Their family names were passed down from father to son in a very male-oriented, patrilinear fashion. Those early tribes had land, cemeteries, and even certain deities especially their own. As this civilization progressed, families combined for strengthening and shoring up power. The Julians and Claudians brought forth a line that would find its way to the top of the Roman heap. The legend had it that Gaius Julius was cut from his mother's womb and thus had the Latin past participle meaning "to be cut" – Caesar – added to his name. Whether or not there was truth to the tale, it made his birth more impressive and full of portent. When this Julius Caesar adopted Octavianus to be his son and next emperor, he also gave him his name. This young man kept the legendary aspect of the name and later became Augustus Caesar.

Now, these Italians may have loved their feasts, but they weren't responsible for the **Caesar salad**. Down in Tiajuana, Mexico, a restaurant owner, Caesar Gardini, came up with the special dish in the late 1940's, originally serving the greens, cheese, and browned bread chunks with a raw egg. "Caesar's," the name of his establishment, became famous for the concoction.

calliope The old circus instrument is fast disappearing in this age of amplification, where a tiny keyboard can synthesize huge sounds by means of a computer program. Some of the models created after Joshua Stoddard's first 1855 calliope could be heard within a ten-mile range and definitely let those far and near know that some event was about to happen. The Greek from which the word was taken means "beautiful voice" and was the name for the muse who presided over the arts and sciences. This Calliope had musical children, too, like Orpheus, the famous singer.

camellia The bushes and trees that go by this name were brought to the attention of Western Europe by a Moravian Jesuit missionary to the Phillipines. George Joseph Kamel described these evergreens in the late 1600's, and botanists gave the native Asian plant his Latinized name about seventy years later . . . long after Kamel could really appreciate the fact. Well, you can call it the **japonica** if you like, another name associated with it meaning "of Japan" where many varieties exist (though some also use this name for the Japanese quince, which comes up in Section Two.)

cardigan The fashion style we mainly think of as button-in-the-front, collarless sweaters has a showy history. Originally a kind of jacket, it was popularized by the controversial, but dashing James Thomas Brudenell who was the seventh Earl of Cardigan. This fellow was determined to be a military type and spent a bit of money to purchase various ranks, a practice that was not uncommon. By the time he was leading his own brigade, he had inherited his father's fortune and used about 10,000 pounds a year to outfit his troops in special uniforms. The "cardigan" jacket was just one of his chic choices that made his troop one of the smartest dressed in the military. The Earl wore the outfit when he led the Charge of the Light Brigade in 1854 at the battle of Balaklava during the Crimean War in which Britain and France fought against Russia over the crumbling Turkish Ottoman Empire. Though he was fifty-seven years old when he found himself placed in command of this ill-fated charge, which saw half of the brigade dead by the time they reached the Russian guns, he showed such madcap bravery in the battle that he was actually first to reach the battery and was made a hero by the British public. Little did they know that after the victorious battle he immediately retired to his yacht to bathe and dine, leaving the troops to fend for themselves. There is more to this fascinating story, but suffice it to say that the feisty Earl of Cardigan died in a riding accident, still active at the age of seventy.

Casanova When some romantic devil is called a Casanova, most of us think of a ladies' man, out for pleasure. According to history, that's just what the real Giovanni Jacopo Casanova was, at least, in his youth. The promiscuous Italian supposedly led the life of a libertine as an adventurous young man. It's hard to know if everything that was said was the truth because he wrote his autobiography as a rather bored and possibly embittered librarian for a German count. He was in his sixties at the time, remembering back to his days as a twenty-year-old . . . . Who mightn't embellish those memories just a touch? After such a reckless, amorous life, Casanova died quietly at the age of seventy-three.

Celsius Though Anders Celsius may have devised a more orderly temperature scale in 1742, I'm one of those who sticks with the German physicist Gabriel **Fahrenheit**, who fiddled with the mercury thermometer while working in Holland in 1714. Besides, it wasn't until 1948 that the "centigrade" scale was officially given the later Swede's name.

cereal So, that morning breakfast food got its name from a goddess? Yes, your corn flakes are called cereal because of Ceres, the Roman goddess of agriculture. Ancient farmers prayed to her for a good harvest, and when grain was plentiful, Ceres got the credit.

chauvinism The movement for equal rights for women brought this term into play quite a bit over the '70's and '80's, usually along with a metaphorical comparison of a male and a swine. The word for a belief in the superiority of one's own group came about when Nicholas Chauvin made a reputation for fanatical devotion to Napoleon I. This former French soldier had such an attachment to the glory days of the lost empire that certain plays of the 1830's used him as a character representing all the overly patriotic nostalgia of French society of the time. A chauvinist got to be the name for all those who took their nationalism or group loyalties to an extreme.

condom Sometimes the legend behind the origin of a word persists even though the proof is either not there or has vanished under the crush of time. The prophylactic item we call the condom was reputed to have been invented by a British doctor of the 1700's. This Dr. Condom or Conton supposedly perfected the original rubber from sheep skin. The story sometimes has it that this fellow was first a British officer who learned of the protective device in India or some other foreign place. Since there is no hard evidence, our inventor remains a mystery. Who knows? Perhaps he didn't want the adverse publicity that moralists of the day would lay upon such a contraption. Today's different mores lead us to have to pay tribute to this contraceptive device without the benefit of the truth about this crafty engineer whose product today graces the drugstores and gas station bathrooms of the world.

D **dahlia** The Swedish botanist of the late 1700's, Anders Dahl, found this flower and its kin while he was in Mexico. Some of these men who bring native plants to the attention of the world get these kind of honors – like J. R. **Poinsettia**, who was the U.S. minister to Mexico when he found his scarlet namesake in the early 1800's, or David Douglas, a Scotsman who roamed the US in that same time period and had that **Douglas fir** take his name. Some plants might wish to have a discoverer's name attached to them as they go through life as yuccas (which comes from an American Indian word) or **pansies** (from the playful changing of a French word meaning "thought"). Then again, a plant like a **gardenia** has such a cultivated-sounding name that we may not think of the Scottish botanist, Dr. Alexander Garden who found and publicized this plant in the 1700's.

davenport This older word got replaced in advertisement with names like "hide-a-bed" and "convertible sofa." That's what a davenport of the early part of this century generally was. Now, some believe that it might have gotten its name from an East Iowa fur trader, but more than likely it was a Captain Davenport of England who was the inspiration for this word. He commissioned a kind of writing desk in the 1850's that had a hinged, lidded top. How this name later got attached to the couch is uncertain, but by the printing of the 1902 Sears Catalog these sofa/beds were listed as davenports. Just for the record, **couch** comes from an Old French verb for lying down and **sofa** comes from the Arabic that refers to carpets that were placed on a raised platform which itself later got the name "sofa." **Divan** also comes from the Arabic and meant "to register" or to account for oneself. It was later applied to the seat used by an administrator when he would hold public audiences.

derby Both the bowler hat and the common name we give a horse or soapbox car race came from the twelfth Earl of Derby who decided to start a major horse race on the Epsom Downs in 1780. Of course, the hat that became the fashion at these yearly English Derbies was called the "derby" after the horse race and the Earl, even though the basic design came from John Bowler, a London hatmaker of the 1700's. The name of the Derby estate came from the Old English for "deer village," in case you're curious. Before I go mad as a hatter (from the use of a kind of hat dye that, when absorbed into the bloodstream, could cause damage to the brain), let me mention another hat. When Sarah Bernhardt took on the role of Fedora Romanoff in the 1880's, she brought us another style of hat. *Fedora* was the name of the popular play and, later, a type of felt hat.

derringer When Henry Deringer invented the small pistol in the 1840's, little did he realize that its popularity would spawn many imitations and that, because of these fakes, a misspelled version of his name would go down in history as the name of the gun. Because Mr. Deringer's workmanship was so well-known, imitators would put his name on their copies. A lot of these bootleg pistols would have the extra r in the brand name. That spelling is the one that stuck.

On the subject of guns, Samuel **Colt** and his revolver were synonymous with quality, but he probably never entertained the notion that his six-shooter would also be associated with a malt liquor. Oliver Winchester's repeating rifle was so linked to his name that many other similar types were also called **Winchesters**.

diesel Rudolf Diesel went through quite a bit in his quest for an internal combustion engine. By 1894, when he came up with a successful engine design, he had failed many times with other trial motors. He first used coal dust to give his machine the explosive force it needed to power itself. Can you imagine your car or truck driver of today pulling up to the pump and getting out to shovel twenty gallons of coal dust: "A fill-up and a shower, please." Strangely enough, Diesel disappeared at the age of fifty-five while crossing from England to Belgium on a *steam*boat.

doily Though there are a few questions about the origin of this lacy kind of napkin that my grandma always had on her chair and sofa arms, a London draper of the early 1700's is probably where this linen and lace covering got its name. This Mr. Doyley or Doily apparently was well-known for his ornamental cloth. Also sneaking into the history is a family by the name of D'oiley who gave the king a special woven table cloth.

dunce John Duns Scotus was a noted man of the church when he presented his theological ideas in the late 1200's. In opposing St. Thomas Aquinas, he took on the greatest philosopher of the Middle Ages, and eventually, this led to his downfall among believers. This was a time when thinkers were trying to come up with a logical proof for the existence of God, using the writings of Plato and Aristotle along with new ideas about the natural world. Not only was Aquinas easier to understand, he was Italian, and this fact also helped the Scotsman to be finally ridiculed. The Dunsmen, as his followers were called, were so obstinate that making fun of them became the standard practice. Centuries later, the "dunce" had become anyone who was thick-headed or just plain dumb. The pointed cap itself was also an exaggeration of the headgear worn by Scotus' disciples.

E | **Easter** Another pagan deity gets into the naming of this, the most sacred of Christian remembrances. The old Germanic goddess of the dawn, Eastre, gives us the name of the holiday and influenced the word for the direction from which she rose, the east. Among the heathens, a feast was held each spring at the equinox to honor the goddess and her bringing fertility back to the land. Yes, newly born hares were at one time offered to the goddess and a tradition of hunting for eggs, symbols of rebirth and common at this time of year, was also part of the original festival. This celebration of the first day of spring had its effect on the early Church fathers as they were marking the particular holy days and when they would be celebrated. They determined that the first full moon after March 21st would mark the date to place the Easter Sunday, which would be the first Sunday on or after this full moon. This was a perfect time for pagans, too, since there would be light into the night if the weather was good. The non-Christian name stayed with the holiday though the religious aspects were quite changed from the Dawn-goddess days. Now was the commemoration of the "dawn" of a new age. Still, our affinity for rabbits and egg-hunts remained.

echo The story of the poor, beautiful wood nymph Echo gives us another of our common words. Jealous Hera was on the prowl, looking for wandering hubby Zeus who probably had more wild affairs with goddesses and humans alike than any of the other gods. Though she couldn't find him playing among the happy nymphs, she decided to wield a bit of power anyway to satisfy her green-eyed anger. She cursed the most talkative of these girls with the command that from thence forward she could only repeat the words that others spoke first. In love with the handsome lad, Narcissus, Echo found it so frustrating to try to communicate with this fellow (who would never give a woman power over him anyway) that she hid in embarrassment in a cave where you can hear her today if you give a good shout. That heartbreaker **Narcissus** had a flower named after him when he was cursed to fall in love with his reflection and died pining for it (himself). From him we get our word **narcissism**. And to top it all off, the curse was placed on him by **Nemesis** – the goddess of righteous anger and vengeance, from whom we get our word for retribution – who was prayed to by one of the gals old Narcissus spurned.

F | **filbert** This variety of hazelnut takes its name from a French saint, Philibert, who headed a monastery in the late 600's. It so happened that his feast day, August 22nd, was set at the beginning of the nutting season. These nuts began to be called "nuts of Filbert" (from Philibert). The **hazel** in hazelnut doesn't come from any mischievous maid of TV fame, but from the Old English for the brown of the nut's shell.

Friday Another goddess gives us the name of the day many of us thank God for. Frigg (who was later altered to Freya), the Scandinavian love goddess, deserved a day named in her honor – at least among the Norse and others of her followers. After all, didn't the god of thunder have his Thor's day (**Thursday**)? Better than if the Roman's choice had won out among future English-speakers, and our fourth day of the workweek had been named Jupitersday. Only the Roman Saturn made it through the calendar wars with his **Saturday**. The sun and moon themselves bring us **Sunday** and **Monday**. The chief of the Norse gods, Wodin, brings us **Wednesday** (Wodin's day) which beat out Mercuryday among the British tribespeople. The Norse god of war, Tiu, was more popular than Mars when it came to giving us our name for **Tuesday**. To tell the truth, the Romans copied their names for the planets from Egyptian ideas and didn't have a real seven day week until Constantine, hundreds of years after Christ. The Hebrews had a seven day week but put their final day of the week at the opposite end from their Egyptian opponents.

G **gerrymander** Our common term for redistricting voting areas for some advantage is actually a combination of two words: a man's last name and an animal. When Massachusetts Governor Elbridge Gerry approved of a district created by the legislature that would favor his party, critics were outraged. They said the voting district was so stretched and spread out that it looked like a salamander on the map. The "gerrymander" as newspapers called the beast, gained quite a bit of attention and led to legislation preventing this kind of arranging of votes. Still, in 1960, a "dumbbell" district was created in California as two heavily populated Los Angeles areas were joined by a strip of beach, forming what looked like a set of barbells. The weight of publicity put a hernia in that idea. Back to Mr. Gerry, he continued his public service, dying in office as Vice President of the United States under James Madison in 1814.

goon Sometimes a word is made up by some writer or artist and it stays in the language. When E. C. Segar created the comic strip character, Alice the Goon, he found how the power of the media can also add to our vocabulary. A goon became any foolish or klutzy person whose actions resembled the cartoon Alice. It also got applied in insulting terms to hired thugs (who sometimes weren't so bright either) and even made its way to the Pacific when the albatross got its nickname (gooney bird) based on its foolish-looking landing and takeoff maneuvers.

graham crackers I'll always remember dunking Nabisco™ graham crackers in milk as I grew up before fast foods and microwaves. Little did I know that I was eating the health food touted by Sylvester Graham in the early 1800's. This vegetarian reformer of diet was laughed at by some, but his notion for using unsifted wheat flour hung around long past his death at the age of fifty-seven. Some of his other causes included the recommending of cold showers, hard mattresses and loose clothing for everyone. I'll stick with the graham crackers.

guy Our informal name for a person, usually male, has a bloody history. Guy Fawkes, a soldier of fortune from England who joined the Spanish army, was hired to try and blow up King James I and Parliament in 1605. He was found in a cellar with his gunpowder, but refused to tell who his colleagues were in this "Gunpowder Plot" until he was tortured on the rack. His anger over the persecution of Roman Catholics, which caused him to take sides against the King, led to his hanging in early 1606. A celebration of the overthrow of this plot grew into a yearly event in England until it became a full-blown holiday. Every November, Guy Fawkes Day found effigies of Mr. Fawkes being burned in commemoration. These dolls were usually dressed in rags or motley; and after a time, when someone was poorly or grotesquely dressed, he was nicknamed a "guy," after the style of the effigies. By the time the word became popular in the U.S., it was the late 1800's and a guy was just any old guy.

H **hermetically sealed** When we hear this we think of laboratories, sterile and scientific kinds of activity. Several hundred years ago the hermetical practices might have been more related to magic and the occult. The "Hermes" from which we get this hermetic was *not* the messenger of the gods we studied in Greek mythology. Instead this was a Greek version of the Egyptian god Thoth who taught alchemy, astrology, and magic. This "Hermes Trismegistus" also supposedly invented a special seal that would magically make things air-tight.

hick It's not a very nice thing to be called, but this name for the naive, rural native came from a pet form of the name Richard, which I'll talk about later. Just as we use names in expressions like "every Tom, Dick and Harry" or "keeping up with the Jones," so names were given to types of people. This nickname was a sort of "Bubba" of over a hundred years ago.

hooch This slang word for booze, usually cheap rotgut, comes from the name of an Alaskan tribe, the Hoochinoo. It seems that these Native Americans brewed some quite potent firewater, and its reputation led the tribe's name to be associated with the sauce of their brewing. Later, it was used for any cheap bootleg spirits. The hootchy-kootchy has a more uncertain origin.

hooker Though this slang name for a prostitute had been around well before the 1850's, a Civil War general helped entrench its meaning into our language. At first, most poor people were called hookers because the clothes they could afford used hooks instead of the more expensive buttons with buttonholes. Since some of the less fortunate tended to help themselves to some of the more wealthy's goods through pickpocketing and burglary, the term came to be applied to less-than-savory characters, including prostitutes. When General Joseph Hooker was given command of the down-in-the-dumps Army of the Potomac, one of his first steps was to boost morale. He gave furloughs and, it was rumored, let his troops have familiar relations with those in the profession older than soldiering. The red-light district in Washington D.C. was even jokingly referred to as "Hooker's division." So the old slang was reinforced with the new by his coincidental name.

hooligan Today, this is more of a light, teasing name for a mischievous person, but the original connotation applied to ruffians and young hoodlums. The name could have originated with an Irish family of Southwark, London, that was well-known for roguishness. Some think it might have come from a group of thugs called Hooley's gang or from a misspelling of another Irish family's name, Houlihan. There's even an old, drinking song that might have given birth to our informal, modern word.

hurricane A tribe of Carib West Indians gave us our name for the severest of storms. Their god of thunder was "Hurakan." Who knows, he might have even been happy that the influence of the women's movement in the `70's caused the naming process of hurricanes to include men's names alternated with the women's, beginning in 1978. It had been a tradition among the mostly male pilots to call storms by women's names, and this was adopted as official policy by the weather service in 1953. Twenty-six years later, in 1979, the first major hurricane to bear a male name, David, struck the American coast.

J **jacket** Somehow or another, most word experts agree that our name for the light, short coat originated with the French masculine name, Jaques. Just as "Jack" has been used to describe a male – giving us lumberjacks or the jack-of-all-trades, Jack Frost and the jack-in-the-box, the jack o'lantern, jack knife, jack rabbit, jackass, and even the playing card called a "Jack" – so the French used this general name to apply to a masculine fashion style. The Scottish version of this common name gives us "Jock," which was attached to the horse-back-riding racer and later to the disc-spinning radio **jockeys** (who are more and more confined to the compact platters). This probably isn't related to the slang for a penis, "jock," from which we get **jockstrap**.

jovial Astrology marks this word, denoting a happy, easy-going person. To be born under the influence of the planet Jupiter meant that your personality would be affected by this seat of happiness. The planet was named after the supreme Roman god, sometimes called Jove, who married his sister and watched over a not-so-contented Rome. Stars and planets had a constant relationship with these gods, which we modern namers continue, calling our rocket missions names like Gemini or Apollo. I won't go into great detail with **saturnine**, which was the gloomy condition of being born under Saturn's influence (though the huge, sexually liberal party that used to celebrate Saturn exists as a word, **saturnalia**, which applies to any unrestrained sexual revelry). With **martial**, a bit later, I'll return to the influences of the gods.

July I've already mentioned how the once-fifth Roman month, Quintilus, was renamed in honor of Julius Caesar. One of his major reforms dealt with the Roman calendar. Around 46 B.C. Julius Caesar obtained the services of a renowned Greek astronomer to fix the date of the spring equinox so that they could arrange to rearrange the year. Romans called that period "the year of confusion" as some eighty days were added to that year to make up for the inconsistencies of the former calendar. 45 B.C. marks the inception of the Julian Calendar which lasted until Pope Gregory XIII readjusted time once more in 1582. It appears that Julius' Greek stargazer was off slightly in his calculations, and Easter was not being celebrated on the right date since the true equinox of spring was occurring earlier and earlier in the calendar year. The Pope added over a week to the year to make up for the lost time and reset the yearly count of days once more. Stubborn Englishmen and their colonists would not adopt the new calendar for over 170 years, and when they finally did, they had to add even more days to that particular year of change. I'm staying away from the Jewish, Hindu, Chinese, and Moslem ways of counting time . . .

jumbo The name of an elephant gives us this word for the extra large size of anything. Jumbo was the biggest elephant anyone had seen, standing twelve feet tall and weighing 13,000 pounds. When

P.T. Barnum bought the pachyderm from the London Zoo, Jumbo became a major attraction of his circus. But where did Jumbo's name originate? Some say the Gullah word for elephant, "jamba," was the derivation. Others say the African magic phrase, "mumbo jumbo," was at its roots, with jumbo referring to a giant, grotesque idol. Whatever its source, the name of the elephant gives us such impossible sounding combinations as "jumbo shrimp."

L **leotard**   One of the most popular garments of the past twenty years, outside of the disposable diaper, is the leotard, which takes its name from a French daredevil. Sort of an Evel Kineval of his day, Jules Lèotard became famous in the late 1800's for his tightrope walking between tall buildings and over waterfalls without using a net. He also became well-known for his skin-tight costumes. His name became teamed with these body stockings, and when dancers or acrobats wore the tights, they were commonly called leotards. Recently, Spandex aerobics outfits have once again made the aerialist's name popular.

lulu   "Watch that first step; it's a lulu" went the famous line. This funny-sounding word is applied to anything outrageous, extreme, or quite remarkable. More than likely, it comes from a pet form of Louise, which I'll talk about in Section Four as being the feminine of a warlike first name. Whoever the first Lulu was that led to the comparisons to everything from beautiful women to home runs isn't clear.

lynch   The arguments are there for several fellows by the name of Lynch getting the credit for adding this word to our language. Charles Lynch, whose brother founded Lynchburg, Virginia, was a justice of the peace who was known for his rather swift prosecution of the law in his area of the Old Dominion state. But it was probably a Captain William Lynch who finally turns out to be the man best known for his severe punishment of lawbreakers. He and his group of vigilantes became affiliated with the tendency to hang first and explore legal niceties later. In its earliest uses, "lynch" was applied to tar and feathering or whipping the violators, as well as the hanging of horse thieves and the like. Later, lynch laws applied primarily to hanging, and this is where the word stands today.

M **magnolia** Once again, the name of a discoverer, this time Pierre Magnol, gives the flowering tree its name. This French botanist lived from 1638 until 1715, and in those seventy-seven years, left his name firmly entrenched in our plant vocabulary. While I'm back among the foliage, let's not leave out the English botanist William Forsyth and his yellow-flowered, Asian **forsythia**; or John L. Macadam whose name is associated with the delicious **macadamia** nut. This Australian chemist shouldn't be confused with the Scottish engineer who developed a street-paving technique of covering a road with small pebbles and binding them with tar. This John Macadam also has a rarely used word for the process, **macadamize**, lodged in our dictionaries.

martial Whether it's the martial arts, martial law or martial music, we look to the Roman god of war, Mars, for the beginnings of these terms. And if you disobeyed a superior in wartime, you could get court martialed. Astrologically, it was believed that Mars, the planet, had an evil influence over people.

Another planet whose god carried influence was Mercury. The quick and changeable personality of a **mercurial** person came from the god of commerce, travel, and thievery. This fast fellow's name not only gives us the word **merchant**, but also **mercy** which was first connected with "pay or reward" in its earliest Latin. The wing-footed messenger was said to be shrewd, fast, and eloquent, all prized characteristics of thieves and politicians. Our metal **Quicksilver**, whose name came from the the Latin, meaning "living silver," is most popularly known as mercury.

masochism Our age has certainly opened itself to a huge range of individual tastes, and masochists are a bit different in their desires. Leopold von Sacher-Masoch first described this condition which depends on receiving abuse in order to achieve pleasure. A lot of us beat our heads against the wall every day, with our shoulder to the wheel and our nose to the grindstone, but very few get that tingly sense of stimulation that the Austrian novelist of the late 1800's described. Of course, there are those of us who might think our bosses are **sadists**, deriving their pleasure from our pain. That term comes to us through the Count Donatien de Sade, known as the Marquis de Sade, who propounded a philosophy of sexual anarchy that he acted out in his real life, ending up in prisons or asylums for over twenty-seven years of the seventy-four he lived. Modern psychology actually was influenced by the French author, who lived around the time of

Napoleon. You can figure out for yourself about the combo-condition, sadomasochism.

mausoleum One of the seven wonders of the ancient world, King Mausolos' tomb was huge and ornate. His grieving wife, Artemisia, built a 230 by 250 foot edifice filled with sculpture and riches. The satrap of the kingdom of Caria in Asia Minor might not have actually been buried in this memorial in Halicarnassus when he died in 353 B.C. Some say this queen so mourned her departed husband that she toasted him every day with a drink containing a bit of his ashes until she died two years later . . . a rather weird wake.

maverick Thanks to a TV series and a departed car brand, this word has an almost romantic connotation today, one of the individualist who carves out a unique path or lives a divergent lifestyle. Samuel A. Maverick was a Texas cattleman of the late 1800's who had quite a scheme for increasing his herd. The tradition of the day was that each ranch had a particular branding mark to distinguish its cattle from those of another ranch, in case a fence broke or a cow or two wandered onto another's land. Maverick asserted his brand was the non-brand, that any steer *without* a brand was his, which, of course, would allow him to claim any wild cattle or an unbranded heifer that strayed his way. If a cow was found roaming with a herd and it didn't have a mark of ownership, it was Maverick's . . . no matter where in Texas this might have been. He got both respect and jokes from his peers, but the notion of doing things a little differently got hooked up with the Maverick name.

May The Italian goddess of the earth, Maia, meaning "she who is great," brings us the name of that great springtime month. Now, I'll let go of all this calendar talk with just the mention that **January** gets its name from the two-faced deity, who looked to the past and future at once and was the god of gates and doorways, Janus. **March**, where Winter and Spring battle, gets its name from the warrior god Mars, who's been mentioned earlier. **April** comes from that Greek love goddess, Aphrodite, whose encouragement to fertility brings the earth to bloom. And **June** brides can thank Juno, that goddess of marriage, for the tradition of weddings in that month.

the real McCoy It's ironic that our slang expression for something genuine or non-imitation comes from a man who used a false name. Norman Selby was a boxer who was well known in the first part of this century as "Kid McCoy." The Irish and Scotch were (and still are) great boxing fans of the day, and their sympathies, cheers, and support could be gathered in a wee bit more easily with a name like McCoy.

Now, there are a few other theories about this phrase. A certain brand of Scotch was made by a Mackay and advertised as the clear McCoy. Scotch drinkers who wanted the best would want to be sure to look out for their brand.

Clans in the land of the thistle were known to be very competitive even within branches of the same family. One Lord Reay of Clan Mackay wanted to be known as the best of the tribe and was known as "the Reay Mackay," which was altered to "the real Mackay," and finally to our present expression. More than likely, a blending of the ideas gives us the final product. Speaking of clan feuds, nothing of the Hatfields and McCoys seems to be part of this phrase.

mentor   This name for someone who passes along learning and wisdom goes back to the trusted counselor of Odysseus. While the lonely Greek was trying to make his way back to his home and wife, the goddess Athena disguised herself as Mentor and taught Odysseus' son Telemachus. Later, a 1699 French play had a character modeled after the Greek version and the word started getting general use as a title for a guide or advisor or guardian of wisdom.

money   Wouldn't you know that from a Roman nickname for the goddess of marriage and the well-being of women comes our modern word for currency? Juno, that Roman deity mentioned above, was also called Moneta by her worshipers. Within her temple in Rome was the mint where coins were pressed. These metallic bits of exchange were called by the goddess' epithet, and the word began its journey through Old French to Middle English to the present, changing form slightly as it was passed along, though "monetary" still bears a strong resemblance to the original Latin.

N **namby-pamby**   This word is still used for the cowardly, those without backbone, and the overly sentimental. When Ambrose Phillips became popular in the early 1700's for his rather weak and over-emotional tales of the sweet goodness of farm life, it was too much for Henry Carey, who wrote a satire on the whole style titled *Namby Pamby*, making fun of "Ambrose" in the title. Authors and their fictional characters have given us many lasting terms like **gargantuan** from the gigantic king in Rabelais' work, or a **scrooge** which obviously comes from the famous Dickens character, or **syphilis** which was named after a character in a 1530 poem by the doctor from Verona, Girolamo Fracastoro, who is claimed to be the first victim diagnosed with the disease and whose poetic character got linked to the terrible infection. Even our word **diddle**, meaning "to waste time," is said to have gotten its start from a swindling character, Jeremy Diddler, in an 1803 comic novel, *Raising the Wind* by James Kenney.

nicotine Ah, the wily French ambassador Jean Nicot who knew how to please the wealthy and powerful with his diplomatic gifts is behind the origin of this word. When he introduced his powdered tobacco to the Portugese court in 1560, he started a regular fad. His gift of snuff to Catherine de Médici of the powerful merchant family brought her great enjoyment, and soon all Europe was using "nicotainia," the "herb of Nicot," as it was called. Even the monks were introduced to the pulverized weed and were very happy at the way it aided in the pleasure of a day of chanting and praying. Nicot was all the rage and seems to have made a fortune importing the stuff. If only Sir Walter Raleigh had been as crafty. Later, however, the Church got rather upset with this constant and addictive use of the powder and began to persecute users and ban the traffic in tobacco . . . a bit like our former Surgeon General Koop's campaign. Science still honored the Frenchman by giving tobacco's genus the name "nicotainia," and levels of nicotine are still an important selling tool for tobacconists.

O **obsidian** A misspelling of a man's name led to this volcanic glass having its present designation. When Latin scribes were copying a manuscript of the great Roman naturalist, Pliny the Elder, several years after the death of Christ, they mistook the name he had given the stone, adding a d in the middle. Pliny had mentioned that an Obsius was the discoverer of the rock and went on to name it "obsianus." Speaking of **volcanoes**, the Roman god of fire and metalworking, Vulcan, gives us the root of this word. The lame and ugly god worked under these mountains at his fiery forge. Even the treatment of rubber to make stronger tires by heating it under pressure and adding sulfur, among other things, was called **vulcanizing**.

ocean One of the giant, elder gods of the Greeks called Titans (from which we get our word **titanic**), Oceanus was the god of the great river that circled the Earth, according to the notions of the world at that time. He and his wife, Tethys, were the parents of all the river gods. Some of the other Titans gave us words that have survived the centuries. Cronus was the god of the universe after overthrowing his father **Uranus**. Cronus was likewise overthrown by his son, Zeus. And this dispossessed father is the likely origin of our **chronic chronological** words. I talked about another Titan, Atlas, in detail in *Where in the Word?* Mnemosyne was the goddess of memory, and we get a word like mnemonics, dealing with memory improvement, from this Titan. She also mated with Zeus to give birth to the muses from whom we get words like **music**, which stood for poetry, literature, *and* music in ancient Greece; and **museum**, which meant "the place of the muses." These inspirers of the arts did not give us the **muse** of **amuse** or **bemuse**. This "muse" that we use for speaking of deep thought came from the Old French, meaning "to sniff about, looking for a scent." This idea of trying to meditate on something not quite certain led to the first musings. "Amuse" was a term for wasting time in its earliest uses.

O.K. The two letters we use to indicate that everything's fine has several possible beginnings, with a president's nickname linked to our popular expression. Martin Van Buren was a powerful figure on the American political scene of the early 1800's, and when he allied himself with Andrew Jackson, he reaped the benefits of the spoils system, which rewarded loyal supporters with appointments to high positions in the government. Van Buren was named Secretary of State during Jackson's first term as president. During Jackson's second term, he was vice president. Van Buren's real power was in his home state of New York where he was known as Old Kinderhook (having been born in the town of the same name). A club of Democrats formed itself around Van Buren, calling itself the O.K. Club. At the same time, a popular slang expression "O.K." had been gaining popularity to indicate a positive disposition, much like the "cool" of today. It's uncertain, but this could have come from the German expression "olle korrect." At any rate, with Jackson's help, Van Buren succeeded Old Hickory as president in 1837, further popularizing "O.K." as a statement of approval. Van Buren's "correctness" was short-lived. Following Jackson's shaky monetary policies, he was met with the Panic of 1837, one of the first major financial crises of the young country.

P **panic** That traveler in ancient Greece who heard strange sounds in the dark woods at night and nearly jumped out of his toga in fright was hearing the noises of Pan, the god of shepherds, who could cause a sense of terror to overcome those crossing through wild and lonely places. The deity with goat legs, horns and ears might have loved to play his musical panpipes across his fields and woodlands, but you might find yourself panic-stricken if you came upon his domain without invitation. He could also cause contagious fear in herds and crowds.

phosphorus This word was created from the Greek name for Venus when she rose as the morning star, the light-bearer Phosphor. If these scientific namers had used the Roman version of this Greek entity, we'd have called the element we find in our safety matches **Luciferus**, since that was the name of Latin light-bearer. He later takes on evil connotations when John Milton uses his name for the angel who leads the revolt in heaven that lands him and his buddies in Hell. Satan is another of his names.

R **rigamarole** A sort of "Dungeons and Dragons" of medieval times gives us this word we apply to nonsense or stupid and complicated procedures. Various characters were part of the game, and verses about them were contained in a scroll. Rageman le bon, or Rageman the good, was one of the more popular characters, and, because of this, the scroll itself got called the "Rageman rolle" in the Middle English spellings of the 1100's and 1200's. The procedures for playing the game appear to have been fairly complicated, leading to the phrase spoken when someone thinks something foolish: "That's just a bunch of rigamarole."

ritzy When something is elegant or very fancy, some will use this word, which comes to us through César Ritz, a Swiss hotel owner of the early part of this century who founded a line of posh boarding houses bearing his last name. Some, like the Ritz-Carlton in New York, had such a reputation for being fashionable that the name became synonymous with class and was used as a slang word, usually by the un-ritzy.

S **sandwich** John Montagu was a gambling man. The Fourth Earl of Sandwich was not very well-liked on the social scene, but he was a man of position, being the lord of the admiralty for many years. Because of that rank, Captain Cook did him the honor of naming the Hawaiian islands after him. The Sandwich Islands weren't where our fast-food bread filler originated, however. Supposedly, during a marathon gambling session the Earl got hungry but didn't want to leave the table. He ordered a hunk of meat to be put between two pieces of bread and was thus able to eat while he bet – a rather chance way for one of our most-eaten food combinations to originate. And, of course some will remember the old advertising technique called the sandwich board, where sandwich men walked the streets with placards slung over their shoulders, touting the wares of merchants in the town. The Earl lived seventy-four years and was blamed for the British loss of the American colonies because of his mismanagement of the navy. Have a Big Mac on us, John.

saxophone Adolphe Sax invented his giant, complex kazoo in 1846, but the Belgian instrument maker didn't see his saxhorns get the kind of respect the concert orchestra might give the oboe or bassoon or even the French horn. If he had lived until the present day music scene, he'd have seen his reed instrument become one of the most-used in popular music.

schlemiel The Yiddish term for a real schmo refers to someone who is constantly botching a job. This bumbler is a true schnook who probably gets his name from a popular Talmudic story from the Middle Ages which was used in teaching and explaining. It seems that Shelumiel had been gone from his home for a year. When he returned he found his wife with a new-born baby. He couldn't quite figure it out and went to the rabbi for help. The rabbi eventually convinced him he had to accept the child as his own and Shelumiel did, much to the ridicule of his neighbors. Another German folktale tells of a Peter Schlemihl, who made a bargain with the devil to sell his shadow for a purse that is never empty. He became an outcast when villagers ridiculed him for being without the gray tagalong. The word could come from the Hebrew "sheluach min `el," meaning "sent away from God," but, in any case, a schlemiel is in danger of mismanaging any task. This is unlike a **schlimazel** who is just unlucky. This poor schmuck probably gets his name from the combination of the German "shlim" meaning "unlucky" and the Hebrew "mazol" referring to stars in a constellation. So the schlimazel was born under an unlucky star. The Hebrew "s-l-msl," means "that which is not luck."

shrapnel Actually, it's sometimes nice when a word is not used as much as it once was. When British artillery officer General Henry Shrapnel invented the projectiles, he was only trying to find an effective killing device that would save *his* men from direct combat and death. The fused metal balls placed inside the explosives would blow up over the enemies' heads, raining metallic terror and injury upon the troops. Later, any exploding shell fragment took the name.

sideburns Ambrose Burnsides might not have been a great general, but he set a bewhiskered fashion that hangs on by a hair to this day. He was relieved of his command of Union forces during the Civil War after the disastrous battle of Fredricksburg and transferred to Tennessee. Here he distinguished himself, but later, after trying to explode a mine under Confederate forces at Petersburg but still losing terribly, he resigned. He went on to become a three-term governor of Rhode Island and a U.S. senator. General Burnsides was well-known for wearing his beard down his cheeks combined with a mustache, but shaving his chin and neck area. The "burnsides," as the style came to be known, was popular. As you've probably noticed, when words get passed from one person to another, changes can occur in spelling and even meaning. The burnsides became the "sideburns" that men like Clark Gable or Elvis made so famous. The hunks of cheek hair *looked* like burns down the side of the face, and this is how the word got interpreted, leaving the military man shaved from the final picture.

silhouette When Etienne de Silhouette raised taxes to fund the Seven Years War as French Controller-general, he was only trying to help. But when he even tried to get King Louis XV to cut back on his spending, he was headed for a fall. After only eight months in office, he left the economy in a shambles, and the short, unhappy career was mocked by the French by nicknaming the cheap shadow-drawings that were popular among the lower classes after him. Add this to the fact that his home was found to contain poorly rendered drawings of this kind and he became the laughing stock of Paris in 1759. None of the mockery remains with the word today.

T | **tantalize** Tantalus was a mortal man, but the son of Zeus and honored by the gods of ancient Greece. He was allowed to eat with them and received their favor. But there was a terrible kind of jealousy within him. He wanted the gods to dine with *him* at a great banquet. They agreed to do so, perhaps with a bit of condescension. Some kind of damning human pride brought out a fury in him. He decided he'd trick these high and mighty gods in the most wicked way. He'd make them into cannibals without their even knowing it. He killed his son and had him boiled in a huge vat and served up to his guest divinities. The gods learned of the plot and punished Tantalus severely. He was to stand forever in the underworld, Hades, in a pool of refreshing-looking water. Every time he would reach down for a drink to cool his burning thirst, the water would recede and disappear. Above him were magnificent fruit trees, covered in pears, figs, apples, and so on; but each time he would grasp for them, they would bob up out of his reach. He would be "tantalized" for eternity, which is how we got the notion of the word. Even a certain kind of liquor cabinet with a lock is called a **tantalus**. As a side note, the entrée child of Tantalus was restored to life and lived happily ever after . . .

tawdry   This word for something of poor quality or bad taste has been somewhat replaced by **tacky** (which was originally a word for a horse of inferior quality or breeding). But "tawdry" gets its start over a thousand years ago with a young woman who, legends say, ran away from a marriage she was forced into and became the abbess of a large convent in Northern England. She became widely known for her good works, but this Audrey had a fondness for lacy, fancy necklaces that had been her fashion passion when younger. When she died in 679 it was from a large throat tumor that she regarded as punishment for her vanity. The kindly woman was made a saint, and her special day became associated with fairs held in that part of England, north of the Humber River. It became a popular tradition among merchants to sell lace neckties in honor of "Seynt Audrie." Over time, the quality of these necklaces deteriorated as did the memory of the Saint's name. St. Audrey's lace became "tawdry lace." Through the passage of time, the word "tawdry" became a descriptor of anything cheap and gaudy.

tontine   You may have only heard this word once in awhile, but it has an interesting background. An insurance scheme was the initial way the word came to us. Banker Lorenzo Tonti, from Naples, Italy, in the mid-1600's, proposed this financial plan involving a group of individuals contributing to an insurance policy that would be awarded to the last remaining survivor. Tontines could be a wonderful way to provide for a child or bring wealth to a particular family, but they could also create devisiveness as members waited for each other to die, trying to outlive one another and collect the ever-growing pot. In this century, tontines have generally been special items like a bottle of brandy that a group of war veterans saves in memory of their time together in war, to be opened by the last survivor.

V **valentine** Two different Christian martyrs named Valentinus, who were both executed for their beliefs, are the possible fathers of the tradition of sending cards of love to those special to us. In the first three hundred years of the Christian church it was not uncommon for outspoken priests and believers to be brutally killed by Roman rulers and others afraid of this new religion. The exact truth of the legends behind the historical Valentines may never be fully known, but one was said to be a priest executed by Emperor Claudius the Goth in 269. This man had been widely liked and was beloved of many children. According to the story, Claudius forbade his young soldiers to marry, thinking this would make them better soldiers. When Valentine was discovered to have secretly married many young couples, he was imprisoned and later beheaded. While he was in the jail many of his devoted young friends wrote him notes that were passed into his cell. The other Valentine was a bishop of Terni who was also beheaded for his beliefs. By the time the Roman Empire had basically converted to Christianity, early Church fathers were constantly confronted by popular pagan holidays and festivals that needed to be transformed into celebrations more in line with New Testament notions. You recall how that happened with Easter, as I described earlier. The Roman purification celebration of Lupercalia was held every February 15th. After a smokey winter indoors, it was time to look forward to spring. In the earliest days, there would be a huge feast and then a kind of purification ceremony. Originally, the feast, in honor of the wolf who raised the founders of Rome, was held to seek protection of the flocks from wolves. Two young men would dress in goatskins and run through the streets, whipping people with strips of animal hide. The belief was that this would also make women more fertile and ease the labor pains of pregnant women. The tradition got to be a bit carnal as young men might chase after these women to attempt to validate the superstition. As Roman life became more civilized, the lustier aspects of the celebration were adjusted to young men selecting the names of young women for their courtship during the feast. Later, Christian church fathers altered the pagan holiday and popularized the saint's (Valentine) feast day which was conveniently one day earlier. Men might choose a young girl to write to concerning spiritual feelings. Later, men and women could choose a saint's name to honor with verse. Needless to say, the excitement of the holiday was shot. There was still feasting on the day before Lent, but the romantic aspects of the period had almost died out until the 1300's. Once again romance got involved in the holiday. For some reason, Europeans believed that birds mated on February 14th. It became a custom for single women to get up before sunrise and watch for the first man to pass their window. It was said that they would marry him or someone who looked like him. Ophelia talks about the superstition in Shakespeare's *Hamlet*. In the 1800's, both efficient postal services and thoughtful entrepreneurs re-established the good saint's holiday with our now-well-known Valentine's cards. The rest is a hallmark of history . . .

 watt We owe this measurement that tells us how bright our light bulbs will be to James Watt, the Scottish engineer who lived out his eighty-three years between 1736 and 1819. The man was quite an inventor, working with steam engines and that new force, electricity. A watt equals the output of one joule per second. Tells you a lot, right? The joule came from James Prescott Joule, the British physicist who spent many of his seventy-one years exploring this sort of thing. To get a joule you take one amp (remember this from earlier in the book?) and pass it through a resistance of one **ohm** for one second. Oh, *that* explains it! It makes me glad I was an English major. German Georg Simon Ohm (who lived sixty-seven years), who was working during this same time frame, gets credit for the measurement that bears his name. And while we're at it, let's not leave out Count Alessandro Volta, the Italian who lived to be eighty-two and studied electricity extensively, giving us the **volt**. With Edison living eighty-four years, Ben Franklin lasting eighty-four years, and Croatian-born inventor, Nikola Tesla going on for eighty-six years, we should look into the relationship of electricity and aging.

Z **zany** The Dark Ages: when the Church ruled the civilized world and the arts were relegated to a religious focus. Theater was banned for four hundred years. After Crusaders returned from their voyages in the 11 and 1200's, a certain amount of enlightenment about the ways of the world was rediscovered. Many of the Greek and Roman classics, housed in great Arabian libraries, were reintroduced. The arts began to focus on things other than the spiritual. Theater made a comeback. What a synopsis of a much more complicated time! I just wanted to give a bit of background for this word that got its birth with the early Renaissance Italian drama form, the *Commedia dell' Arte*. During the 1400's and 1500's, the common man of Italy was entertained by a group of stock characters performing variations of a never-ending sit-com. The foolish father, Pantaloon, would try to protect his sweet and flirtatious daughter, Columbine, as Pierrot struggled for her love, and the clownish Harlequin played trickeries. Harlequin and his servant friends, like Scapino, made foolish and bumbling plans much to the amusement of the crowd. Another of these characters was the Zani, a ridiculous fool from whom our circus clowns get many of their time-worn routines. The name came from an Italian pet name for Giovanni, their "John." There will be more on that name later in the book.

By the way, our word **pants** comes from the father's name. Pantaloon was named for the patron saint of Venice, St. Pantaleone who was a doctor who died as a Christian martyr in 305 A.D. When Commedia dell' Arte was popular, Venetian merchants were known as stingy traders, and so Pantaloon was mocked with huge-waisted trousers for his skinny frame. Eventually, the trousers themselves bore his name, and the shortened version got applied to more stylish garb.

zombie How many of us have stayed awake for that late, late show on TV to watch the B movie zombies stalk the innocent girl and her boyfriend? These living dead with their robot-like walk get their name from the snake god of West Africans, Haitians, and Gulf-Coastal African-Americans. The voodoo spell that creates these walking corpses may actually have some connections with certain real poisons that can cause people to seem dead, only to have them return, benumbed, to roam about. The alcoholic beverage that has the same tag as our scary friends was named much later for its similar effects

SECTION TWO

Words from the Names of Places
(Real or Imaginary)

A **artesian well** Water that gets trapped underground between two impermeable layers of rock can be under a lot of pressure, enough to bring it to the surface without a pump. Such was the case in Artois, France, the former name of a northern province. The Old French name, Arteis, gives us this common term for any well of this type.

attic As a child, I would occasionally have to go up into the hot, stuffy attic for some stored relic and wondered why on earth this storage space was above the house in such an uncomfortable location. The answer comes from Greece. The land around Athens was called Attica. During the golden age of classical architecture, it was common to put a low wall or story above the cornice of the façade in front of the roof. This style of construction became popular, and the room beneath the roofbeams got the name of the Greek people who invented the space which, in ancient times, had square columns surrounding it.

B **badminton** It was probably an Indian game called "poona" brought home by British officers in the 1860's that was the inspiration for our popular lawn game of badminton. It got its name from the country seat of the Duke of Beaufort in Gloucestershire, England, where the British version of the game was in vogue. Unlike tennis, badminton could be played on just about any flat, grassy surface where a net could be staked out. The sport was also serene enough for ladies of the day to enjoy.

ballyhoo This word for shouting or clamor probably sprang from a place in Ireland. Ballyhooly was located in County Cork, Ireland, and could be the location that sparked the term for outrageous, sensational advertising or hubbub, possibly from fairs and festivals that were held there.

baloney When we say someone is full of baloney, we are not usually meaning that that individual has been heartily dining on sandwich meat. The more formal spelling, bologna, is usually applied to the food and gets its birth in the city of Bologna, Italy. Here, in the north part of the country, it became traditional in the 1850's to take the odds and ends of meats left over from the slaughter and season and smoke them and stuff them into large sausage casings. Just as fast food restaurants of today have had to face rumors that the quality of their patties might be suspect, so did bologna get a poor reputation for its ingredients. It was said that some bologna might contain asses' meat. This slighting of the sausage led to its use in English for anything of inferior quality. In the 1920's it was first applied to a boxer who was a disappointment. Apparently, he got the stuffing beaten out of him.

Other cities also made their mark with meat. The **frankfurter** was originally made in Frankfurt, Germany. Our common name for these bun dwellers doesn't have a derogatory story attached as did bologna. They're called "hot dogs" because of a vendor who thought the frankfurter looked like a dachshund. A cartoonist popularized the joke. The German love of sausage gives us another name for the bun-length dog. The **wiener** came out of Vienna, Austria. The "Wienerwurst," as it was first named in German, meant "Vienna sausage." Hamburg, Germany, was noted for a way of cooking ground meat. This **Hamburger** steak, as it was first called, gives us that special sandwich that has seen billions sold.

bayonet The wicked blade that made rifles have a secondary function as a kind of spear and allowed hand to hand combat while retaining control of a soldier's most important weapon was first manufactured in Bayonne, France. This southern seaport town brought forth the initial knives that could be attached to the muzzle end of a musket.

bedlam   The noisy uproar and confusion we think of in defining bedlam probably fit very well the place where the word got its birth. In the 1600's, the Hospital of St. Mary of Bethlehem in southeastern London was a well-known insane asylum. In those days, the mentally ill were not well-treated and a visitor to "Bedlam," as the Londoner commonly called this place, would find screaming, moaning and a babble of confusion among the sometimes naked, unkempt inmates. That nickname, a dialectical version of "Bethlehem," became synonymous with the racket of the madhouse and was passed on with that definition attached.

Bible   Literally meaning "the Book," the name for one of the most widely read religious texts came to us from the Greek. The ancient Phoenician port of Bublos or Byblos was famous for its export of Egyptian papyrus, the paper used in the earliest books. The name of the city was applied by the Greek merchants to the paper itself and came to mean "book" in their language. When Greek scholars first translated the Hebrew version of the New Testament, it came to be known by the unassuming, yet all-encompassing name it bears today, coming through the Latin to the French to the English with little change. St. Jerome's Latin translation of the good book was the standard for the western Roman Catholic Church, while the Greek text was the acceptable one for the Eastern Orthodox followers.

bikini   Though the first two-piece bathing suits were fairly demure by today's skimpy standards, they created quite an impact on the beach. Several theories exist as to why these bathing suits were named for a particular atoll in the Marshall Islands called Bikini. One idea is that the islanders themselves had very brief attire, and when they were being moved from their home, their native style inspired a national swim fashion. Another idea concerning the name deals with the reason these gentle islanders were relocated. Their little spot in the water was used for atomic bomb testing. When the bikini bathing suit became the hit of the summer season, it was compared to the atomic impact of the island explosions. As a kid, I had always thought a "kini" was a foreign word for some part of the anatomy that needed to be covered up somehow, and when there were *two* places, you needed a *bi*-kini.

bohemian   The artistic, nonconformist lifestyle that has been commonly associated with a bohemian way of existence got its name from the province in western Czechoslovakia because it was believed that the Gypsies came from this region, and everyone knew what a care-

33

free, unconventional way of life they had. Though they did use the large forested area for a refuge and temporary camping space, this was not their homeland. The original people who lived there were of Celtic ancestry. The Boii, as they called themselves, meant "fighters." The Romans adapted the tribal name to their language, and so "Bohemia" meant "land of the fighters," not very close to a beatnik or hippie mode of living.

An interesting sidelight comes with the name of this region when trying to trace the African-American slang term for a white: "**honky**." Eastern Europeans were given a lot of disparaging ethnic nicknames as they tried to fit into American society as immigrants. One of the terms for a slow-witted laborer from Bohemia or Hungary was "bohunk," which combined the first parts of the names of each of the regions. Later, this was shortened to "hunky." This slang ethnic slur for an ignorant white seems to have carried over into Harlem where "honky" derogatorily described any white person and is still used to this day.

bourbon A kind of whiskey that was distilled from a corn mash took the name of a place where some of the very best of its type was popularized. Bourbon County, Kentucky, made fine sour mash corn whiskey, and the reputation of this sipping liquor spread the name of the county far and wide. Over time this type of booze itself was called by the county's name. Places can easily get associated with food and drink. We all know that most **Scotch** is made in Scotland. And it is also thought that the syrup of butter and brown sugar that also comes in hard candies that we call **butterscotch** was originally made in Scotland. **Gin** takes its name from a plant that also names a city. Geneva was the Middle Dutch name for the juniper berries which named the Swiss town and the distilled spirits made in the area.

bronze Man's oldest known alloy is this mixture of copper and tin. It more than likely gets its name from the ancient Italian seaport that was located in the southeastern part of the boot and was called Brundisium. The Latin for "copper of Brundisium" is the root from which we get today's word. In its first form any mixture of copper with tin, zinc, lead or other metals was called bronze, and it was usually used as a verb describing the process of covering something with the metal. By 1200 there was a distinction between brass and bronze, and the word finally got into the English language in the 1600's.

Brunswick stew Our modern Brunswick stew is generally composed of pork or chicken along with other ingredients which might include corn, onions, tomatoes, and more. The meal was created in Brunswick County, Virginia, where the primary ingredient was either squirrel or rabbit, cooked until falling to pieces, along with onion as the main flavoring. I'll talk more about some of our favorite foods and their relationship with places later in this section.

bunk I'm sure Buncombe County, North Carolina, didn't deserve to have this word for nonsense derived from its name, but it happened over a hundred and seventy years ago. Felix Walker was a member of the 16th U.S. Congress and represented this area of the Tar-Heel State in the early 1800's. Around 1820 he got a reputation for constantly making long-winded idiotic speeches, in which he would include the comment that this was a "speech for Buncombe." The term "bunkum" got humorously associated with anything full of wind and stupidity, signifying nothing. The shortened version of the word is still popular today.

Now, the **bunco** squad, composed of those police officers who investigate frauds and swindlers, gets its name from a different source. A bunco was a con-game played on an unsuspecting mark and had its roots in a Spanish card game, "banca," where one of the gamblers acted as the "bank."

C **cajun** A kind of cooking that I truly enjoy comes from that group in Louisiana called by this name. Many of you know the story of how the British gained control of the French part of what is today Canada, which was at one time called Acadia. They renamed the area Nova Scotia and New Brunswick in 1755 when they exiled the French colonists for refusing to swear allegiance to the British crown. Henry Wadsworth Longfellow told of their plight in the poem "Evangeline." Some stayed in Maine where you'll find the Acadia National Park. But most traveled down the U.S. coast until they settled in the steamy bayous of Louisiana where their French ancestry got mixed into the native population. They still remembered their place of origin, however, but these Acadians wound up with the altered name "cajun" from the English translation of their pronunciation. A parish in Louisiana still has the name Acadia.

calico Today, we seem to associate this word most with the multicolored cat spotted with orange, black, grey, and yellow. Most people know the name comes from a kind of brightly colored cloth. Originally, this cloth came into England totally white, imported from the Indian city of Calicut. This "cloth of Calicut" was then dyed in the

English factories and sold with the misspelled name of the Indian city as its brand. The town in India has been renamed Kozhikode, but the cloth and cat retain the original name (as do a spotted black crappie, the calico bass; a speckled bug, the calico back; and the mountain laurel, sometimes called the "calico bush").

Another name for a cat, the **tabby**, also comes to us through a reference to cloth. A suburb of Baghdad, Al-attabiya, was known for a watered silk woven there. Certain domestic cats with stripes or spots that looked similar to the fabric got the nickname from the French version of the Arabic place name, "tabis." The suburb itself had been named for a Prince Attab who had lived there. For some reason, an old maid or gossip is also sometimes called a tabby. How catty.

And on the subject of felines, the **Siamese** cat was developed in the Orient in the area we now call Thailand that was Siam.

Well, now that I've mentioned Siam, I *have* to bring up other uses of the ancient name. The great circus stars, Chang and Eng, who were the first "Siamese twins," gave us their home country's name as the label for this birth condition. Even plumbers have taken advantage of it by naming a double headed outside water faucet a siamese. And you aquarists are probably familiar with the Siamese fighting fish found in the tropics of Asia.

canary The little colorful songbird we call by this name originally came from the Canary Islands. These islands themselves weren't named because of the green and yellow popular housepets. The Latin origin, taken up by the Spanish, meant "Isle of the Dogs." The **canines** that were first bred there were huge and had a wide reputation. A kind of wine was also made there and called canary. And a court dance of the 1500's fashionable in England and France was also called the canary.

cantaloupe Other fruits of this kind have simpler names like "honeydew" or "watermelon," but the cantaloupe has an origin that has religious overtones. The popes of yesteryear had many estates and villas where they might go for meditation, rest, or relaxation, away from the politics of the Vatican. One such villa in Cantalupo, Italy, was the location where the first of the tasty melons was grown. The sweet orange pulp of this food can be found everywhere today, from the breakfast table to the salad buffet, in slices, balls and chunks. It was named hundreds of years ago in honor of the pope's residence.

canter Speaking of religion, when Canterbury, England, became the center of church government and worship in 597, it was common practice to make a pilgrimage to southeastern England to visit this cathedral city in Kent. Wayfarers on horseback took an easy pace that became known as the Canterbury gallop, a slow and undisturbing gait that let them tell a tale or two on the way, if they were of a mind.

champagne New Year's Eve celebrants couldn't do without it. The sparkling wine found at weddings and romantic dinners got its start in France in the area the Romans called Campania, meaning "field." The place gained fame when those Romans defeated Attlila the Hun there in 451 A.D. But its popularity bubbled over in the 12th and 13th centuries when, for those 200 years, fairs were held in the region known then as Champagne. One of its greatest products was the cork-popping stuff that tickled the noses of its consumers. A little bubbly has come a long way.

chartreuse This yellow-green color takes its name from a French monastery, La Grande Chartreuse, near Grenoble. The reason for the relationship of this place with a color had nothing to do with the plants of the region or the hue of the monks' habits . . . . But one habit of the friars was to make a liqueur. These Carthusian monks were famous for their greenish or yellowish concoction, and the name for the shade came from this.

cheddar A village in Somerset, England, became well-known for its smooth, hard cheese that had wide variations in flavor. It was common for special cheeses to be named for the place where they were first perfected. The fancy, mold-ripened, soft, white cheese called **brie** was first made in northern France in Brie. **Camembert**, which softens inside as it ripens, was made in a town in Normandy of the same name. **Gouda** first came from a hamlet in the southern part of Holland which gave the cheese its name, and **Edam** produced a namesake cheese in northwestern Netherlands. A whole country gets the credit for **Swiss** cheese. Switzerland is also responsible for a meat dish, Swiss steak; a vegetable, Swiss chard; and even a light cloth called swiss.

coach A town in Gyor, Hungary, is where we owe the origins of this word for both a vehicle and an act of teaching. Kocs was the place where the first horse-drawn wagons of this type were manufactured and through alterations in spelling as the brand name got passed to German and then to French, we get the coach, a closed, four-wheeled carriage. When trains adopted the name for the railroad passenger car, it eventually led to the low-priced accommodations we today call "coach" fare.

The athletic overseer we call a coach got earliest use in the 19th century as university slang. A special tutor was called a "coach" because he helped "carry" the student through the exam period.

The Dalmatian that we think of as a fire dog was originally called a "coach dog" because it was the fashion to train them to run behind a coach.

cocker spaniel The droopy-eared dog that is still very well-liked as a pet takes its name from an occupation *and* a place. The dog was first bred to hunt woodcocks. It takes the second part of its name from "Spanish," from where it was supposed to have come. The **Great Dane** was actually developed in Germany, not Denmark. In the 1800's Ludwig **Doberman** bred the dog which takes his last name. The "pinscher" part of the name comes from the English "pinch," referring to the bobbed tail and ears. Watch out for the tiny, but vocal **Chihuahua** which comes from that northeast province of Mexico bearing the same name. And of course, it's obvious where the **German shepherd** gets its name since it was developed in that country, but Britishers call the breed **Alsatian**, after the territory in northeastern France that has been both German and French, Alsace-Lorraine. Being a "dog person," I could go on and on: from **Irish Setter** to **Samoyed** (Russian, meaning "of Lapland") to **Scottish terrier** to Pekingese that most know as **Pekinese** (from Peking, China) to the **Labrador retriever** (from Newfoundland), but I'll stop dogging this trail for now.

cockney A native of the East End of London gets this name, and we generally think of the lower classes and the strange accent of the cockney. If you were within the sound of the bells of the Church of St. Mary Le Bow in the center of London, you were in cockney land. Originally, you were a true city slicker if you were a cockney. It came from the Middle English for "cock's egg" and referred to an effeminate or foolish child, a pampered brat of the inner city who had everything he could want. His effeminate affectations were mocked by the notion that he came from a rooster's egg, a very difficult proposition unless the rooster had some strong female attributes. Some say the name also had a reference to the imaginary land of luxury and ease, Cockaigne.

cologne Our fragrant liquid's name first came to our language around 1709 when the German town of Cologne became renowned for mixing alcohol and various scented oils. In days when baths were seldom taken, the "water of Cologne" was widely used to cover less pleasing odors that might drift up from the body while interacting with polite society. **Perfume** gets its beginnings from the burning of incense, the *fumes* of which spread pleasant smoke to cloak more nasty aromas. **Incense** itself goes back to the Latin "to set on fire," from which we also get **incendiary**.

colossal It's hard to decide whether this is most associated with a place or a person. The Greek term for any huge statue was most widely known to apply to a 120 foot statue of Apollo that guarded the entrance to the ancient harbor of Rhodes, southwest of Turkey. The Colossus of Rhodes was one of the Seven Wonders of the World. When the Romans borrowed the Greek word, they took it to mean anything huge and named their giant arena the Colloseum. We still use this term for the large amphitheaters we call **coliseums**.

Conestoga wagon Some of the younger readers may still have studied the wagon trains of the American pioneers. The heavy, covered wagon with its wide wheels was the 4-wheel drive of the Old West, getting settlers and their belongings over some pretty rough terrain. It was named for a valley in Lancaster County, Pennsylvania, where the town of Conestoga had a wagon-building operation. The town was named for the Conestoga Indians.

copper After optic fibers take over the phone lines and zinc dominates the metal of the penny, we may have fewer and fewer uses for this fine conductor of heat and electricity. Brass and bronze will probably keep this metal's uses alive, though. The word for the reddish-brown element comes from the Greek name for the Isle of Cyprus: "Kuprios." In ancient times, this was the best source for copper, and this reputation gave the important metal its name.

D **dagger** There are so many times when a word's origin is obscure or uncertain, but when word experts argue, I enjoy wondering at the theories. The disagreement about the naming of this small knife has some believing that the Romans *could* have started the journey of this word into English with the Latin, "daca," which referred to a "Dacian knife." Dacia is the ancient name for Romania and as this knife's label shifted from Italian to French to Middle English, it could have transformed from

"daga" to "dague" to "daggere." Others will say the evidence isn't strong enough for them to take a stab at it, but I thought I'd slice into the theory with you anyway.

daiquiri The popular rum drink gets its origin from the town in Cuba where the beverage got its start. Daiquiri, Cuba, made the rum used in the first, tartly sweet cocktail. Another south-of-the-border drink can't be left out here: the Mexican district of **Tequila** will always have its name remembered for distilling liquor from the century plant. The **Margarita** doesn't seem to have any connection with the Caribbean Isle of Margarita, near Venezuela. The name comes from the Spanish for Margaret, which I'll talk about in Section Four.

denim The fabric of those blue jeans comes our way via France where the rough cloth was first known as "serge de Nims," from the city of Nims where the coarse weave originated. In the late 1600's the English were using the cloth for clothing. **Serge** was originally not such a tough material. The Latin origins referred to the Seres, the Romans' name for the oriental people we would call Chinese, who made silken garb. Back to denim, the first trousers made of this were probably seen in the late 1860's. Before that, pants called "**jeans**" got their name from a twilled cotton made in Genoa, Italy, and had a Middle English spelling of "Jene." The Genoans probably learned their technique from the Egyptian clothmakers.

It seems that some marketing mischief might have been responsible for the naming of **corduroy**. Duroy was an old name for the coarse, woolen fabric made in western England. Somehow this was used in advertising the cloth, but it was altered to "cord du roy," which was claimed to have been the attire of the kings of France and meant "the king's cords." This might have sold an extra bolt or two, but no real connection has actually been found to France.

dollar The good old American greenback actually got its start in a Czechoslovakian town. In the mid-1500's Joachimstaler was known for its silver mines. The "Taler" was a coin made from the ore of these mines and was a medium of exchange throughout that part of Europe. In the melting pot of the early American colonies, the taler or daler, as it became known, was a name applied to many coins, including Spanish "pieces of eight." After the American Revolution, there was discussion concerning what the new country would do about the kind of currency it would use. Certainly, the rebellious Americans did not want to employ the British pounds, shillings and pence. In 1782 Thomas Jefferson suggested that we adopt the dollar, as it was then spelled, as our main unit in our monetary system. Congress made it official in 1785.

donnybrook The renown of a suburb of Dublin still lingers with this word we use to describe a chaotic fight or free-for-all. Back in the early 1800's, yearly fairs were held in this Irish location, and their fame was known far and wide. Unfortunately, one aspect that seemed to become a tradition of these fairs was the outbreak of wild fights among the feisty Celts. By 1855 the fair was actually canceled because of these brawls. The name of the suburb, however, became permanently allied with fighting.

duffel bag How many soldiers and sailors have carried their lives about with them in this all-too-familiar canvas sack? The original blanket fabric took its name from a town near Antwerp, Belgium. Duffel became famous for its woven woolen cloth with nap on both sides. Heavy cotton, called "duck," was later used in the bags, but the town's name stayed attached.

G **gauze** Where blinded Samson pulled down the pillars of the temple, killing himself and his captors, is the place most associated with the filmy cloth we now use mainly for bandaging. Gaza is the town in the notorious strip of the same name. This Biblically important city was known for the finely woven cloth used for curtains, then cool clothing, and, of course, surgical dressing. The Philistines in Judges 16 probably needed plenty of gauze after Samson, since there were three thousand people on the roof of that temple and many more inside when the strongman brought down the house.

H **hack** I'm not talking here about what you might do to a tree with an ax or to hair with dull sissors. No one who takes scribbling seriously wants to be called a hack writer, and even taxi drivers can get insulted if you accuse them of driving a hack. Long ago, the town of Hakeneye, England, was famous for its horses. This horse raising became such a business that people began to hire ponies from this area. Over time, the use of any hireling or drudge became compared to the use of Hakeneye's horses. The idea behind a "hackneyed expression" also derived from this English town's horsey reputation. When a horse was used for everyday riding or daily labor, it was common to say it was hackneyed. When words and expressions were equally over-employed, they, too, were said to be hackneyed.

I **indigo** The dark blue dye takes its name from the Greek for the place from which the dye was first brought into the Western world. "India" came through the Greek from the Persian translation of the Sanskrit word for "river." The Indus was one of those, giving its name to the prominent province of Sind and also to the religion of the area, Hindu. A plant first gave us the dye the Greeks called "Indikon pharmakon" or "Indian dye."

italics With the invention of the movable-type printing press in the 1400's, the world changed. Not only did the Bible become available to huge numbers of people, but great works of literature were also able to be printed and distributed. Though poor Gutenberg had to sell *his* press to pay his debts, most printers became powerful, respected citizenry. One such person was Aldus Manutius who founded the Aldine Press in Italy in the late 1400's. When his company printed an edition of Virgil in Venice in 1510, it dedicated the volume by the most famous of Roman writers to Italy and introduced a special right-slanted type that was thereafter called italic print. Today italics, formed as a copy of the Renaissance script, usually sets off words, passages, or titles within regular type. In these times, that regular type is called **roman** because a student of Gutenberg's, Nicholas Jensen, perfected the style based on Roman inscriptions. It eventually replaced **gothic** style that was at first the most popular typestyle of the first presses, called "black letter," "Old English," or "church style," and still seen on the mastheads of many newspapers.

J **jersey** The largest of the Channel Islands of England is responsible for this word that football players are very familiar with. The knitted pullover shirt has gone through many transitions from the first sweaters worn by the fishers of Jersey. Those originals were woolen garments worn on the chilly Channel waters. From this island we also get the brown-colored dairy cow, the Jersey. One of the other Channel isles gives us the **Guernsey**, another popular breed of dairy cow. Guernsey Island was also known for a snug wool shirt worn by the sailors there. If their style had gotten more notoriety, we might be hearing about football guernseys. Just to follow through with dairy cows, the **Holstein** was originally bred in a district of the Netherlands, Friesland, but gained most of its popularity as a strong, high-production dairy cow in the German area of Holstein (which had been part of Denmark).

K **kaolin** The French took this Mandarin Chinese word as the name for the fine clay used in everything from ceramics to paper-making. The translation of the Chinese is literally "high hill" and was the name of the mountain where the gray, white or yellowish stuff was first found. It's also sometimes called "terra alba," meaning "white earth."

L **lesbian** The use of Lesbian to describe a female homosexual didn't appear in English until 1890, and it was capitalized, in reference to the island of Lesbos where one of the greatest of all Greek poets resided in its Golden Age. Sappho had many female disciples that she taught at her island residence and, apparently, at a temple to Aphrodite. Though little of her poetry survives, she was noted for her lyrics expressing love toward her fellow women. Though the Greeks saw nothing bothersome in this, early Christian churchmen seemed to, and there was a general destruction of her work in church libraries. Since these were just about the only libraries, Sappho's volumes of poetry are all but lost. Her home, however, lives on in the word that today most commonly describes female homosexuality. By 1960 the capital letter was replaced by the smaller case "l."

limerick "There was a young lady from Georgia . . ." Many of us have concocted limericks, the five line humorous poem that can sometimes get a bit ribald. The name for this light verse seems to have come from the town of Limerick, Ireland. First noted in Edward Lear's *A Book of Nonsense* in 1846, it was popular at parties to make up little crazy poems, and at the end of each verse the crowd would say, "Will you come up to Limerick?" Why, I'm not sure.

limousine How does the luxury vehicle gets its name from a goat's hair cloak? In central France is an area called Limousin, and here cart and wagon drivers had a practice of wearing protective garments that flowed loosely around them and could keep them warm and dry in the wet winters. When some of the earliest cars were designed with enclosed cabs for the passengers and an open front area for the driver, the idea of protection from the elements gave it the name of the cloak. In 1902 when the word was first seen in English, the chauffeur might even have to stoke a steam engine and so the cab was a guard from the smoke too.

lumber Once again, there is argument as to the origin of this name now applied to wood. Wordsmiths give two possibilities. First, a Swedish root meaning "to move or walk heavily," which we hear when talking about someone lumbering up the stairs clumsily, could be part of the roots of the word for boards. However, another British use of the word, "to clutter with unused articles," may have come from a place in Italy. In 568 A.D., a Germanic tribe invaded northern Italy and settled in a region named after them. These Lombards of, of course, Lombardy went on to gain a reputation as bankers, moneychangers, and pawnbrokers. In fact, a lombard was a name for a pawnshop. Here is truly where you can find the cast-off goods cluttering the floors and walls. Disused articles of furniture were dominant in pawn shops of old, before the heyday of the color TV, stereo and VCR. So here might be where the idea of the sawmill product we today call lumber got its start. It could even be a combination of the two notions. By the way, "Lombard" originally meant "long beard" in Latin, describing the rough Germanic tribesmen. And the center of financial dealings in London took its name from these Italo/German bankers. Lombard Street is known for its banks and stock exchanges.

M **magenta** When Napoleon III led his large force of French and Sardinians against the Austrians at Magenta, Italy, in 1859, one of the worst of battles ensued. Some 9,700 men were killed or injured and 4,600 were never accounted for. It was said that the field was stained with the blood of the clash. A large vault was built there containing remains of 9,000 of the casualties. When the purplish-red dye was discovered soon after, it was called magenta, reminding all of that bloody conflict. The city of Magenta itself had a warlike background, being named for Marcus Maxentius, a Roman general who lived there for a time and later became Emperor in 306 A.D.

magnet A bit of magic is wrapped up in the origins of this word that eventually led to that modern "power," electricity. Some of the first lodestones were found in Thessaly, a region in central Greece, in a metal-rich area called **Magnesia**. Yes, that is where we also get the name of our laxative product. These magnesia stones had the strange power to attract or repel certain

metals and, when suspended, would consistently point in one direction, a handy quality for the traveler across unknown seas. The Middle English translation for **lodestone** is "guide stone." Later, in the mid-to-late 1300's, magnets were thought to be part of the ingredients of the "philosopher's stone." When alchemists were searching for that elixer that would prolong life, change lead into gold, and cure all ailments, the stone of magnesia was thought to be one of the components. Though the philosopher's stone was never quite discovered, scientists of the early 1800's found that magnets and electrical currents could make interesting companions, and this has led to the electric motor that helps refrigerate your food, pump your water and create energy from the force of steam or water spinning a turbine . . . Kind of magical at that. If you're wondering if that Thessaly was the place where Paul sent his letters to the Thessalonians, the answer is no. That city, today also called Salonica, is about eighty miles northeast of what was once Thessaly. Oh, and one other laxative product, magnesium sulfate, we call **Epsom salts** because of the mineral springs in this English town where the stuff was found.

marathon Tragedy mixed with happiness is the basis for the creation of this word for the 26 mile, 385 yard-long race. For over fifty years the Persians and Greeks battled each other, until 449 B.C. During one of the campaigns in 490 B.C., the Athenian general Miltiades defeated the Persian army on the Plain of Marathon in eastern Greece. He sent one of his best runners, Pheidippides (some legends say), to Athens with the news of the victory. That gallant run, which was close to the distance of the modern race, ended in the death of the messenger from exhaustion. And the battle was not over. Miltiades had to push his tired troops back to Athens to successfully defend it from the Persian fleet. In commemoration of the run, the race was incorporated into the modern Olympics in 1896. When King Edward VII wanted to see the start of the race from his Windsor Castle home at the 1908 Olympics the length of the marathon became official. It was 26 miles, 385 yards from there to the Olympic stadium in London. The race ended just as regally in front of the royal box at the stadium. So a monarch's will was imposed upon a race commemorating the preservation of the oldest democracy.

mayonnaise Once again, victory in war creates a word that is very common today, found right there on your slice of bread. It is believed that when a French chef came up with the fragile sauce, combining raw egg yolk, olive oil, lemon juice, and other seasonings, it was named in honor of the victory of the Duke of Richelieu in

1756, who captured the city of Mahon on the western Mediterranean island of Minorca. With spelling regularity being fairly nonexistent, our modern word for that potato salad mixer came to us not as mahonnaise. Now, **Hollandaise sauce** has a less martial origin and was just a French name for a Dutch sauce very similar to mayo. **Béarnaise sauce**, with its tarragon and shallots, comes from Béarn in southwestern France. **Bordelaise sauce** gets its flavorful reputation from Bordeaux, France, where the wine of that country is added to the brown mixture. Now, I'm not certain about the origins of **Tartar sauce**, but the combination of mayonnaise and pickles, onions, olives and capers has something to do with the Tatars (also called Tartars), the horde that mixed with the Mongols and brought Genghis Khan an empire that extended from the Pacific Ocean to eastern Europe.

meander   The hill country of what is now western Turkey has a very winding river. The Greek name for this snakey stream gives us today's word for wandering aimlessly. Phrygia was the ancient name of this land of the rambling river.

When someone meanders along he may also be **lethargic**, indifferent to where he is lazily traveling. "Lethargy" comes to us from another river, this one mythological. When it came time for the dead souls to leave the underworld, Hades, and return to new lives above, they would drink from the waters of Lethe, the river of forgetfulness so that they would not remember their past lives as they began anew.

As long as we're hanging around ancient Greece, let me mention **laconic**. Not quite as commonly used, this word for someone who isn't very talkative comes from the early name for the Pelopponesian penninsula where Sparta was capital. Here, if a boy was not of the slave or merchant class, he was taken at the age of seven to live in a barracks and trained to be a professional soldier until he was twenty, learning intense discipline, loyalty, but no real intellectual pursuit (so as not to be softened). At twenty he could marry (though he couldn't live with his wife until he was thirty), usually a woman also trained from childhood to be the wife of a soldier and a mother of soldiers. Needless to say, this lifestyle was not very conducive to lots of gab. In fact, thinking for yourself could get you in trouble in this society. It was, truly, a **Spartan** existence.

milliner   Once a much more important profession, the hat-maker has gone the way of the girdle and garter as far as fashion goes. Modern society seems to be much more oriented toward the baseball cap and the beret. The milliner gets the name from Milan, Italy. Natives of this city were known to be very successful at establishing import businesses for ladies' finery and were also well-known for their fine straw hats. Originally, a Milaner, as the occupation was first called, had laces, ribbons, and other accessories that might be suitable for ladies' apparel. The specialty became hats, and the spelling altered through time. Italian cities give us other words like the triple flavored ice cream, **Neapolitan**, from Naples, **Parmesan cheese** from Parma, and **Venetian blinds** from Venice. I've already mentioned Bologna, Cantalupo, and Genoa; and I'll talk about other cities of Italy as we go along.

morgue   Our name for the place most often associated with the unidentified dead bodies rolled out on the slab in detective stories comes from a particular place in Paris. Le Morgue was well-known as the building where dead bodies were kept prior to burial or cremation. When this kind of location became commonplace in our urban centers, the Parisian name was applied, just as the famous London prison, the **Clink**, gave us our slang for jails.

P **peach**   Georgia and South Carolina peach growers can look to ancient Iran for the origin of the name of this fruit. Actually, the Romans named the peach for Persia, which encompassed more than just Iran. In Latin our peachy-keen food was the "persicum malum" or Persian apple. No, **impeach** was *not* a way of getting rid of politicians by throwing rotten fruit at them. The term we use for removing a rotten apple from office comes to English through the Old French which was influenced by a Latin verb meaning "to put in chains." **Impede** comes from the same root.

piker   Older folks will probably know this word for a stingy cheapskate, though it isn't used nearly as much today. It was quite a derogatory slang word in its beginnings in the California gold rush days. It seems that a certain group of Missourians from Pike County got quite a reputation for their miserliness and unwillingness to risk. The roaring gold-mine-camp days of the '49ers were marked with gambling, and a piker was known to hold the cards close to the chest, bet low, and fold quickly.

polka   The ever-bubbling Lawrence Welk probably kept the polka popular in this country, though it had its source in Poland which gives the dance its name. The Czechs passed the name to the French and Germans from whom we took it. In Polish it just means "dancing woman." Apparently the Poles loved their dances because the more stately **Polonaise**, named by the French for Poland, comes to us from them. A **mazurka** is another Polish dance derived from the province of Mazovia.

R **rhinestone** The rhinestone cowboys of the glittering days of mechanical bulls in country bars might find it interesting to know that their artificial gems get their name from the river Rhine where the first ones were made. Strasbourg, France, on the Rhine River, first crafted these sparkling fake jewels. Known for its glassmaking and paté, this town was passed from the Romans to the French to the Germans and back to the French with the Huns getting in their brief conquest too. **Rhine** itself is a Germanic word for "river," which also gets associated with a dry white wine.

romance Ah, romance! Well, the influence of Rome spread far and wide in ancient times, and though today, we most associate this word with love and affairs of the heart, a romance was originally a long tale of heroes having chivalrous adventures, told in "the Roman manner." These medieval stories were very popular and usually *did* involve brave knights rescuing distressed damsels. In some way or another, the idea of love and the pursuit of "happily-ever-after" became the public perception of the word, though it is still used literarily to describe a class of fiction where good predominates over evil . . . not always the case in a love story today. Romance languages like French, Spanish, Italian and Romanian are all based on the Vulgar Latin of Rome. If you take a Roman holiday, you get your enjoyment from the misery of others . . . a meaning that came from the tradition of ancient folk taking a jaunt to Rome to watch gladitorial contests. I'll mention a few more Roman stories in Section Four.

S **sardine** The fishers of Sardinia, the large Mediterranean island, probably were responsible for giving the name to the lowly herring and other little fish going by the name of sardine. The island kingdom played a large role in the uniting of Italy as Victor Emmanuel II and his grandson brought a country, divided by Napolean, the Austrians, and the popes, into a reorganized kingdom . . . sardines in one can.

scalawag Though the miniature Shetland ponies have delighted circus audiences in modern times, they were considered quite useless when they were first taken note of. One of the Shetland Islands of

England, Scalloway, was known for its small horses and cattle, and this is probably where the term for a good-for-nothing person got its start. A scalawag was worthless, like the animals. During the Reconstruction in the South, a white Republican got the name applied to him, and the connotation was that of a scamp, rogue, and rascal. They were almost as bad as carpetbaggers, the name applied to Northerners who came South to find profit from misfortune during the same time period, travelling with suitcases made from floor covering.

seltzer The first seltzer water came from a natural mineral spring near Weisbaden, Germany. "Selterser Wasser," as it was known in German, was found at the springs of Neider Selters. Most of our modern seltzer is filtered water, pumped with carbon dioxide to give it the effervescent quality of the natural product. Our soda water gets its name from the barilla plant, as it is called in Spanish. The medieval physicians burned it to obtain sodium carbonate which was mixed with water as a tonic. They used the Latin "soda" to describe it.

shanghai Not many sailors wanted to be on board a ship bound for the dangerous treaty port of Shanghai, China, during the mid-1800's, when the angry Chinese attempted to stop the lucrative importation of opium by the British. The drug was ruining the lives of many, but the British government wanted the right to trade in it. To get seamen to man ships bound for that region, it was a common practice to kidnap them, sometimes drugging them or knocking them senseless. They would wake up aboard ship and be forced to work. The word got attached to any situation where you were tricked or forced into something unpleasant.

sleazy There is some disagreement about the origin of this word we use today for cheap, low-class, or in poor taste. More than likely, a very flimsy cloth made in Silesia was at the source of its creation. This region is now mainly in Poland with Wroclaw as its major city. Supposedly, the cloth was of such poor quality that all it was used for was the linings of coats and inexpensive material for pockets. A tailor could save money on these parts of the jacket or pants by using the cheaply made Silesian cloth. As with many words, the passage from mouth to mouth distorted its original spelling.

While we're back in the fabric area, let's not leave out **muslin**, a sturdier cotton weave used for sheets or clothing patterns, which gets its name from the city in northern Iraq, Mosul. The Italians first called the cloth "mussolina" or "cloth of Mosul." The wall hanging we call an **arras**, most famous for a hiding place for Polonius to overhear

Hamlet and there be mistakenly stabbed, gets its name from a city in northern France, Arras, which, in the 1400's, had a reputation for its fine tapestries.

suede When you live in a cold northern clime, you tend to become good at ways of keeping warm. You learn to knit sweaters and tan animal hides for sturdy coats . . . or you open a naugahide factory. The Swedish people had a reputation for keeping the cold out, and one of their products was a kind of leather glove that became popular in France. "Gants de Suede" or "gloves of Sweden" were all the fashion. Eventually, any gloves made of similar leather were called suede, and finally, the leather itself was given the name as it came into English use in the late 1800's.

T **Tabasco** As you've seen, the places where substances are first encountered are sometimes honored in our vocabulary by having that location become the name of the substance. When Americans and Europeans first swallowed the spicy sauce in Tabasco, Mexico, the location became linked with the pungent peppers. It is today a brand name for the wonderfully fiery condiment.

Just so, a certain fibrous hemp was famous in Manila, Philippines, and its use in paper-making gives us **manila folders**. I'll talk about that capital city's name in Section Four.

A fine citrus fruit was exported from the port of Tangier, Morocco, and will now forever be known as the **tangerine**. Well, some will call it the **mandarin orange** because some of these juicy fellows were also imported from China. And though Mandarin Chinese is the predominant language of China, the word "mandarin" actually came from a Sanskrit word meaning "counselor." From this root we also get the Hindu magical prayer, the mantra. The Chinese Mandarins were powerful public officials.

tarantula A strange Italian epidemic gave this wicked-looking spider its name. The hairy creatures were common in southern Italy in the 1400's when bizarre disorders began to occur in people, especially those living around the seaport town of Taranto. Part of the sickness they developed involved an uncontrollable urge to dance. The **tarantism**, as it was called because of the commonness of the disease in that area, was believed to be caused by the bite of the big spider, henceforward called the tarantula. A vigorous spinning dance was even invented as a remedy for the illness. The **tarantella** was created to get the ailing ones "danced out." The disease is no longer common, though the dance is still performed, and the spider still carries its name of blame.

turkey   When a breed of guinea fowl was imported into Europe from Turkey, the bird got the name of that place of origin. The large avian was part of the Christmas tradition as early as 1575. As early American colonists settled the new world, they came across our wild birds in abundance, and one of these looked somewhat like the guinea hen. They called this bird a turkey, and today, the North American variety bears the name and *not* the earlier import. Hunters will tell you that the wild turkey is one of the most challenging of prey, and its early reputation for intelligence led Ben Franklin to propose it as the symbol of our country, though the eagle won out. In its domesticated state, however, it has a renown for its seeming stupidity and panicky nature. This later fame led critics to compare a poor theatrical performance to the bird. By the 1960's, a person who was considered stupid or incompetent was called a turkey. Now, though "talking turkey" refers to honest deliberation, it probably doesn't have too much to do with the gobbler and its strange vocalizations. More than likely, this phrase dealt with bargaining in the marketplace where the birds were sold. If you've ever danced the turkey trot, you'll have an idea of how to move like the fowl . . . probably a closer approximation of animal movement than the funky chicken or fox trot.

Going back to that other name for the first turkeys, the **guinea** fowl – they were so named because they first came from the Guinea coast of Africa. But the guinea pig comes from South America and should have been called the Guiana pig instead, since that's its home. Well, the mix-up just adds to the confusion about them: they're not pigs, but rodents. The poor things will always have that rather negative connotation of being the first to try something out or be experimented on, since that was one of their early functions as laboratory imports. Now, the British coin that was worth one pound, one shilling was called a guinea because it was made from gold mined in African Guinea. But why is an offensive term for an Italian also "guinea"? This is probably a derogatory comparison of the darkness of some Italians to the black people of the African country. Bigotry takes many forms: "**wop**," another slang slur for the Italian comes from a word meaning "dandy," in reference to some of the overly dressed, upper-class individuals of that country. I'll mention "**dago**" in Section Three with the name Jacob.

All right, before I leave this one, let's go back to Turkey. That beautiful blue or blue-green mineral made up of copper and aluminum was first found in Turkestan and today bears the name **turquoise**.

turtle The slow-poke reptile who can hide away in its shell and rarely sticks its neck out has had some rough times in its relationship with humans. In early Christian times, for example, the turtle was considered evil and a sign of the devil. Why? This goes back to the name of the animal. "Turtle" is a variant of **tortoise** which came from Tartarus, the Roman name for the underworld. An evil beast of that region of the dead was sometimes compared to the rather wicked-looking turtles. By 400 A.D., that association remained, translated into the Christian notions of the time. There was probably some combination of tortoise with a French word meaning "twisted," referring to the turtle's legs and this gives us the common name. Marylanders, especially, may wonder about **terrapin**. This name for turtles *doesn't* refer to the fact that they are also land dwellers, pinned to terra. No, this is an Americanization of an Algonquin Indian name for the animal. Today, we're trying to preserve certain varieties by requiring fish nets to have escape hatches. And, of course, a younger generation seems to revere a mutated, adolescent, martial-arts version of the creature . . . "Slow, but steady wins the race."

tuxedo At the verge of the gay '90's a hundred years ago, there was an exclusive country club in New York where style and elegance were the trademarks. It was there at Tuxedo Park that the monkey suit was first introduced. The strange **cummerbund** that sometimes accompanies the tux was brought to us through the Hindu people who took it from the Persians for whom it was a fancy band around the loins. "Waist band" or "loin cloth" is what the translation would be.

V **vaudeville** There are several notions as to the origin of this word for the once-popular form of entertainment of songs, comedy, and other stage antics that can now be found mainly in the casinos of Las Vegas and Atlantic City. It produced our legends of 20th-century comedy from George Burns to Bob Hope to Milton Berle, the Marx Brothers, and Abbot and Costello. Most likely, the name for the wide-ranging variety shows came from a valley in

France. In the 1400's, popular humorous songs were all the rage in the Vire Valley of Calvados, Normandy. These "chansons du Vau de Vire" or "songs of the valley of Vire" gave us our beginnings of musical comedy and the light theatrical entertainment that the general public would flock to see.

WHAT IN THE WORD?

SECTION THREE

Meanings of First Names

A **Aaron** This name is not as common as it once was and probably for good reason. The biblical Aaron gets a mixed review. This brother of Moses became the first priest of Israel and his name's meaning fits that rank: it's Hebrew for "he who is exalted." It seems that Moses wasn't really much like Charlton Heston. He was very shy and a poor speaker and let his brother do the talking for him. Though Aaron could speak well, apparently he was not very good at thinking for himself. Twice he was involved in serious rebellions. Once, when Moses had gone off to speak to God, Aaron was convinced by the people to make an idol, the golden calf (similar to Egyptian and Phoenician god figures), for them to worship and perform fertility rites for. Though Moses convinced God not to kill the Israelites for this sin, he himself commanded the Levites to grab their swords and destroy the rebels. In one afternoon there were three thousand men killed in the camp, certainly straightening out the idolaters. Later, Moses' sister **Miriam** convinced Aaron to turn against Moses because Moses had married an Ethiopian woman. Well, her name in Hebrew does mean "rebellion." For this little revolt Miriam was struck with leprosy for seven days. Aaron didn't get punished in either case. In the end, he and his tribe became the priesthood of Israel, and in a symbolic test, Aaron's rod (the staff representing his tribe), miraculously flowered and bore almonds to show God's favor. He died at the age of 123.

The modern Aaron I think of first was the poor Aaron Burr who tied with Thomas Jefferson in the 1800 presidential election. The New

Jerseyite was made Vice President thanks to his enemy, Alexander Hamilton, who convinced the House of Representatives to put Tom in the highest office. Hamilton even kept him from winning the governorship of New York four years later. Their conflict led to the duel that saw Hamilton killed. It was downhill for Burr from there as he was later tried for treason for plotting to colonize the Southwest to form a new country allied to Spain. Though he was found innocent, he didn't figure in politics again.

Abbot If your first or last name is Abbot, you can trace the source to the Aramaic, "Abba," which meant "father." With a capital "A" it was used for God and with a small "a" it was a title of respect. The abbots who head monasteries get their name from the same source. But no, music lovers, the Scandinavian group of the `70's, **Abba,** weren't alluding to the Biblical reference. The two men and two women got the name of their group from the initials of their first names. They might have been called Baba or Baab if things had turned out differently.

Abel The story of the first murder in the Bible made this name prominent. It comes from the Assyrian through the Hebrew and means "son." Sometimes names become tainted because of stories associated with them. For instance, who would name their child **Cain**? Even the Hebrew meaning, "creature," isn't very pleasant, but his role as the murderer of Abel makes the name one of wickedness. And we even call a scheming woman a jezebel after the Phoenician princess who became a queen of Israel when she married Ahab and was known for her wild and heathen ways. Ahab himself has a name that goes down the tubes when it is attached to the obsessive captain in *Moby Dick.* Though there are plenty of Matthews, Peters and Jameses running around, how many people do you know by the name of **Judas**? His name came from the son of Jacob and Leah, Judah, and meant in Hebrew "praised." The "iscariot" part of Judas' name refers to an anti-Roman group among the Israelites, the Sicarii, who hoped for a major rebellion against the Latin overlords.

Abigail This Hebrew name means "my father is joy," which is a nice commentary on parenthood. The main Biblical Abigail was the wife of David who saved her first husband, the fool Nabal, from being killed by David. Her wise words to the future king were remembered. Soon after, her husband died and David married her. He must have been in a marrying mood for at the same time he married Ahinoam. His first wife, Saul's daughter Michal, given to him as a gift for slaying Goliath, had been taken from him just as easily by her father who had exiled David. Now, in the early 1600's an abigail was a name for a lady's maid. It started with a play in 1616, *The Scornful Lady*, which had a serving maid character by that name.

The Abigail most familiar to me is Abigail Smith who married John Adams and wrote wonderful letters. The second First Lady lived seventy-four years, but her husband, John, outlived her by eight years and died at the age of ninety-one. Those of you named **Gail** or **Gayle** get your name from Abigail, but there is a Teutonic **Abby** which means "fair harbor."

Abner The alleged inventor of baseball, Civil War general Abner Doubleday, got his reputation for the American pastime from old friend A. G. Mills, who said Abner came up with the game in Cooperstown, N.Y., in 1839. Well, we'll give him credit though there are many doubts. Abner means "my father is light" in Hebrew and doesn't refer to a parent's dietary habits at all. The Biblical Abner was a warrior loyal to Saul until Saul's son accused him of sleeping with one of Saul's concubines. This made Abner mad, and he decided to ally with David, a final blow to the House of Saul.

Abraham At ninety-nine years of age this Hebrew patriarch was told by God to change his name. It had been Abram, meaning "high father," and now it would be "father of multitudes." God made a covenant with the "new" Abraham, and to seal the deal, so to speak, Abe and all males in the tribe would have to be circumcised, a bit of a painful showing of an outward sign of loyalty, making the future Israelites different from the Assyrians and Babylonians. From then on a male child of eight days of age and any conquered or purchased men would lose the foreskin to that covenant. Abraham lived seventy-six more years.

Abraham Lincoln is our most famous modern namesake.

Ada This was once a popular woman's name and has two sources of origin. Pet forms of names are the kind of shortening and changing about we do to get Dave from David or Bill from William. Ada was a pet form of **Adelaide**, **Adele** and **Adela**, all of which come from the Old High German, meaning "nobility" or "noble one." Another form of Ada comes from the Hebrew, **Adah**, meaning "ornament" or "decoration," applied to things of beauty. **Alice**, **Alison**, **Alysia**, **Alyson** and **Alicia** all trace their roots to the same Germanic beginnings of Adelaide. Names get pulled this way and that in their spellings as they go from one language to another . . . as confusing sometimes as Alice in her madcap wonderland.

Adam In Hebrew, this name simply means "man" and was derived from another word meaning "earth." After all, it was a dusty birth for the first man. After his tragic experience with his first two sons, he had no heir until, at the age of 130, he "begat" **Seth**, which in Hebrew means "appointed." Adam had more children after that, but they go unnamed. At the overripe age of 930 he passed away. Old Seth lived only 912 years.

The economist Adam Smith comes to mind when thinking of modern Adams.

Adolf The Old High German for "noble wolf" is what this name means. It was a very popular first name until the late '40's. After the defeat of Adolf Hitler and the revelation of the atrocities committed in his name, it wasn't a name with much value attached. Only part of the original meaning of the name seemed to fit anymore, and even that did a disservice to the poor mammal.

Adrian This was a Roman family name whose greatest namesake was the Emperor Adrian or Hadrian, the powerful wall-builder and patron of the arts. "Black earth" is the Latin meaning and gives the Adriatic Sea its name also. Now, **Adrienne**, the feminine name, comes from the Germanic for "bold."

Agatha This name goes back to the Greek word for "good." Agatha Christie was certainly good at detective fiction. With over eighty books and plays to her credit, Dame Christie will be the Agatha thought of most in this century.

Agnes The Greek word for "chaste" or "holy" gives us this feminine name. The play and movie *Agnes of God* has brought it back into the public eye, though actress Agnes Moorhead might have popped in your mind, too. Some will argue that Agnes comes from "Agnus Dei" which was a lamb symbolizing Christ.

Alan There are actually two Alans: the one with one "l" and the one with two. Now, there is a bit of dispute as to their difference in origin. Alan goes back to a Celtic root meaning "harmony." Some say Allen has a Latin beginning, meaning "cheerful." Some spell the name with an "e" in the second "a" spot. Not too harmonious a description . . .

Lots of Al(l)ans come to mind: Actors Ladd and Hale, *Candid*

Camera's Alan Funt, and Robin Hood's Alan-a-dale. **Alanna**, by the way, is the feminine form of the Celtic original.

Albert

This Germanic name basically means "noble and bright." The feminine Alberta is a variation, as is **Albertine**. When the German Prince Albert married his first cousin, Victoria, who was also half-German, he was continuing the link between his land and the throne of England. English kings had had a large German connection since the early 1700's when the area of Hanover, now part of Germany, became linked by marriage to the throne. A series of George's ruled. Victoria was the daughter of the fourth son of George III, the king during the American Revolution who later went mad. At first, Albert wasn't popular among the people who were a little fed up with all these Germans in their royal line. But, because of his devotion to his wife and his diplomatic prowess, he won them over. The prince helped to keep a moderate approach when, during the Civil War, a couple of Confederate ambassadors were forcibly removed from a British ship by a Union captain. The initial British reaction was to declare war on the U.S. and recognize the Confederacy, but Albert, along with Secretary of State Seward, helped avoid this response. Thus, the husband of the granddaughter of the king most responsible for the birth of the United States helped to keep that union from dissolving.

Alexander

The young man who ruled the world for a short time is the most famous of all Alexanders and so is called "the Great." This Greek name means "defender of men," and the Macedonian conqueror both defended *and* fought with them during his brief thirty-three years. He founded the city in Egypt named after him, **Alexandria** . . . but there is no connection to the brandy Alexander. There were plenty of other popes, czars, and kings named Alexander, but I think of one who brought us a device even more powerful than these rulers: Alexander Graham Bell. **Alexis** is a shortened version of the name.

Alfred

The Old English original that gives us Alfred meant "elf counsel." Did that mean he was a counselor to elves or one who was counseled by them? I don't know. The British king known as Alfred the Great made the name very popular as he conquered the Danes and brought peace to oft-invaded England. Did you think of Alfred, Batman's butler, or Alfred, Lord Tennyson, the poet? What's it all about, Alfie?

Alma

This Latin feminine name means "nourishing" or "cherishing." Yes, we get our "Alma Mater" from the same root. The school anthems we sing refer to the institutions themselves as "nourishing mothers." In an age of avoidance of feminist language perhaps we should change this to "Alma Persona."

Alphonse This is a Germanic name meaning "eager for battle," though today it doesn't seem appropriate for a fighter. The great lines of kings of Portugal and Spain take the version more attuned to their languages: Alfonso. **Alonso** is another variation.

Alvin Most of our awareness of this name comes from hearing it shouted by Dave to the mischievous chipmunk. The name goes back to Germanic root meaning "noble friend." Well, Alvin, Simon and Theodore *are* friendly, though it's hard to see nobility in their pranks.

Amanda A pretty name that has brought us a wealth of "**Mandys**," this name goes back to a Latin root, meaning "worthy of love," though some think it is related to the French word for almond. Another name that comes from the same basic Latin beginning is **Amy**, meaning "beloved" and can also be seen as **Aimée**. **Amigo**, Spanish for "friend," has that same basis as those other amicable, amiable, amorous words revolving around love and friendship.

Andrew A strong, masculine name, Andrew goes back to the Greek and means "manly." In the Bible he was one of the Apostles, the brother of Simon Peter and the patron saint of both Scotland and Russia. The nickname form, "**Andy**," has less punch, but certainly fits the more comic orientation of a man like Andy Griffith or the fictional Andy Hardy. **André** is the French version and **Andrea** is the feminine form.

Angela Obviously, the Greek word for messenger, which gives us "angel," is at the root of this feminine name worn prominently by those like actresses Angela Lansbury or Angelica Houston. The male version is seen as **Angelo** or just plain **Angel**.

Ann, Anita, Annette: See **Hannah**

Anthony There are a lot of Tonys and Anthonys out there, which makes sense since the name means "flourishing" in Latin. It was the family name of a large Roman clan. The famous Antony who romanced Cleopatra was one of this ancient family's prominent members, spelling it in its original form. Unfortunately, he didn't flourish as his love for the Egyptian queen led to his eventual defeat by Octavius (who became Augustus) and his suicide. Now, Saint Anthony also lived in Egypt but was an opposite to Marc, living alone as a hermit until he attracted a crowd of others who wanted to lead the simple life with him, thus beginning the first monastery. Eventually, he had to get away from the crowd and go off into the desert . . . . Probably not the kind of character you'd see Tony Curtis play.

Archibald The Old High German means "bold and true" or could be translated as one who is proper *and* bold. The comic book character, **Archie**, was bold in his day and probably seems pretty proper next to mutated reptiles on the half shell. Kowabunga, dude.

Arnold There are fewer Arnolds today than in the past, but the most prominent definitely fits the Germanic origin: "strength of an eagle." I think Mr. Schwarzenegger qualifies.

Arthur This name gets a lot of good press from the legendary British king of the sixth century and probably comes from the Celtic, meaning "bear." Another opinion is that it means "eagle of Thor." That latter translation might sound nicer to the light-footed Arthur Murray or the ukelele-strumming Arthur Godfrey. Arthur Conan Doyle of Sherlock Holmes fame and playwright Arthur Miller might like "Bear" better. It definitely fits **Art** Carney.

Augustus We know most of the males of this name as **Gus**, except the great Pulitzer Prize-winning playwright, August Wilson, who has a shortened version pronounced like the month. The name means "imperial" or "magnificent" and goes back to the Latin of Roman times. I don't think anyone called the early Christian church father, Augustine, St. Gus. Several Polish kings went by the full name. **Austin** is a shortened version, and **Augusta** is worn by women. Both are seen as names for cities (see Section Four).

Let's wrap up the A's with a few of the more obscure, just to make sure you're not left out: **Alastair** means "unforgetting" in Greek, and we won't forget the *Masterpiece Theater* host, Alastair Cook. **Aldo** is Germanic, meaning "experienced," which actor Aldo Ray certainly became as far as the movies go. **Almira** is of Latin birth, meaning "at whom we wonder." **Althea** is another name of Greek origin and means "truth." **Alton** is Germanic and means "old village." **Ambrose** goes back to the Greek, meaning "immortal," from which we get that food of the gods, **ambrosia**. **Anabelle** comes from a Latin beginning, referring to beauty. **Anatole** is Greek for "sunrise." **Angus** has Celtic beginnings and translates as "of great virtue," but is primarily used for a county in Scotland and a type of cattle. **Ardel** and its variants have the hard-working Latin origin, "industrious." Those named **Arleen** or something like that should see **Eileen**. **Ashley**, once considered a man's moniker, but now very popular among females, has Germanic roots and refers to a grove of Ash trees. Since I already spoke of the saint in another section (see **tawdry**), I didn't make a special section for **Audrey**, which in its earliest Germanic form meant "noble helper." I think the great actress and helper of the poor, Audrey Hepburn, would have understood. **Averils** out there should be happy to know their name has the Teutonic root for "courageous." **Avis**, whether a woman's name or a rent-a-car company, has Latin beginnings, applying to birds, as in aviation. **Axel** is not seen much anymore but has a Germanic source and means "heaven reward." In these wrap-up sections I'm sure I'll leave out a friend or relative, but I'll try to stay with the most used in our language.

B **Barbara** The Greek beginnings of this word has the meaning, "little stranger," and from that same root we get **barbarian** which was applied by the Greeks to anyone foreign. Sorry about that, girls. Renaissance woman Streisand spells hers **Barbra**. **Babette** is a pet form of the original. I don't think that Mr. Bush uses such a nickname for his Barbara. Ms. Hershey and Ms. Stanwyck also come to mind when thinking of famous Barbaras.

Barnard We also see this name as **Bernard**, and it goes back to Germanic roots and means "bold bear." The visions of the most famous female namesake, Saint **Bernadette**, are responsible for the shrine to the Virgin Mary at Lourdes, France. Her full name was Marie Bernarde Soubirous. The peasant girl who lived her thirty-nine years in the mid-to-late 1800's wasn't made a saint until 1933. Now, Saint Bernard of Clairvaux lived almost 800 years earlier. This mystic condemned the logic mixed with Christianity of Peter Abelard, the tragic Parisian who set the stage for Aquinas. Saint Bernard was a very influential figure and sparked the Second Crusade in 1147, which ended in dismal failure. The name of the dog goes back to a hospice in the Swiss Alps run by brothers of St. Bernard who used the dogs to patrol the snowy altitudes in the area.

Barry The Irish give us this popular name which probably means "good shot." Now, the famous mistress of Louis XV of France who literally lost her head during the French Revolution probably got her honorary title from Bareges, France. Comtesse du Barry was actually an illegitimate child who found favor in the court by offering her favors.

Bartholomew Simon Peter was not the only disciple with two names in the Bible. Saint Bartholomew is also sometimes called Nathaneal. Maybe he liked that second name better. Bartholomew means "born of furrows" in Hebrew and seems to refer to the farming life, while **Nathanael** or **Nathaniel** means "God has given" in that same language. Bartholomew only gets brief mention in Matthew, Mark, Luke, and Acts, but as Nathanael he reveals a bit more personality in his initial slight cynicism about the Messiah before he actually meets him. There are definitely more famous Nathanaels than Bartholomews, such as Revolutionary War General Nathanael Greene. **Nathan** was originally a separate Hebrew name, meaning "he gave," and a Revolutionary war hero like Nathan Hale, who had but one life to give, takes his name from the Old Testament prophet who scorned David for his adultery with Bathsheba, but later helped her get her son, Solomon, lined up to succeed to the throne.

Basil Both the spice and the first name go back to a Greek root meaning "king." **Basilica** also gets its origins from this base. Besides Saint Basil who was a Greek Christian leader in the church's early days, there were several Byzantine emperors named Basil. I always liked Basil Rathbone who could be heroic as Sherlock Holmes or villainous as he fought Errol Flynn's Robin Hood, acting the part of the Sheriff of Nottingham.

Beatrice Danté's love for a Florentine woman of this name led to the composition of *The Divine Comedy*, one of the greatest of Italian poems. When she died, twenty-five-year-old Danté devoted himself to philosophy and religion and, years later, wrote of the journey through the afterlife in which Beatrice leads him to heaven. The Latin root for "blessed" gives us this name as well as other words for blessings like "**beatitudes**." Ah, if Aunt **Bea** could only have been such an inspiration for the likes of Barney Fife and Opie. **Benedict** is a male name based on the same root. In Shakespeare's day a benedict was a longtime bachelor who decides to get married, based on a character in *Much Ado About Nothing*. It's doubtful if Saint Benedict ever thought of marrying, though the liqueur made by the monks of his order has probably been used to toast a few unions. Americans don't offer much of a benediction to famous traitor Benedict Arnold who made the first name unpopular in the U.S.

Benjamin The Biblical Benjamin's rather tragic birth led to the founding of the twelfth tribe of Israel and to the death of Jacob's favorite wife. Rachel died as she bore this second and, later, favorite son for Israel, who reminded his father of his beloved wife. Just as she was dying, she wanted to name the boy Benoni, which meant "child of my sorrow," but Jacob changed the name to "child of my right hand." The name was a sign of good fortune, as most right hand men seem to have. However, much later, Benjamin didn't seem so lucky when his brothers had to carry him to Egypt to serve as a hostage in the rather harsh trick that Joseph played on those other ten siblings who had tried to get rid of him many years before. Just plain **Ben** means "son" in Hebrew, if you haven't guessed. Benjamin Franklin, now sitting on the hundred dollar bill, is one of America's most famous Bens. Benjamin Disraeli converted to Christianity at the age of thirteen and eventually led England as Prime Minister in its glory years in the 1870's. There is a Ben Hur mentioned in the Bible, but he is an officer of Solomon, not the imaginary figure of movie fame.

Bernice The Greek for "bringer of victory" was originally the name of an Egyptian city founded by Ptolemy II, the son of one of Alexander the Great's mightiest generals, who claimed Egypt after his commander's death. Berenice is in ruins now, but was once part of the glory of Greece in Egypt.

Bertha Those of you named Bertha, **Berta** or **Bertina** get your appellation from the Old High German, meaning "the bright one." A certain type of lace collar called a bertha takes its name from Queen Bertha who was the mother of the great French ruler, Charlemagne.

Bertrand All of you **Burts** out there could find your name's origin in this French form of Bertram which goes back to a Germanic word for "bright raven." Philosopher Bertrand Russell comes to mind. You could get the shortened version from **Berthold**, another Germanic name meaning "bright and bold." Playwright Berthold Brecht was both of those. Or your name could come from **Burton** which is a changed-about form of Breton which came from Briton, an inhabitant of Britain. **Bret** also takes his name from the same acknowledgement.

Beverly Once both a man's and woman's name, it is primarily feminine today, seen on the likes of opera great Beverly Sills. The Middle English original means "beaver meadow." Beverly Hills is not exactly *that*, but you will see fans gnawing through obstructions to see their favorite stars there.

Brenda This popular name might have come through the Old Norse to a Shetland dialect and originally mean "flaming sword." The males out there named **Brendan** have a version of that root. Singer Brenda Lee was a popular representative of the name.

Brian The Celtic for "strong" is the meaning of the first name worn by such vigorous figures as Canadian Brian Mulrooney or actor Brian Keith. Some spell the name **Bryan** or **Brien**. The first unifier of Ireland, Brian Boru, lived a long life but was murdered soon after putting together the first national state in 1014. Divisions continue on the Emerald Isle.

Bridget And Old Irish fire goddess is at the root of this name. Later, one of the patron saints of Ireland was Saint Bridget who led the Irish Roman Catholics in the 500's. There was actually another Saint Bridget, a Swedish Catholic who founded the Brigittine order of nuns. Ms. Bardot and Ms. Fonda will probably never be named saints, but they both carry on the name with its original fire. **Biddy** is a variation of Bridget that referred to the fire goddess and was a slang term for fiery women (See Section One).

Bruce The Celtic for "ruler" was made most famous by Robert the Bruce who fought two English kings to earn the right to be named the king of Scotland in 1328. One of our "rulers" in the music world is the "Boss," Bruce Springsteen. Bruce Jenner will always hold a special place to fans of the Olympics.

Not to shirk some of the less-used "B" names, here are a few more: **Barnaby** or **Barnabas** has Hebrew origins and means "son of consolation." It wasn't a consolation prize when the apostle Barnabas sold his property and gave the money to the other apostles. **Beauford** comes from the French for "fine ford." **Beauregard** is another French name for "fair view." **Belinda** goes back to the Latin for "graceful." **Belle** has a French birth and is the feminine for "beautiful," as **Beau** was a popular masculine name for "handsome." **Bentley** has Germanic roots translating as "winding meadow." **Beulah** has Hebrew beginnings and means "married," referring to the promise in Isiah of a holy nation and sung about in Gospel songs as Beulah-land. **Blake** is a Germanic name whose root means "dark" and is related to **Bruno** and **Brenna**, which mean the same thing. **Blanche**, on the other hand, means "white" in its original Latin form, as does **Bianca** which came from the Italian. **Bonnie** is of Latin beginnings, meaning "little good one" . . . not too applicable to Clyde's outlaw partner. **Boris** is obviously Russian and means "fight." All of you **Brad**s out there could go back to the Germanic root that gives us **Bradley** ("broad meadow"), **Bradshaw** ("broad forest") or **Bradstreet** ("broad way"). **Brigham**, the most famous of whom was Mr. Young, goes back to a Germanic phrase: "town by the bridge." **Brock** has the animal, the badger, to thank for his Germanic name. **Broderick** has the unflattering meaning of "plague of the king" in its Germanic beginnings, while **Brooks** has an easily understood meaning "little stream." You Wangerians may want to know that **Brunhilda** has a Germanic meaning: "brown maid of battle." **Bud** and **Bubba** are childhood forms of "brother." **Buck** originates as a variant of Huck, Hank, or Henry. And **Burgess**, as in the name of actor Meredith, has a Germanic root meaning "Freeman."

C **Caleb** The only members of the original Hebrew desert wanderers to make it to the Promised Land were Caleb and Joshua. I'll talk about Josh later. In Hebrew, Caleb means "faithful like a dog" and the Biblical Caleb was certainly that. When Moses sent spies to check out the land of milk and honey, Caleb was one of the twelve. He and Joshua were the only two who gave good reports. The others whined about the strong, walled cities and the giants who lived among the people there. Caleb felt that if God had promised the land to the Israelites, it shouldn't be any problem to go in Hebron and the lands around it. After Joshua's death Caleb took over as leader. At that time he was eighty-five years old and said he felt as strong as when he was forty.

Calvin The Latin word for "bald" gives us this first name, and though a man like President Calvin Coolidge did get pretty thin on top, it is not a prerequisite of the name. Mt. Calvary gets its name from the same root, but it was aimed more at the smooth skull shape than the lack of hair.

Camille This first name and its variant, **Camilla**, have their birth in Roman religious rites. In those days, a noble youth who assisted in the temple was called a "camillus." The very best of these helpers were virgin girls of pure character, and the feminine version of the name became popular among all classes of people.

Candace The Latin for "glowing" is appropriate for an actress like **Candice** Bergen, whose name has a spelling variation. She's definitely had a bright career. The root also gives us **candid** which refers to whiteness. In Roman days this translated as truth and purity.

Carl The Germanic term for a man gives us this first name and was usually applied to a freeman, not one subservient to another. There have been many manly Carls from baseball great Yastremski to political leader Carl Vinson. The feminine **Carla** is seen quite a bit, though the girls of this name may not feel it complimentary to refer to them as "manly." Other languages took a fancy to the name and **Carlos** and **Carlotta** are two results. The Medieval Latin got hold of the German original and out came **Charles** and **Caroline** and the variants: **Chuck, Charlotte, Carol, Carrie, Carrol, Karl** (which is much closer to the Germanic original), and **Charlene**. The Frankish king, Charles the Great, who became Holy Roman emperor Charlemagne in 800 A.D., made the name a popular one for kings of France, England, Spain, Hungary and Sweden, to name a few of the countries with Charleses as rulers. He did much to band the Holy Roman Empire into a power, but his legends outweigh his achievements. Our modern Prince Charles is creating his own history. Now, **Cary** isn't related, but probably goes back to the Greek for "nut" or "kernel." Though actor Cary Grant played some crazy roles, not many would think of him as nutty.

Casey When Casey struck out in Mudville it didn't diminish the significance the name would have in baseball. Charles Dillon Stengel took the nickname and put it in the record books as he managed the New York Yankees to seven world championships in twelve seasons. His sense of humor helped him in the early days of the Mets of the same city during 1962-65. The name has a Celtic origin and means "brave."

Cassandra Some of you **Sandras** and **Sandys** may take your shortened name from this one. Others get theirs from Alexandra. The original Trojan Cassandra was a daughter of King Priam. She refused the love of Apollo even though he had given her the gift of prophesy. He couldn't take back the present, but he added an extra ramification: no one would believe her. So she knew the Greeks would overrun her city, but could convince no one that inside that wooden horse was destruction. When the Greeks yanked her from the temple of Athena in Troy, she knew she was headed for her death in Greece. The meaning of the name in that language is "winning love."

Catherine, Cathy, etc.: see **Katherine**

Cecil The Roman culture was built upon a league of families that later became the ruling clans of the Empire. The family of Caecilus was one of those. Their name in Latin meant "blind" and came from a root which meant "one-eyed." I don't know the story behind the naming of the family, but it doesn't seem to have any relationship to the Cyclops, the race of one-eyed giants who lived on Sicily. Certainly, a movie director such as Cecil B. DeMille wasn't blind to the ways of giving an audience a good story. I remember watching the cartoon characters, Beanie and Cecil (who was a dragon). The feminine versions of the name range from **Cecilia** to **Cicely** to **Celia** and even **Cely**.

Christopher: The touching story of the saintly man who carries the child across the river and almost can't make it because the child seems extremlely heavy gives us the legend of St. Christopher whose name in Greek means "bearer of Christ." The story goes on to explain that the child turned out to be Jesus who was carrying the world in his hands. The piggybacking saint was probably a martyr of the third century. He became the patron saint of travelers because of the tale, and his likeness appeared on medals worn by the faithful who looked for his protection across the sometimes raging rivers of life. The Catholic Church cast great doubts on this story's authenticity, and St. Chris and his feast day were dropped in 1969. The story of sacrifice and generosity still has its value. Other names that gave homage to Christ are **Christian** ("follower of Christ"), **Christina** and **Christine** ("little followers of Christ"), **Christy** (shortened from Christine), and **Christiana** (which was also the former name of Oslo, Norway). And I can't leave out **Kristin**.

Clara The Latin meaning of this name can be interpreted as "bright" or "beautiful." We would all probably agree that Clara Barton was bright, but I'm not sure if this founder of the Red Cross was beautiful. The French version of the name, **Claire**, is seen often, as in Claire Bloom. **Clare** has been used as both a masculine and feminine name, as in St. Clare who founded an order called the Poor Clares with the help of St. Francis of Assisi in the 1200's. **Clarence** has its roots here and in the dukedom of Clarence, which gives its name to a four-wheeled, closed carriage. The Duke of Clarence, who later became William IV of England, made these carriages popular in the early 1800's.

Claude This first name also has its roots in the family names of Rome, the ancient clan of **Claudius**. Probably the most famous Claudius was Tiberius Claudius Drusus Nero Germanicus who was known as Claudius I and ruled rather well for about thirteen years starting in 41 A.D. His physical condition fit his name which in Latin means "lame." He had a type of paralysis that affected all of his physical aspects. Movie star Claude Raines comes to mind when I think of modern wearers of the name, as does **Claudette** Colbert. French painter Claude Lorrain also helped give the name popularity. **Claudia** and **Claudine** are other feminine versions of the name.

Clyde This name means "strong" in its Greek origins and seems to fit the powerful horses, the Clydesdales. Actually, they get their name from a Scottish valley where the Clyde River flows into the Firth of Clyde.

Constance Many of you **Connies** derive your name from this Latin-born handle, meaning "steadfast." Yes, we get **constant** and other words on **constancy** from the same root. Other variations of the name include the masculine version, **Constantine**, worn most famously by the emperor, Constantine I, who adopted Christianity and changed the face of the Roman Empire. Connie Francis has had her ups and downs but made the shortened version of the name popular in the 50's.

Cynthia On the island of Delos in Greece the goddess of the moon was born on Mount Cynthus. This birthplace gave this maiden-goddess one of her names. She was also called **Artemis** and was the virgin ruler of the hunt. In fact, she had many names: **Phoebe** (Greek for "shining"), **Selene** (from the same language, meaning "bright"), **Luna** (the Roman name for the moon), and **Diana** (see **Diane**). The deer and the cypress are sacred to her. She was also associated with the witch-goddess Hecate. But **Cindys** out there shouldn't worry about the connection. It came much later.

There are a lot of seldon-used "C" names to mention. I wondered where a man like **Cameron** Mitchell got his first name. It's Celtic for "crooked nose." **Carleton** isn't related to Carl, but means "country town" in its Germanic roots. **Carmen** is a very operatic feminine name which traces itself to the Latin for "charming one." **Carmine**, on the other hand, can either come from the Hebrew "vineyard" or from the color name for a type of red. **Casper**, as in the Friendly Ghost, goes back to a Persian word for horseman. Another spelling is like that of **Caspar** Wineberger, former Secretary of Defense. **Cedric** has a martial Germanic meaning: "general." **Celeste** has the much more peaceful Latin root for "heavenly" as its translation, as does **Celestine**. **Chadwick** gives us **Chad** and is of Germanic origin, meaning "village haven." **Chloris**, whose most famous representative is Ms. Leachman, comes from the Greek green goddess of flowers. **Chlorophyll** has a similar ancestor. **Clarice** and **Clarissa** have a Latin birth and mean "famous." **Clark** referred to clerks who, in their Germanic concept, were scholars. Clark Kent might have been the perfect name to fit that image as the disguise for Superman. **Clifford** is a fairly popular name deriving from a Germanic land name: "ford at the cliff." **Clinton** has a similar landmark origin: "hill town." **Clint** Eastwood might not find that worth a fistfull of dollars . . . or it might make his day. **Clorinda** is Persian for "famous." **Colin** gets his name from the Greek for "triumph." **Conrad** has a Germanic birthplace and means "wise counsel." **Consuela** also has a similar meaning, but is Latin. Fans of the late Mr. Twitty of country music fame might like to know that **Conway** is Celtic for "wise." **Cora** is a Greek name, meaning "maiden," but **Corey** is Germanic for "chosen." **Cornelius** and the feminine version, **Cornelia**, mean "crowned" in Latin. Remember **Cosmo** Topper of the movie and TV stories of ghosts and comedy? His name is Greek for "orderly." Hmmm. **Craig** is a popular name that goes back to a Celtic word for a rocky crag. **Crystal** has a logical Greek meaning: "clear." **Cyrus** is a Persian name for the sun. Most recently, Cyrus Vance was in the "sun" of governmental duty.

D | **Dale** From Dale Evans to Dale Robertson, both men and women have been called by this name which goes back to the Old English word for a valley. **Delle**, **Del**, and **Della** (as in Ms. Reese) are other variations. Just so, the Scots used their old Gaelic word, **Glenn**, as a name that referred to people and valleys. So, the **Glens**; **Glynesses**, **Glennas** and **Glynns** are all of this origin. In such rocky country a valley was where life was found, where food could be grown and where protection from the torments of nature could be had. Glen Campbell, Glen Miller and Glyniss Johns are familiar representatives of the name. Scotch drinkers will know of the valleys of Glenlivet and Glenfidditch.

Daniel The Biblical Daniel actually had two names. When he and three of his associates were taken as Jewish hostages to Babylon by King Nebuchadnezzar, they were given pagan names by their tutors who wanted them to learn the ways of their captive country. Daniel means "God's judge" or "God's Prince" in Hebrew, and the name he was given was Belteshazzar or "prince of Bel" (a pagan deity) in Chaldean. Names were very important to people of that day, representing the person by their meaning. Daniel went by his Hebrew name during his captivity, but most remember his three friends who survived the king's furnace as proof of their God's power, by their pagan names: Shadrach, Meshach and Abednego. Daniel, who is most remembered for surviving a night with the lions, has a distant ancestor, plain **Dan** whose name means "judging," given to him by Rachel because, though she was barren, she gave her handmaiden to Jacob and that woman bore him a son, answering Rachel's prayers. Daniel Webster is a well-known American Dan. **Danielle** Steele has given the feminine version of the name some notoriety.

Daryl Larry, Daryl and Daryl of TV's "Newhart" may have thrown a bit of negative connotation on this name which has a Germanic birth. It means "dear little one" and is seen also in the feminine **Darlene**, **Darline** and also Daryl (as in actress; Ms. Hannah). Racing's Daryl Waltrip brings more respectability to the name than "Daryl and his other brother, Daryl."

David Here's a chance for me to look at my first name. The Hebrew meaning is "beloved," and the most famous David is obviously the king whose many exploits made him legendary as a man who was not only wise, but also foolish and very human. His mistakes may not be as well known as his triumphs, but his ability to own up to his errors led his line to be the ancestors of Jesus. From musician to warrior to lover to king, the story of David is one of drama, tragedy and joy. He lived seventy years, forty of them as king. Other famous Davids include Mr. Niven, David BenGurion, Israel's first Prime Minister, and good old Davey Crockett.

Dean A fairly popular name in the fifties, Dean goes back to the Greek for "ten." The original term was one of authority in church or academic settings. A priest who was appointed to oversee a number of parishes or an officer of a college set over a group of departments was and is a familiar use of the name. Dean Stockwell and Dean Martin may not strike you as priestly or ivory-tower bound, but they are good examples of the name that spring to mind. Girls will find **Deana** and **Deanie** as feminine versions.

Deborah The Biblical Deborah was a prophetess of Israel who had to scold one of its rulers into battle. By so doing, this judge of the people of the Promised Land brought them a great success on the battlefield. Her name is Hebrew for "bee" and is related to industriousness. One of my favorite Deborahs is actress Kerr. **Debbie** is a shortened form as in Ms. Boone or the very busy bee, Ms. Reynolds.

Denise Drinking wine can have its good effects, making you cheerful and light and medicinally helping the heart, if used in moderation. It can also have its bad effects when used to excess. So, too, the Greek god of wine, Dionysus, was both the happy, inspiring god who led men and women to write plays, songs and poetry, and the mad god who led some down paths of drunkenness and insanity. Denise comes from the Greek: "servant of Dionysus." **Dennis**, **Denis**, **Dion**, and **Dionne** are a few of the variations. The god of revelry has had his name attached to the patron saint of wine country, Saint Denis of France; actors like Dennis Morgan and Dennis Quiad; and even cartoon characters like Dennis the Menace. Do they serve wine at **Denny**'s?

Diane This name, along with **Diana**, was mentioned earlier as a name for the goddess of the moon and basically came from a Greek root meaning "to shine." A famous Diane of the past was Diane de Poitiers who was mistress to King Henry II of France in the mid-1500's while being friends with his wife, Catherine De Medici. Our modern namesakes of this ancient goddess of forests, animals and women in childbirth include Diana Rigg, Diane Keaton, and, of course, Princess Di.

Dinah I first heard this name in a song that referred to a woman who seemed to have someone in the kitchen with her who liked to play a banjo. Actually, the name goes back to Biblical times and is related to the same root that gives us **Dan**. Dinah was the seventh child of Jacob and Leah, the daughter of Laban whom he was tricked into marrying before Rachel. Dinah's name means "judgement." She was later raped by a foreign prince who then fell in love with her and wanted to marry her. Jacob made a bargain that if all the men of this prince's city were circumcised, he would agree to the marriage. But two of Jacob's hot-tempered sons, Simeon and Levi, got their swords and killed all the men of the town. It seems the prince's men weren't in any condition to fight after the recent operations that they had undergone. I'm sure most of you out there with a little age thought of vivacious Dinah Shore when this name came up.

Dolores This feminine name gets its meaning from a Latin root for pain or sorrow. The seven sorrows of the Virgin Mary are called "the dolores" and gave the name a strong religious underpinning. Now, Dolores Del Rio didn't cause male eyes much sorrow.

Donald Most recently, Mr. Trump has given this name wide public use, even being called "the Donald." The name has its origins in the Gaelic, meaning "mighty in the world" . . . Fitting for the Trumpster, but not necessarily for the duck of the same name. Many whose nickname is Don, like Drysdale or Ameche, may take their name from a shortened version of Donald, but others may get theirs from the Spanish or Italian title, meaning "sir" or "lord." Don Juan or Don Corleone (of "Godfather" fame) are examples of this Don which also gives us **Donna**, as in Ms. Reed. Donna comes from the Italian for "lady" and is also seen in **Madonna**, meaning "my lady," something Ms. Ciccone doesn't get accused of too often in her "material girl" world of glitter, dance, truth or dare. Infamous Don Juan seduced the ruler of Seville's daughter, killed the man in a duel, and then was dragged to Hell when the statue of that commander came to life at a party where it had been brought in mockery by the notorious libertine. Don Knotts would have had him arrested.

Doris When the Dorians invaded Greece about a thousand years before Christ, they kept their language and culture separate from the other Greeks. This is where some of you named Doris got your name. Others might trace their name to the sea nymph, Doris, who was the daughter of Ocean and wife of the Old Man of the Sea, Nereus. Before she married this gentle god of the Mediterranean she vied with her sister, Galatea, for the hand of Polyphemus, the giant cyclops. Doris Day stands out as one of the most well known bearers of the name.

Dorothy When the *Wizard of Oz* made this name a household word, Dorothy became a very popular girl's designation. It goes way back to the Greek, meaning "gift of god." **Dolly** is a pet form of the name. Come to think of it, Ms. Parton has several outstanding gifts . . . as a creative songwriter and singer. The word we mainly now use for the child's toy, **doll**, also comes from a pet form of Dorothy. **Dorothea** and **Dora** are other versions of the name. From Dolly Madison, the outstanding First Lady of James, to Dorothy Parker, writer and wit, there are many who have used this name or a variation of it.

Douglas This Gaelic name means "dark" or "grey" and is also the name of the capital of the Isle of Man. That's where its use as a last name gained prominence. Douglas MacArthur had his dark days as he fought in World Wars I and II, the Korean War, and with President Truman. He also ran for president himself two times. **Dougs** of the world might cringe at the antics of the fictional Bob and Doug McKenzie.

There are other "D" names that you'll find here and there like **Damon** whose Roman origins tell the tale of the friendship between him and Pythias that was so strong Damon allowed himself to be held hostage for his condemned friend and by this won their freedom. **Daphne** gets her name from the Greek for "laurel," the plant of victory which the nymph who was running from the amorous advances of Apollo decided to turn into. **Dawn** takes her sunny name from the obvious promise of a new day, going back to Germanic roots. **Deirdre**, seen in actress Hall, is an Old Irish name, meaning "one who rages." A famous Irish princess of this name killed herself when her husband was murdered. **Derrick** has Germanic origins, meaning "ruler." **Delmar** has a Latin root, meaning "of the sea." I think of the Beatles' song about **Desmond** and Molly Jones when I hear this man's name meaning "potent in the world" in Latin – Obla-di, Obla-da. **Dexter** means "right-handed" or "clever," related to dexterity which deals with being good with the hands. **Doyles** out there have Celtic roots in their name which means "dark stranger." **Dudley** is also of Celtic origins and translates as "fair field," with actor Moore being one of our best known. **Duncan** is Celtic for "dark haired," something you wouldn't want to see in your cake mix. **Dwight** was made famous by President Eisenhower and has a Germanic meaning: "wisefellow." I liked **Ike**.

E | **Earl** The British ranking system for royalty can seem fairly complicated. An earl is above a viscount, but below a marquis. A viscount is above a baron which is lowest on the totem pole. The marquis is right under a duke which is the highest of the nobility. In other European countries an earl would equal a count. The Old English roots of this name refer to a warrior or chief. Former baseball manager Earl Weaver was certainly a warrior of the diamond, and Earl Warren was definitely a chief – Supreme Court Justice, that is. But what rank was the Duke of Earl?

Ebenezer As I remarked before, sometimes a name gets a bad reputation and falls out of use. When Charles Dickens gave Scrooge the first name Ebenezer, he forever associated it with the skinflint. The appelation comes from the Hebrew and was the name given to a commemorative stone that the prophet Samuel set down to mark his thanks for God's help in a victory of the Israelites over the Phillistines. It means "stone of help."

Edward The early tribes of England constantly had to guard their homes from invaders, whether they were vikings, Danes, Scots, Picts, or Norman French. Names grew up dealing with the safekeeping of the clan's goods. The Old English name, Edward, means "one who guards the family possessions." **Edmund** is similar to this, meaning "protector of the family goods." **Edgar** is more war-like and speaks of "a spear for the family possessions." **Edith**, though feminine, still keeps on the same path with its meaning, "one who will fight for the family possessions." **Edwin** and **Edwina** are a bit less violent, meaning "friend of the family possessions." Many Edwards were kings or princes in England, from the "Black Prince" of the 1300's to Edward VIII who left the throne in 1936 to marry non-royalty, American Wallis Warfield Simpson, and become the Duke of Windsor. From Edward R. Murrow (journalist) to Edward Arlington Robinson (poet), the name has been a popular one. Some of you **Eds** and **Eddies** might take your name from the other "Ed-" names. Edgar Bergen, the great ventriloquist and father of Candice Bergen, could have been called "Ed." I doubt the great British philosopher and politician (they once were compatible) Edmund Burke had a "Hey, Ed!" shouted to him by Samuel Johnson. If the English had listened to him, America might still be under British rule. Now, those of you wondering about **Edna** should know that it has no relationship to those Old English names. It actually comes from the Bible from the name Adna, which in Hebrew means "delight," like the poetry of Edna St. Vincent Milay.

Elaine, Eileen, Eleanor, Ellen: See **Helen**.

Elizabeth One of the more famous of Biblical names, the story of Elisabeth, the mother of John the Baptist, is found in the first chapter of Luke. When the angel Gabriel told her husband that the old, childless couple would have a son, he didn't believe it and for that was struck dumb until after the birth. "God is my oath" is the Hebrew meaning of the name and it's derived from a root meaning "seven" because the Jews swore oaths on the sacred number seven. Many rulers have been named Elizabeth. There was an empress of Austria who was assasinated at the age of sixty-one in 1898. A czarina of

Russia held the name and ruled her country in the mid-1700's. A queen of Rumania in the early part of this century was a writer in her spare time, but used a pen name. And, of course, two English queens have had the name. The extraordinary Elizabeth I, who ruled for forty-five years, took England into a period of greatness. The present Elizabeth II rules at a time when the monarchy has more celebrity and symbolism than power. **Betty** (how about White and Grable?), **Betsy** (Ross, right?), **Bess** (as in Truman), **Bessie** (jazz great Smith fits), **Liz** (Ms. Taylor's nickname), **Liza**, **Eliza**, **Lisa**, **Lizbeth**, **Beth** and **Lisette** are a few of the many variations on the name.

Emily One of the old Roman families gives us this name, which has a less-than-flattering Latin translation of "one who imitates or emulates." The very original Emily Dickinson does not fit that meaning. The Belle of Amhurst had only seven poems published during her reclusive lifetime, but her drawer full of letters and verse has influenced American literature since her death in 1886. **Amelia**, **Emilia** and **Emiline** are variations of the name. **Emil** is the masculine form. To tell the truth, the Romans generally thought of the name as referring to one who imitates or emulates the good or best. No, **Emma** does not have any relation to the Latin. It is Germanic and means "whole" or "universal." **Irma** and **Erma** are related to this, as is the combination name, Emmylou.

Eric There are many names that are derived from words that refer to a king or ruler, and this name from the Old Norse is one of them, meaning "honored ruler." The discoverer of Greenland, Eric the Red, comes to the fore when thinking about famous Erics. He was the father of one of the first explorers of America, Leif Ericson, who landed on a place, probably near New England, that he called Vinland around 1000 A.D. Some may remember the wise journalist, Eric Severeid. Author **Erica** Jong is the most prominent of the female users of the name.

Ernest We all know the importance of being earnest and still use the word in its Germanic root meaning, "serious" or "truthful." Both Hemingway and Borgnine have demonstrated that translation in literature and entertainment respectively (*Marty*, not *McHale's Navy*). **Ernestine** was more popular years ago as a girl's name than it is today. Now, the "earnest" that we use in "earnest money," the advance payment to bind a contract, comes from a Hebrew root, meaning "he pledged." That may be where a few of you **Ernies** get your name.

Eugene The Greek, meaning "well-born" or "noble," gives us this name, which is more popular today in its shortened form, **Gene** (as in cowboy-star Autry). **Eugenia** is the feminine version that gives us **Genie** (not the one you dream of that comes out of bottle). This first name was one of the few used to name a city: Eugene, Oregon (from one of its greatest benefactors). Several popes have also been named this, as was a great general of the Holy Roman Empire, Eugene of Savoy, who led troops in many battles in the early 1700's.

Eve The Biblical Eve is our most well known of all those of this name. The Hebrew for "living" gives us this feminine name for this first Old Testament mother. Poor Eve gets a lot of bad publicity for being so easily tempted and taking that first bite of the apple. What the heck, without her we might still be lazing about in the garden with not a stitch on . . . **Eva** (as in Gabor), **Evelyn**, and **Evalyn** are three faces of the name. There is no relationship of this name with the coming of night we call "eve." This goes back to an Old English idea that the day and night are even as the sun goes down.

Here are some more "E" names for you. **Effie** comes from Euphemia, a Greek name, meaning "well spoken of." **Egbert** was once a popular name, and its Germanic root means "bright sword." **Eli**, such as in actor Wallach, comes from the Hebrew and means "the Lord is God." **Elias** and **Elijah** are usually the forbears of the shortened version. **Elliot** has seen more use lately, what with G-man Ness and actor Gould, and gets its beginnings from the Celtic word for hunter. **Elsie** is sometimes a form of Elizabeth, but also has a Germanic origin, meaning "good cheer." **Elvira**, which means "manliness" in Latin, has had a kind of comeback as a girl's name, thanks to the Oak Ridge Boys' song and the buxom horror movie moderator's pseudonym. All you **Manny**s out there probably get your nickname from **Emmanuel**, the Hebrew for "God is within us." **Errol** Flynn fans may be interested to know that his name means "wanderer" in Latin. **Estelle** gets her name from the Latin for "star," as do those of you named **Stella**. **Esther** is a Persian version of the same meaning. **Ethan** was a fine name for Vermont Revolutionary War hero Ethan Allen. The Ethan of the Bible was actually a very wise man who even had a Psalm (89) written for him. **Ethel** got good use when actress Barrymore used it which is an Old English name, meaning "noble counselor." **Evangeline** has the Greek language as its mother and means "little bearer of good news" from whose root we get evangelism.

F **Fay** There are two different origins for this popular name. one comes from a Middle English root, meaning "faith." The other goes all the way back to a Latin word for fate that had changed to "one who had magical powers" over its thousand-year use and was applied by the English to fairies, sprites, and elves. **Faye** Dunaway has a variation of this name. On screen she *does* seem to have a bit of magic going for her.

Florence The girl's name and the city in Italy both come from the same Latin root, meaning "flowering" or "blooming." Maybe it was because she was born in Italy that English nursing pioneer Florence Nightingale was so named. In her ninety years of life she became legendary both on the battlefields of the Crimean War and in hospitals across England. I don't think there is any Italian connection with actress Florence Henderson, but her name pops up when thinking of **Flos**. Other similar flowery names are **Flora** which is from the same Latin and was also the name of the Roman godess of flowers, **Florabel** (beautiful flower), **Florella** (little flower), and **Florinda** (flowering). I'll talk about Florida later.

Floyd This first name is a changed about form of Lloyd, and both names come from the Welsh word for grey. I'm not sure why inhabitants of Wales would want to name their children after so bland of color, but hues play a prominent role in many names. Floyd Patterson, the great heavyweight champ, caused many of his opponents to see grey . . . then black. Lloyd Bridges' name jumps up when thinking of those with that name. From *Seahunt* to *Airplane*, there haven't been many grey moments for his career. Lloyd's of London, the famous insurance firm, began when underwriters of merchant ships began gathering at Lloyd's Coffee House in London in the late 1600's. It was a sometimes dangerous gamble to offer to guarantee the cargo of a sea-going vessel in those days, but good profits could be made. Two or three partners in a venture could make the risk less worrisome. At these coffeehouse gatherings an association was formed that made the risks of loss even less. The eventual company kept the name of the coffeehouse.

Frank It is much more common to hear Frank as a man's first name rather than its relative and sometimes parent, **Francis**. Football legend, Frank Gifford, has had that name heard across the nation on many a Monday night. Though you'll sometimes hear him called Francis Tarkenton, that football great who also crossed over into TV-land likes to be called **Fran**. The names were almost titles of respect in their earliest use. Over the centuries, France has been a country almost constantly at battle with the German people. One of the most successful invasions of that European country occurred in 500 A.D. when Roman rule in what was then Gaul was withering. The Franks, who were a Germanic tribe, fought and drove out the Latins. Whereas Romans generally made slaves of the people they conquered, the Franks granted full freedom to those under their protection. This idea of freedom was so associated with the tribe that the Latin language used "frank" to mean "free." So, when someone speaks frankly, they can talk honestly, without restriction. When a representative to Congress uses franking privileges, he or she can mail something at no cost. It even used to mean "to be able to come and go freely." If the Romans had done their etymological homework, they would have discovered that the *Germanic* meaning of the word was "javelin," one of the primary weapons of the tribesmen. Well, being too frank can be similar to having a spear stuck in you (or in someone else). When the West Frankish empire became France in 870, Francis or Frank was common name for a freeman as were **Frances**, **Francesca**, and **Francine** names for free women "of France." A number of saints have been named Francis, the most famous being the son of the wealthy merchant from Assisi who gave it all up for the life of poverty. The founder of the Jesuits was another Francis, St. Francis Xavier. From Frank Lloyd Wright to Francis Scott Key, the name has been a popular one. A once-popular woman's nickname, **Fanny** (as in funny-girl Fanny Bryce), came from Frances through **Franny**. Unfortunately, the same nickname got applied to the buttocks in the sexist kind of way that names of people get associated with parts of the anatomy, and this variation on the name is heard much less today. **Franklin**, as in President Roosevelt, also has its ties to the conquering Germans and referred to "free land," an estate that was held without dues, a feudal term that has also become a common last name.

Frederick Freds of the world, be proud! Your name has a heritage that goes far back to the Old High German, meaning "peaceful ruler." **Fredericas**, forgive me. Though your name means the same thing, it wasn't applied to girls for quite some time. Fittingly, many kings and emperors have been named Frederick. The one called "the Great" was probably the most famous of these. Though his father never thought much of him, he surprised everyone by becoming a military wizard and a patron of the arts, making Prussia one of the greatest powers of the Western world by the late 1700's. On the gentler side, Fred MacMurray comes to mind when thinking of famous Freds. **Fritz** is another variation of the name.

There are many less-used "F" names. **Fabian**, the teen star of the fifties and sixties, got his name from the Latin for farmer, though the name is also attached to the British organization that was interested in promoting socialism in the late 1800's, The Fabian Society. Obvious names like **Faith** or **Fawn** I don't need to say much about. **Felix**, like that crazy cat, and his feminine counterparts, **Felicia** and **Felice**, come from the Latin, meaning "happy." **Ferdinand** was once a popular name worn by kings of Bohemia, Hungary, and Spain and comes from the Germanic for "adventurer." **Fifi** seems so French, but probably comes from the Hebrew root, meaning "addition." **Fletcher**s out there get your name from the Old English that is still used for an arrow maker. **Frasier** and its several variations have Latin origins that referred to those with curly hair.

G **Gary** There are many variations on this first name and an assortment of meanings associated with it. "Gar" was an Old English word for "spear," and a spearman was a "Garvey." This was altered over time to Gary. **Garrison** (as in Keilor, the wonderful storyteller from "Woebegone") is also at the root of some Garys and comes from a related Germanic root, meaning "protection," from which we get the name of the fort and other words like **guarantee** and the Frankish "**garage**." Most of these **Garry**s add the second "r." **Gerald** and **Gerard** sometimes give us Gary as a nickname. They are related to the first idea and mean "bold spearman." Of course, Gerald Ford, our thirty-eigth president, took the name of his stepfather and was actually born Leslie Lynch King, Jr. **Geraldine** translates as "little one with a bold spear."

Geoffrey Most of us see this name today as **Jeffrey**. It has an origin in the Old High German describing a place of peace. Geoffrey IV wasn't exactly peaceful. He was a warrior of the twelfth century who conquered Normandy and fought in the Crusades. Geoffrey of Monmouth brought us the first real stories of King Arthur as he collected the legends in the mid-1100's. **Jeff**s out there see your name worn by actors like Hunter and Bridges.

George Though George has had much royalty associated with the name, including six kings of England and a couple of Greek rulers, it has a humble beginning in the Greek language and means "farmer." I don't know if I could visualize George C. Scott behind a plow or George Plimpton pushing a tiller, but George Washington actually had a farm at Mt. Vernon. The father of our country did, at one time, resign from the military to devote all his time to his plantation (though he was probably rarely seen weeding in the garden), but he left Martha for the Revolution after a number of years down on the farm. All the **Georgettes**, **Georginas**, **Georgias**, and **Georgianas** can trace their names' meaning to the old Greek agrarian.

Gloria Obviously, the word "glory" comes into play with this name. The Latin for splendor and brilliance has long been a common feminine name. Gloria Swanson, of acting fame, is one of the most well known.

Gregory The Greek word meaning "watchful" is at the root of this name. It has long been associated with Christianity as Saint Gregory I spead the Gospel after the Roman prefect converted in the late 500's. Since then, there have been fifteen other popes besides him named Gregory, including Gregory XIII who reformed the calendar (see **July**). There was also an anti-pope by that name in the early 1100's. His election was not considered official. The last pope made a saint was Pius X who was pope from 1903-14. Gregory Peck may not be a saint, but his acting talent has inspired many.

There are many "G" first names in use. **Gabriel** has been a popular one and **Gabes** out there will be interested to know that God's messenger, the archangel, got the name from the Hebrew, meaning "man of God." **Gabriella** has been used as a feminine version. **Gardner** keeps the garden, according to the Germanic origins of the name. **Garth** was the Old Norse name for a yard or garden. **Gavin** and its brother, **Gawain**, go back to a Welsh name, meaning "hawk of May." **Gay** used to be a very popular female name and the original Germanic root meant "impetuous" or "sudden." Later, this referred to the impetuousness of a happy person and happiness itself. **Gaylord** (baseball pitcher Perry is a modern example) referred to a happy ruler. Changes in the connotation today find it used less as a first name. See **Jennifer** for **Genevieve**. **Gertrude** has a war-like Germanic birth, meaning "spear strength." **Gilbert** goes back to Celtic and Old Irish and speaks of a "bright pledge or promise." **Gina** Lolabridgetta certainly wasn't little, but her first name in Latin dealt with little things. **Godfrey** has Germanic roots, meaning "God's peace." **Golda, Goldie** or **Goldy** have the obvious Germanic reference to gold. **Gordon** comes from the Celtic for "upright man." **Graham** (as in author Greene) is also Celtic, meaning "stern-faced." "Pleasing" or "thankful" gives us the Latin meaning of a name worn by the likes of **Grace** Kelly, who was certainly pleasing, and one we are thankful to have been able to watch. Both President Cleveland and the Sesame Street character get the name **Grover** from a Germanic root describing a woodsman. The King Arthur tales made **Guinevere** a popular name. It's Welsh for "white phantom." Some of you **Guses** and **Gussys** might take your name from **Gustave**, Germanic for "staff of the good." **Gwen** Verdon, actress, and **Gwendolyn** Brooks, poet, get their names from the Celtic for "white-browed."

H **Hannah** Though she only appears in the first two chapters of the First Book of Samuel, the Biblical Hannah played an important role in Jewish history. Because she was sad about being childless, she made a vow to God that, if she could have a son, she would dedicate herself to Him. He granted her request (and later added three more boys and two girls), and she gave birth to Samuel, the great transitional prophet between the rule of judges and kings. I'll speak more of him later. Hannah's name means "grace" in Hebrew. The Greek version is **Anna** which led to the **Anns**, **Annies**, **Annettes** and **Anitas** getting their versions of the name. The English pet form of the name is **Nanny** which led to a variation, **Nancy**. That Nanny wasn't the one applied to a child's nurse, but *was* used for the nanny-goat. The reign of Queen **Anne** of England brought the Parliament into greater power in the early 1700's, and they wound up giving the throne to the German House of Hanover when Anne's death left no heirs. Henry VIII had two Annes among his six wives during his long reign in the 1500's. Anne Boleyn lost her head as his second wife. but, in getting her, Henry created what became the Church of England so he could get divorced from wife number one. Anne of Cleves was from a powerful German family, but after marrying her as wife number four he found her boring and a bit ugly. He divorced her before the year was out. Csarinas, princesses, and queens have been Annes and Annas, yet the humble progenitor of the name, Hannah, has not had many famous wearers. Nancy Reagan has been our most recent world-famous namesake, though some have questioned her graciousness.

Harold "Army commander" is what the Old Norse root of this name means. An accident led to one of the biggest changes in government in England and involved that country's most famous Harold. When Harold, the Earl of Essex, was shipwrecked on the coast of France, he was forced to take an oath supporting William I's claim to the English throne. Harold actually wanted to be king himself, and he succeeded to the throne in 1066. That pivotal year saw William (whom we know as "the Conquerer") invade England to make the new king live up to his former vow. Harold was killed at the Battle of Hastings after a near victory. This Norman conquest forever changed England *and* our English language, as Norman French was imposed by the new rulers and hundreds of new words entered our vocabulary. Playwright Harold Pinter has led his armies . . . of fans of his work. Some of you **Harry**s out there derive your shortened version from Harold, others from Henry.

Harvey Conflicting sources give this name's meaning as either "bitter," from the Breton, or "noble warrior," from a Germanic root. Most Harveys would probably prefer the latter translation. Remember Harvey Kuen and his baseball prowess? And, of course, there is the giant rabbit of the play bearing the name who forever gives the first name an amusing quality.

Helen Here is another feminine name that has launched a thousand variations: **Ellen, Eileen, Elaine, Ella, Nell, Eleanor, Lenore,** and **Leonora** . . . just to name a few. The most famous Helen of history was the beautiful Greek daughter of Zeus and Leda, a mortal woman. When she was stolen from her new husband Menelaus by the Trojan prince, Paris, that famous war broke out that we study in Homer's *Iliad*. Paris felt he had the right to her because Aphrodite had promised him the fairest mortal maid in all the world. The wimpy Paris actually fought Menelaus in single combat, but it wasn't much of a battle. Eventually, Helen was returned, but not until one of the greatest cities in Asia Minor lay in ashes. Now, the ancestor of the Greeks, who are also called Hellenes, was a daughter of the two survivors of the Greek flood story. Those of you who are more familiar with Noah will find the parallels interesting. Men had become wicked and Zeus decided to get rid of them by flood. He and his brother, the god of the sea, caused nine days and nine nights of pouring rain, covering the earth in water until only the peak of Mt. Parnassus remained showing. Two humans had been kept safe: Deucalion, the son of a god and a human, and his wife Pyrra, also of similar heritage. Deucalion was commanded by his father Prometheus, who knew the flood was coming, to build a wooden chest, stock it with food and get in with his wife. They landed safely on the mountaintop and later gave birth to Hellen. "The bright one" is the Greek meaning of Helen. Helen Hayes has certainly been a shining star of screen and stage. I also think of Eleanor of Aquitane, queen two times over, once to Louis VII of France and then to Henry II of England, whose children, John and Richard the Lionhearted, play such interesting roles in history. There are so many who bear variations of the name that I could go on about them until you cried, "Nevermore!"

Henry   Most of us think of the many Henrys who ruled England when the name is thought of historically, but what of the seven Henrys who were Holy Roman Emperors or the four Henrys who were kings of France? Well, maybe Shakespeare helped us remember the English kings a bit better. Many will recall Prince **Hal** and his faithful companion, Falstaff, when they think of the battling Henry V. I've already mentioned the rather selfish Henry VIII and his habit of removing heads from wives he did not like. Henry Fonda stands out as royalty of the American cinema. Hank Williams was one of the more famous to wear one of the nicknames that come from the first name. **Henrietta** comes from the French form of the name, Henri. **Harriet** and **Hattie** are versions of that feminine variation. Henry comes from the Old High German and means "ruler of the house." **Huck** is another of the nicknames, but not when it comes to the shortened form of Huckleberry we're familiar with.

Herbert   President Hoover is one of our more famous Herberts. This mining engineer from Iowa had a tough time in the top office as his administration ran through the worst years of the Depression. Though his first name means "bright army" (from Old High German), the thirty-first president was primarily a peacemaker who helped bring food to the hungry in the aftermaths of both World War I and II. He died at the age of ninety in 1964. Herbie got strange use as a Volkswagon with a mind of its own in several Disney movies of the 60's. **Herb**, another shortened version, has no relation to the plants used in medicine and cooking. Those herbs get their name from the Latin.

Humphrey   Though it is rarely used today, it will stand in our minds as the name of Academy Award winner Humphrey Bogart. "Home peace" is the Germanic meaning of the root of this name. There was not much of that in the movie roles he played, but in his private life it seems to be something he enjoyed.

Let's look at some other "H" names. The Germanic **Hamlet** is hardly ever seen, but the play's protagonist has a name that refers to a village. Related to it is **Hamilton**: "hill town." **Harrison** (as in actor Ford) has an English meaning: son of Henry. **Heather** is a popular girl's name these days and relates to the untilled land where the heath and its pretty flowers grow. **Hector**'s Greek meaning is "someone who holds back." **Hedda** (remember gossip columnist Hopper?) and **Hedy** (and actress Lamar?) come from the Germanic for a guard. **Heloise** is the French variation of the Germanic **Eloise** and means something like "healthy and wide." No hints intended. **Herman** is another name from the Old High German referring to a man of the army and not to **hermits** (Greek: "one of the desert"). **Hester** got a bad rap about her rep in *The Scarlet Letter* by Hawthorne. Her name means "star" and is a variant of Esther. **Hiram** was a Biblical king of Tyre who supported David and Solomon and whose name meant "lofty" in Hebrew. **Holly** obviously comes from the plant which has an Old English meaning: "to prick" (think of its leaves). The Latin for "keen-eyed" gives us **Horace**, as in journalist Greeley. **Hortense** was once a fairly popular girl's name, going back to the Latin for "gardener," from which **horticulture** is also derived. **Howard** Cosell is the most famous of recent namesakes of this moniker, meaning "castle guard" in its Germanic beginnings. **Hugh**, and **Hugo** get their meaning from the Germanic root, meaning "to comfort," that gives us **hug**. **Hubert** is from the same source, meaning "bright Hugh," certainly fitting for the very brilliant Mr. Humphrey.

I There are only a few common "I" first names, so let's give them a run down here. **Ian** we'll talk about when we get to **John**, as we will **Ivan**. **Ida**, as in Ms. Lupino the actress, probably comes from the Old North French, meaning "work," though some relate it to the Greek word for "happiness." **Ignatius** is found in the names of several saints and popes and probably comes from the Latin for "fiery." **Imogene** (remember Sid Caesar's Coca?) gets her name from the Greek language: "born of love." **Ina** more than likely comes from the Latin, meaning "little one;" whereas, **Inez** has Greek roots, meaning "maiden." **Ira** derives from the Hebrew and translates as "watchful." **Irene** has graced many, including actress Dunne, and comes from the Greek, meaning "bearer of peace," like the theological practice of promoting peace called **irenics**. **Iris** was a Greek goddess of the rainbow from which we get the names of part of the eye that gives its color and the colorful flower. Iris was also a messenger of the gods who, dressed in her multicolored robes, arched through the sky on errands. **Irwin**, as in author Shaw, is a variation on **Erwin**, a Germanic name that means "victorious lord." **Isaac** was given his Hebrew name, meaning "laughter," because his very aged mother laughed when she was told she would bear a son. Some of you **Ikes** get your nickname from this, as do **Zacks**. **Isadora** Duncan, the great dancer, had a first name that means "equal gift" in Greek.

J **Jacob** The Biblical Jacob had a life filled with trickery. First, he was born hanging on to his brother Esau's heel, sort of pulled out of the womb at the same time and, thus, got his name which means in Hebrew "he who takes by the heel." Later, he got his brother to sell his right as firstborn for a pot of soup. Later still, he and his mother, Rebekah, fooled a nearly blind Isaac with a bit of goat meat and fur into thinking Jacob was the hairy huntsman older brother which led to Isaac's giving his blessing to the disguised Jacob. This infuriated Esau to the point where Jacob had to run away and stay with Rebekah's family. There he fell in love with his cousin Rachel, but after working seven years for her hand, was tricked on his wedding night into marrying her older sister. He worked another seven years for the second wife he had hoped would be first. This same father-in-law tried to trick him again when Jacob said he would work for him if he could have all the brown sheep and speckled goats that were born to the herd. The father-in-law agreed, but quickly removed all the off-color animals from the flock to prevent interbreeding, thus starting the son-in-law with nothing. Jacob turned the tables by placing spotted and streaked objects about the drinking troughs to influence the white sheep and black goats to bear variegated offspring. He got his new name, Israel (Hebrew: "he who striveth with God"), by wrestling an angel and pulling a hamstring in the process. Finally, he was tricked by his sons into believing Joseph was dead, and Joseph tricked them all back by keeping Benjamin hostage under false accusations.

All of you **Jims** out there get your name from the Anglicized version of Jacob, **James**, which came out of the Late Latin variation, Jacomus. Most will recognize King James I because of his important support of the translation of the Bible in 1611, which still bears his name. The French **Jacques** comes from this name as do many **Jacks**, though some of these latter nicknames come from John. The radical republicans of the French Revolution were called Jacobins because they first met in the Church of Saint Jacques. All of you **Jimmy**s can also find several saints named James. Two were of the twelve disciples, one the son of Zebedee and the other the son of Alphæus. Some argue that this second James might be the brother of Jesus; others say that that James is separate and was the author of the book of the New Testament bearing his name. On a more negative note the slang for a Hispanic person, **dago**, comes from the Spanish Jacob, **Diego**. **Jake** is a more pleasant form of the highly popular Jacob.

Jason This Greek name has become quite popular lately. The name means "healer," and its most famous historical bearer was the Jason who led the Argonauts on the quest for the Golden Fleece and who later married the magical Medea. As it turns out, the hero was a bit too ambitious and threw Medea aside to marry a daughter of the king of Corinth. Medea got her revenge by killing the two boys she had borne Jason as well as the princess bride-to-be. Because of this, not many girls have been given the name Medea.

Jennifer Some of you **Jenny**s reading this get your nickname from this Celtic first name which means "white wave." Others trace your shortened version to Jane which I'll talk about later. Jennifer has become a very popular first name for girls. Jennifer O'Neal is an actress/model whose name I think of when I hear this first name. Older folks might associate the name with the actress Jennifer Jones.

Jeremy "Uplifted by the Lord" is the Hebrew translation of the progenitor of Jeremy, **Jeremiah**. This Old Testament prophet was in and out of trouble with the rulers of his day because of his very political prophesies, even getting sealed up in a large jar once for his predictions. Many Jerrys get their nickname from the Biblical original, though many others are linked to Gerald or the name below. Let's see, Jeremy Irons is the latest greatest Jeremy . . .

Jerome Other Jerrys get their moniker from this name which comes from the Greek, meaning "holy name." Because of the World War II slang, "Jerry," meaning German, the nickname derived from this and other first names suffered in popularity for a while. Originally, Saint Jerome made the name famous through his good work in the early Catholic church. This man lived up to the meaning of his name, translating the Bible into its first coherent Latin form from the Greek and Hebrew. Where "jerrybuilt," meaning cheaply or poorly constructed, came from is uncertain, but has no reference to St. Jerry's painstaking labor on the Vulgate Bible.

Jessica Here is a name that has seen the original masculine version drop in common use, while the feminine version has flourished. Those of you who read the original David and Goliath story closely will remember David's father Jesse, whose Hebrew name means "wealthy." The work of the Missouri bandit of the same name who, with his brother Frank James tried to *get* wealth through robbery, led to "Jesse" falling into disrepute. Through modern bearers of the female version like Jessica Tandy or even the fictional Jessica Fletcher (of *Murder, She Wrote* TV fame) the name is popular among women. There is some speculation that a separate "Jessica" came to us through the Hebrew name "Iscah," which meant "imprisoned."

John This first name is probably the most widely used in the western world. The original Hebrew root from which we get the word meant "the Lord is gracious." The first John we run across was known as "the Baptist" and was beheaded by Herod not because of his preaching, but because he scolded this puffed-up fellow for marrying his niece and brother's wife which made the woman angry enough to have John's head on a platter. The disciple John, also known as the Beloved Disciple, was one of the closest of the twelve to Jesus. He was given care of Jesus' mother Mary as Jesus died on the cross. From those biblical Johns came a tradition of popes taking the name, twenty-three all together. Kings of England, France, Hungary, Poland and Portugal also bore the name. The Dutch version is seen as **Jan**; the Russian form is Ivan whose feminine form is **Yvonne**; **Juan**, **Juana**, and **Juanita** are Spanish variants; while **Ian**, **Shawn**, and **Sean** are Celtic. Jane is one of the feminized versions of the name which came to us through the French, **Joan**, which derived from the Latin. **Joanna**, **Janice**, **Janet**, **Johanna**, **Jean**, **Jeanette**, **Jennie** and **Jenny** (which is also a name for a female donkey – no offense, **Janey**) are diverse forms of the name John. **Jack** is a nickname which also originates with this first name. So, all you **Johnny**-come-latelys will see this common name on every John Doe (though this anonymous character is also called "Richard Roe") who might put his "John Hancock" on a document. Civil War Johnny Rebs were Johnny-on-the-spot when it came to a fight, and some might have liked their John Barleycorn (whiskey). The name is so common that we refer to bathroom toilets and customers of prostitutes as "johns," both originating from the more revered version. Legendary Johns of recent history include Johnny Appleseed, based on John Chapman, who wandered the Midwest sowing his fruit tree seeds, and John Henry, the steel-driving African-American who may have also been based on a real person. "**Johnson**," one of the most common last names, comes from "son of John." **Jonathan** actually comes from a slightly different Hebrew root, meaning "gift of the Lord" or "the Lord has given." The first recorded Jonathan was a son of Saul in the Bible who became David's best friend, which eventually set him against his father. Jonathan was such a popular name in the American colonies that during the Revolutionary War, British soldiers called all Yankees "Jonathans." Later, England would call their independent rebel country "Brother Jonathan."

Joseph This son of Jacob was given a name that means "He adds (or increases)" in Hebrew. This first child of Rachel was born to her after long infertility that she worked hard to remedy, including using mandrakes, a plant supposed to act as a love potion and fertility enhancer. After that failed, the credit had to be given to God for the addition. The story of Joseph being sold into slavery by jealous brothers shows that even the early Israelites were full of bickering and envy. There are numerous **Joes** and **Joeys** out there who share the name that was also born by Mary's husband, most famous from that Bethlehem birth. Well-known **Josephines**, such as Napoleon's consort or the singer/dancer, Ms. Baker, made the name a popular one among women.

Judith Though this biblical character is unfamiliar to most Protestant students of the Bible, she was a popular figure among the early Jews and Christians. Her name in Hebrew means "praise to God" and is derived from the tribe of Judah from which we also get **Jew**. Her apocryphal book of the Bible tells of the beautiful widow, Judith, who saves her city by killing an Assyrian general waging war against it. A popular **Judy** came from the famous puppet show, Punch and Judy. The mean husband got his start in Italy as "Punchinello" (meaning "little turkey cock" because of his big beak of a nose). From that character we get the expression "pleased as Punch." From Judy Holliday to Judy Garland, modern bearers of the name abound . . . though Punch has fallen by the wayside.

Lots of "J" names vary in popularity. **Jasper** is Persian for "lord of the treasury" and had more use than **Jasmine**, the name for the flower that also originated among the Persians as **Yasmin** and also gives us **Jessamine**. The prophet **Joel** told of a plague of locusts and got his name from the Hebrew, meaning "the Lord is God." **Joshua** was one of the only two original wandering Hebrews to cross into the Promised Land, and he became one of Israel's great leaders. It's no

josh (from the name) that the translation of the appellation is "the Lord is salvation." **Joy** and **Joyce**, you get your names from the Latin root referring to gladness or merriment. The Roman goddess of marriage and women gives us **June**, while her husband, Jupiter, is responsible for **Julius**, **Julia**, **Juliana**, **Jules** and **Juliet** – all meaning "descended from Jupiter." **Justins** and **Justines** go back to the Latin for their names' meaning: "one who pronounces the law." They have the Roman Emperor Justinian, who brought order to Roman law, to thank for their names' survival.

K **Katherine** Well, **Kathy**, if you're reading this, you'll know your name came from Greek roots and means "pure." The Romans liked the name, passed it on to the French who brought it to the English. From **Kate** to **Kathleen**, examples of variants of this popular name abound. Miss **Kitty** of "Gunsmoke" fame takes her pet name from one of the forms that also give us **Katerina** and the "C" versions like **Catherine**. The Russian girl who took the name and became Catherine the Great made it popular throughout Europe. There was the influential Catherine d'Medici, who may finally be remembered for popularizing snuff-dipping and massacring French Protestants; and Katherine of Aragón, who was the first wife of Henry VIII and inadvertently caused the English Reformation. Ms. Hepburn can't be left out as a memorable **Katy**. **Karen** also gets her name from the same Greek root which also gives us the formal name for a laxative, "**cathartic**" (purifier), and the term for the cleansing of emotions, "**catharsis**."

Kenneth The Scottish origins of this name mean "handsome." One of the most famous historic **Kens** is found in 9th century Scotland. Kenneth I united the country and is considered its founder. **Kenny** Rogers may not be Scottish, but many would consider him handsome.

Let's look at other "K" names. **Kay** has been both a masculine and feminine first name and derives from the Greek word for "rejoicing." **Keenan** is a good Celtic name meaning "sharp" or "wise." Yes, **keen** also derives from this. **Keith** can trace his name to another Celtic word for "windy." **Kelvin** and **Kevin** have two paths that lead to the present: the Latin Calvin (See page 69) or the Germanic root meaning "fighting friend." **Kemp** probably gets his name from the Germanic borrowing from Latin which, early on, meant "warrior" and likewise gives us "**champion**," but also had a Roman application to a "field" and brought us "**campus**" and "**camp.**" **Kendall** goes back to a tribal Celtic word for "chief of the valley." **Kirk** has Old English beginnings as a word for a church. **Knut**, which we most associate with football coach Rockney, has an early bearer, Canute the Great who became king of England, Denmark and Norway around 1000 A.D. It means "club" in its earliest Danish. **Kurt** has Germanic roots, though the Germans were probably influenced by the Latin root which meant "to cut short" and referred to brevity, a popular trait among early men. Today, this kind of shortness of speech has connotations of rudeness seen in the word "**curt.**"

L **Laura** In ancient times, many evergreen plants were revered for their ability to stay potent and alive when all else seemed barren during the winter months. The laurel was one of those plants which appeared to conquer death, and it became a symbol of victory. In Roman times heroic generals, athletes, and artists were crowned with wreaths of laurel. The name of the plant was also given to newborns as a sign of triumph, fertility, and luck. You Lauras, **Laurels**, and **Laurettes** are joined by **Lawrences** and numerous other variations. Famous **Larrys** from Sir Olivier to that one of Arabia are popular examples. **Lora** and **Lorenzo** also join the crowd.

Laverne This name got notoriety with the popular TV sit-com *Laverne and Shirley*, though it had fallen out of popularity as a common feminine name. The Latin roots refer to spring from which we also get the "**vernal**" equinox and other fancier spring words. Some could argue that Laverne might have other origins, tracing its roots to another Latin base for a native slave, "verna," from which we get the word for the language spoken by the natives, "**vernacular**," whether they be Samoans or Brooklynites or lawyers . . .

Leo Leo's name is well known for its Latin parentage, meaning "lion," because of the fame of the horoscope member. Several saints and numerous popes and emperors bore this name. One holy See, Leo I, persuaded Atila the Hun not to attack Rome; another, Leo III, began the Holy Roman Empire after crowning Charlemagne its first ruler; and another, Leo IX, was responsible for the breakup of the Eastern and Western branches of the Catholic Church. **Leon** was a popular Spanish form of the name. Other names tracing roots to the king of the beasts are **Leonard**, a Germanic offshoot which means "bold as a lion," **Leonardo**, **Leona**, and **Lenard**. **Lionel** was a name oriented to the hunt and meant "lion club." The **leopard**, by the way, got its name from the belief that it was a mixed breed. A "pard" was the ancient name for large cats, and the spotted beast was thought to have mated with a lion, giving it its hybrid name.

Lewis This spelling of the name goes back to the original Old High German, meaning "famous in war." The name was appropriate for a fighter and the French took it, spelling it "**Louis**," and gave it to a whole line of kings, some fighters, some not. The first of these was the son of Charlemagne. Other Louis-namesakes had such nicknames as "the Stammerer," "the Sluggard," and "the Fat." Louis IX was the one we know as Saint Louis (See in Section IV) and had quite a life in the 1200's, going on crusades, keeping peace in France, and improving the economy. His 56 years of life were full of travel and yet were also ones of sound administration and wise rule. There were eighteen French Louis altogether. The feminine **Louise** and **Louisa** come from the same root. Other **Louies** can trace their nickname to variants like **Ludwig**. **Louella**, **Lew**, and **Lou** are still fairly common forms. (See Louisiana, Louisville)

Linda This popular feminine name has two possible paths to modern usage. One set of Lindas can trace their name to **Melinda**, from which we also get **Mindy**, going back to a Greek root for "honey-like." Others may come from **Belinda** which is most likely from the Latin for "graceful." **Lindy** is one nickname. Linda Evans wears the name well as does Linda Ellerbee.

Lucy Actually, Lucy was the first form of this name which in Latin means "bright." **Lucille** came along later, along with **Lucinda**, **Lucia** and other variations. The masculine form, **Lucius**, is not used nearly as much. *I Love Lucy* will probably be remembered for generations as an example of the comic genius of Lucille Ball. Strangely enough, **Lucifer** also comes from the same Latin root, originally the name for one of the Roman gods, "the light bearer." His name was later one of those given to the archangel who led the revolt in Heaven. **Luke** is a Greek form of Lucius.

Many "L" names come in and out of popularity. **Lambert**, from the Germanic for "bright lamb," isn't in much use today; nor is **Lancelot**, whose legendary name meant "warrior" in its Germanic origins and lives on in the King Arthur tales through the brave, but amorous knight. **Lavinia** has fallen out of common use, though the name, based on the Latin root for "cleansed," was once widespread. **Lazarus** had its day as a first name, but this Hebrew for "God's help" is no longer seen very much, nor is a feminine biblical name, **Leah**, also from the Hebrew for "languid." **Lee** and **Leigh**, which were once mainly masculine names have made a comeback in popularity for boys and girls. The Old English origins refer to a meadow sheltered from the winds. **Leila** has Arabic beginnings as "dark beauty." **Lemuel** comes from the Hebrew, meaning "devoted to the Lord." **Leroy** has a French birthplace, referring to "the king." **Leslie** has Old English roots as a name for a wooded valley or dell. **Lester** is also from the Old English for a "meadow camp," from which we also get place names like Leicester or Glouchester. **Letitia** and **Letty** were once more common, but the names, whose Latin base means "gladness," are rarely seen today. **Levi** Strauss might be known for a type of jeans, but levis have Hebrew beginnings that relate to "joining" or "uniting." **Lillian** and **Lilly**, on the other hand, are still popular and come from the name of the flower which was a sign of purity and beauty. Most **Lina**s come from the shortening of Carolina (see Charles). **Lloyd** has Celtic roots meaning "brown," while **Lois** goes back to a either a Greek word for "desired" or from **Aloys**, Germanic for "famous maid of war." Take your pick. Whatever **Lola** wants, Lola gets . . . maybe because she has Germanic roots meaning "manly." **Lorna** has Old English parents which we see in **forlorn**, meaning "lonely." **Lorraine** goes back to Latin for "sad." **Lucretia**, Latin for "lucky one," got a bad reputation as a first name from Ms. Borgia of the late 1400's who apparently had quite a few lies told about her, probably because of her Machiavellian brother, Cesare. **Lydia** gets her name from the Greek reference to a woman from that ancient country in Asia Minor. **Lyle** is an Old English variation of "little." **Lynn** is either masculine or feminine and has the Celtic language as its base, with "lake" as its meaning.

M **Madeline** Poor Mary Magdalene has suffered from being associated with the repentant prostitute who washes Jesus' feet with her hair and her tears. Somehow, that story got mixed up with another incident where Mary of Bethany, sister of Lazarus, anointed Jesus with oil soon before his crucifixion. Then, *both* stories were associated with the woman from Magdala who was one of the first at the tomb to see the stone rolled away and later to converse with the resurrected Christ. Admittedly, this Mary Magdalene had had seven devils cast out of her earlier in her acquaintanceship with Jesus, but whatever that exorcism was about, it didn't involve the oldest profession. Mary Magdalene *did* follow Jesus around, as did a number of women, but this was mainly to help him and his disciples with food and other needs. The Hebrew word for "watchtower" gives us Magdalene, which later variegated into **Madeleine**, **Madelon** and **Madeline**. Because of the tradition of the tearful, repentant prostitute, we get the word "**maudlin**," derived from the Old French variation and meaning "overly sentimental." Some of you **Maud**s get your name from this, though others come from **Matilda** which has Germanic sources and means "mighty in battle."

Malcolm The early missionaries to the pagan tribes of Northern Europe and Britain were very brave and pious men who risked death daily in their attempts to convert the warlike clans. The Celtic Picts were no exception, sometimes painting themselves blue before battle to strike fear into their enemies' hearts. When an Irish missionary calling himself Columba (from the Latin for "dove") came into this part of Scotland in the 500's AD, his faith so impressed the warriors that eventually the whole of Northern England converted to Christianity. One of the names that came out of that conversion was Malcolm which means "servant of St. Columba." Actually, part of the name translates as "bald" because servants in those times shaved their heads. When Malcolm Little became Malcolm X, he too led a religious movement within the black community of the 50's and early 60's.

Margaret The Greek word for pearl is at the root of this name that has been borne by a variety of royalty in its time. Two Danish queens, one of Scotland, one of France, and several queen consorts have had the name Margaret. There have been writers like Margaret of Valois, who fought against her husband, Henry IV of France, in the mid-1500's; or Margaret of Navarre, who managed to turn out seventy-two stories during that same general time period. And I can't leave out our Southern romance writer, Margaret Mitchell.

A bit removed from Tara comes another word from the same root, **margarine**. Our butter substitute got its name from the pearl-colored acid from which the spread was first obtained.

All of you named **Margarite**, **Margot**, **Marjorie**, **Mags**, **Maggie**, **Madge**, or **Marge** take your names and nicknames from that first mother-of-pearl, as do some of you **Megs** and **Megan**s, though some of you take your name from forms of **Magna**.

Mark More than likely, the Saint Mark who wrote the second gospel was a Palestinian Jew who was educated in Roman ways and served Peter until that disciple's death and then wrote his account from the many sermons he had heard and translated for Romans and others on his journeys with that fisher of men. The writing of his gospel probably took place in the late 60's A.D. John Mark, as he was known in biblical accounts, was the son of a Mary (which Mary isn't clear). Whether he got his last name through Hebrew or Roman influence makes a difference in meaning. The Roman "Marcus" comes from the name of the god of war from which we get the name of the planet, **Mars** (red as the blood of war), and words like **martial** (as in court martial and martial law) and other "warlike" words. The Hebrew "Marc" means "bitter." **Marcia** comes from the Latin war god as does **Marcella**, **Marcelle** and **Marsha**. The patron saint of France, St. **Martin**, has a name that also comes from that god of conflict, but this gentle hermit was anything but a warrior. His feast occurs on November 11th, and that mid-November warm spell we call "Indian summer" is called "St. Martin's summer" in England. The bird was also named for the saint from the fact that it migrated from England about the time of his feast day.

Martha The biblical Martha was another of those women who loved Jesus and wanted to serve him. This sister of Lazarus and Mary of Bethany tried to perform her service in very practical ways, bustling about the kitchen and seeing to the physical comfort of her guest. When her sister didn't help out, but instead sat listening to Jesus, Martha complained, as might many an over-burdened mother at the holiday season. Jesus gently pointed out that there are sometimes more important things than having the perfect household. It seems that these three siblings were special to Jesus, so much so that when the sisters grieved to him about their brother's passing, they got a miraculous resurrection of Lazarus as a result. Martha comes from the Aramaic and means "lady." Historically, we see the name on ladies like Martha Washington and Martha Graham. I've always wondered who was responsible for Martha's Vineyard.

Mary There are six Marys mentioned in the Bible. We've spoken of Mary Magdalene, Mary of Bethany, Mary, Mark's mother, and, of course, the mother of Jesus. There was also a Mary who was the mother of James and Joses and who may have been a sister to the most famous of the Marys. A final Mary is mentioned in Romans as a Christian woman living in Rome. The name is derived from Miriam, which we've spoken of earlier as the Hebrew for "rebellion." So many modifications of the name exist to make it one of the most widely used of feminine names. **Maria, Marie, Marietta,** and **Mariette** are obvious versions, but how about the Scottish **Maisie** or the Celtic **Maureen? Molly** is another variant. **Marilyn** and **Marion** mean "little Mary," while **Marlene** means "like Mary." Put Mary and Ann together for **Marian, Marianna,** and **Marianne**. The English had two Queen Marys. Mary I so cruelly persecuted Protestants in the 1500's that she is remembered in the drink "bloody Mary." Mary, Queen of Scots was another exciting gal, but neither of these famous Marys is responsible for our state's name. I'll talk about that in the next section.

Matthew There is still an argument as to whether the tax collecter-turned-disciple actually wrote the first gospel. It is obviously aimed at Jewish converts to give them the faith that their new beliefs followed Old Testament predictions, but whether the apostle, sometimes called Levi, penned it or not is in doubt. The name, Matthew, means "gift of the Lord" in the Hebrew. Kin to this name is **Mathias**. When the remaining disciples decided to replace Judas Iscariot, they prayed and cast lots, and the winner of that lottery was Mathias, who had been a companion of the group and had witnessed the resurrection of Jesus.

Michael Until Mr. Jordan and Mr. Jackson, the most well-known Michael around our house was the fellow who is implored to row his boat ashore. The first mention of Michael is in reference to the archangel, who appears several times in the Bible. The guardian angel of the Jews has a name that comes from Hebrew, meaning "who is like God." He first appears to Daniel to tell him a prophecy. Later in the book of Jude, the angel is mentioned as being in contention with the devil. And in Revelations, he and his band of angels toss the dragon (the devil) out of heaven. There is even a church festival in his honor on September 29th. Numerous Byzantine emperors, circa 800-1200 A.D., were named Michael, as were several Rumanian heros, including Michael the Brave. **Mike, Mickey, Mick,** and **Michelle** owe their names to the Hebrew original.

There are numerous "M" names that also need to be mentioned here. Let's start with **Manuel** and **Manuela**. We generally see the majority of the bearers of these names coming from Hispanic background, but the meaning is Hebrew: "God with us." **Manny**s out there probably knew that. **Marvin** has Celtic roots, referring to "high hills." **Mason** is pretty obviously connected to stone working and comes from the Old French. It originally just meant "to make." The first freemasons came from the guild of stone workers in the Middle Ages. These valued laborers developed their "union" into a huge, secret society that still exists today. **Matilda** has Germanic origins and means "mighty in battle" – no waltzing for her. **Maurice** takes his name from a reference to the northern African Moslems known as Moors, as does **Morris**. The usual translation is "dark," though that couldn't be said about Mr. Chevalier. **Mavis** was once a popular name and orginated from the song thrush with that same Old French title. The many of you named **Max** may get your nickname from **Maximillian**, Latin for "the greatest," or from **Maxwell**, which has Germanic beginnings and means "big spring." **Maxine** derives from the Latin "little great one." **Maynard** means "mighty" in its Germanic parentage. **Melanie** goes back to the Greek for "dark one." From the same root we get the pigment that makes our skin dark, **melanin**. The bees' business has a lot to do with the following Greek names: **Melicent** (or **Milicent**), "honey-sweet"; **Melinda**, "honey-like"; and **Melissa**, "honey bee." So all of you **Millies**, **Mindys**, **Minnies**, and Lindys can brag on your sweetness. **Melvin** goes back to an Old English name and was applied to a "friend of the council." **Mercedes** was the car maker's daughter, and when Mr. Benz decided to honor his new vehicle with her name, he probably altered its popularity permanently. The name means "mercy" or "reward" in Latin. **Merle** and **Myrl** take us from the bees to the birds: the thrush, to be specific about their Latin derivation. **Mildred** has a nice Old English meaning: "mild strength." **Miles** and **Milo** are other forms of the root for "mild," which Mr. Davis never was musically. **Millard** hasn't been used much since President Fillmore, but the thirteenth president's name meant "grinder" in its Germanic form. Our most famous **Milton**, Mr. Berle, might be interested to know that his name comes from "mill town" in its Germanic beginnings. **Minerva**, the Latin goddess of wisdom, is best known for her being shown up in a weaving contest with the mortal girl, **Arachne**. After causing this girl's suicide, Minerva felt guilty and changed the girl into a spider so she could keep weaving . . . not much consolation for you arachnophobes. **Miranda** has gotten to be a popular girl's name and not because of the Supreme Court case that forced police to read rights to an arrestee. Her Latin name means "worthy of wonder." **Mona** has Irish origins and means "noble." **Monica** is more hard to trace and probably comes to us from Africa through Late Latin, though it could get to us from the Greek for "alone." **Morgan** has a Celtic birth and means "dweller by the sea" – the Pacific for Ms. Fairchild. **Mortimer** has Latin roots and refers to a "bitter place by the sea." **Moses** is probably Egyptian in origin, which makes sense since that's how the biblical Moses was raised. It means "child." **Muriel** goes back to an Old Irish beginning: "bright sea." **Murray** also deals with water in its Celtic origin and refers to "a great body of water." **Myrna** probably has Greek origins, meaning "sorrowful." **Myron** was named for the sweet perfume, myrrh, and in Greek was the name given to "something delightful." And **Myrtle** gets her name from the plant, which, in its Greek form, was a symbol of beauty.

N **Nan, Nancy, Nanette**: see **Hannah**

Natalie The Latin roots of this name can be seen in other words like **native** or **nativity**. "Little one born" is the translation of Natalie, **Nathalia**, **Nathalie**, and other variations. Apparently it was common to give this name to a child born on Christmas. Natalie Wood stands out as one of the most famous in recent history.

Nathan Appropriately, the Hebrew translation, "he gave," certainly applies to one of the great American Nathans, Nathan Hale, who would have been willing to lose several lives for his country. Now, the prophet Nathan was pretty important in Israel during the time of David and Solomon, scolding the former for his dealings with Bathsheba and later helping her get the latter on the throne.

The other form of this name, **Nathanael**, we've already mentioned as one of the disciples of Jesus. His name means "gift of God" in Hebrew. The Revolutionary War provides us with the most heroic of American Nathanaels, General Greene.

Neil The Old Irish word for "brave" is at the base of this common first name. Neil Armstrong stands as one of the courageous as he will be remembered for his command of the Appollo 11 lunar-landing trip that led his to be the first feet on the moon. Though Mr. Diamond and Mr. Sedaka may not seem quite as brave, they represent the name (that is also spelled **Neal**) well in the music industry. **Nelson**, by the way, means "son of Neil."

Nicholas It was probably the Bishop of Myra in Asia Minor who gave us the story of Santa Claus. During the fourth century A.D., he was well-known for helping the poor, especially children. The most famous story associated with him deals with his giving three impoverished girls dowries, so important to women of that day. It was said that he threw three bags of gold through their open window in order to help them while remaining anonymous. He also became the patron saint of sailors and was prominent among the Dutch sea-going folk who gave us the variation, Santa Claus. One of his other names, **Kris Kringle**, came from the German "Christkindl" which means "Christ child." There is another Saint Nicholas known as Nicholas the Great who was pope from 858 to 867. And, of course, there are the czars of Russia: Nicholas I (r. 1825-55) and Nicholas II (r. 1894-1917). The latter we remember as being overthrown in the Russian Revolution. It may well have been the strange peasant-turned-courtier Rasputin who, more than anyone, added the last straw to the backs of the Russian people, causing the revolt. While the czar was off fighting World War I, Rasputin's power over the czarina led to appointments of some of the most corrupt of his cronies to high government posts.

You **Nicks** and **Nicoles** out there might also have a relationship with the metal nickel which actually takes its name from the German mythological water sprite, Nix. Copper miners were often disappointed by nickel ore, which looked like copper but wasn't, and so blamed the mischievous imp. The legend of the dwarfish demon who could sometimes be half-human and half-fish led to Nick being one of the nicknames for the devil. Well, one thing leads me to another: no, **nickname** has nothing to do with this. The original Old English was "an ekename" which meant "an additional name." And **nix**, meaning "nothing" or "to wipe out," doesn't have devilish origins since it comes from a different Germanic root. Now, the bread pumpernickel does have reference to the devil. It was so named because it was so hard to digest and translates from the German as "the devil's gas." I hope that doesn't offend you **Nickys**, **Nicolettes**, or **Nicolles**.

Noel Noel actually means "birth" in the Old French, but was always capitalized to refer to Christmas. It has been a popular name for both women and men. Noel Coward stands out in my mind as one of the most famous.

Norman Fans of the TV show *Cheers* will always associate the name with the bulky, beer-drinking, buffoonish character glued on the barstool. Had you been in England in the 1100's and 1200's, you might have had very different feelings for this name, which in Old English means "north man" and is also seen in **Norseman**. When, in the 900's, Scandinavians invaded that part of France still called Normandy, that is definitely the direction from which they came. About a hundred years later, they *went* north to conquer England. If you were a Norman in England during the time of their rule, you were of the elite. If you were not, you were subjugated. Naming a child Norman might get you a favor from the ruling class. Ironically, that area of France was the site of another invasion hundreds of years later when, in 1944, some of the distant relations of the Norman conquerors hit the Normandy beaches to wrest control from the Germans.

Now, **Norma** is not allied with the Norsemen who so loved battle. Her name derives from the Latin for a square or pattern used by carpenters and draftsmen, from which we also get the word **normal**. Because the carpenter's tool could be used to set standards, shape, and align, there could be sameness in measuring building materials. Things would be "normal." The word also got applied to humanity and models for what was right and true. The Ecole Normal was a French school created to teach teachers, and from this model, many other normal schools grew.

Other "N" names of significance need to be included. **Nadine**, **Nadia**, and **Nada** have Slavic origins and mean "hope," such as that gymnast brought to her Rumanian countryfolk. **Napoleon** had its most famous bearer in Mr. Bonaparte. His first name derived from the Greek: "lion of the new city." The mother of Ruth was named **Naomi** which in Hebrew means "pleasant to behold." **Nell**, **Nellie**, and **Nelly** are variations of Helen. **Nettie** and **Netty** are Germanic names, meaning "neat." **Neville** seems especially British, as in Mr. Chamberlain, but it's Latin, meaning "new city." **Newton** is similar in meaning, but Germanic in origin and means "new town," which Mr. Gingrich ha tried to make of Washington. **Nigel** translates from its Medieval Latin origins into "little black one." We'll talk about this root in Section Four with **Nigeria**. **Noah** is most famous as the name of the ark-builder who was the first to save endangered species, including himself. Actor Noah Beery may be familiar to a few old timers out there. This first name means "rest" in Hebrew. **Nola** is Celtic for "white shouldered." And **Nora**, **Norah**, **Norine**, and **Norita** are all versions of **Honoria** (Latin for "honorable") or Leonora (See).

O | **Oliver** There are two paths by which this common name reached its present form. One route deals with the olive tree, a symbol of peace. "The bearer of the olive branch" was a peacemaker, as this name meant in its Latin beginnings, and a good name for a child. A more warlike track comes to us from an Old English root, meaning "elf army." From Charles Dickens' young orphan scamp, Sir Twist, to modern-day director Stone, the name has widespread popularity. The female version has been given a bit of negative shading by the skinny, somewhat whiney **Olive** Oyl, who seems to always bring out Popeye's violent streak. **Olivia**, however, has fared better because of the likes of Ms. DeHaviland.

Orlando This name is an Italian version of **Roland**, which comes from Germanic origins, meaning "famous in the land." One of the favorite stories of knights and chivalry is "The Song of Roland." Shakespeare liked the Italian variation of the name for his play *As You Like It*, as did the mother of baseball great Cepeda.

Orson This name has Latin parents and refers to a "litte bear," not far from describing the late Mr. Wells but not nearly applicable to Mr. Bean. You see a version more closely linked to the original root in a name like **Ursula**, which also means "little bear." Before actress Ms. Andress, the most well-known Ursula was the saint whose legend tells of her death at the hands of the horde of Huns while she was doing her holy work in Cologne around the fourth or fifth century. Killed with her, the story reports, were 11,000 virgin followers. Almost a thousand years later, an order of nuns devoted to the education of girls was founded. The Ursaline order still exists. Finishing off the bearish name, you will also find its Latin form in the other names for the constellations, the Big and Little Dippers, **Ursa Major** and **Ursa Minor**. **Orsino** and **Arsinio** probably also get their names from the same root.

Oscar The legend of the secretary who first sees the motion picture award statuette and claims that it looks like her Uncle Oscar is one that may be questionable, but it does make for good press, and Hollywood is certainly known for that. The Academy of Motion Picture Arts and Sciences' use of the familiar, friendly name for its award probably led TV moguls to alter their award from **Immy** ("image orthicon tube") to **Emmy**, Broadway bigwigs to use "Tony," and advertisers to employ "Cleo." Oh, yes, the name Oscar has Old English origins and means "spear god" . . . the only reference to this today might be the skewering of a certain brand of hot dog for roasting.

"O" names may not be quite so common, but interesting ones abound. **Odette** has musical roots in the Greek, meaning "little song." **Ogden** Nash made quite a smash with poetry that bore a lash. His first name comes from Germanic roots and means "dell of oaks." **Olaf** is a popular Scandinavian name used by several kings of Norway and even a saint. The name means "champion." **Olga** also got its start in Norway as **Helga** then traveled through the Russian, still meaning "holy," and was last most prominently displayed on gymnast Corbet. **Opal** takes her name from the gem that traces its origins to the Sanskrit where the root meant "precious stone." The opal was a sign of hope in ancient times. **Ophelia** was a popular name before Shakespeare's suicidal beauty in *Hamlet*. The Greek translation of the original is "helper." **Orville** Wright and his brother will always be given the credit for opening the sky to human flight. This bicycle maker's first name means "golden city" in French. **Osmond** comes from a Germanic language base and refers to "one whom the gods favor." **Ozzies** (and Harriets) out there might be interested to know that **Oswald** means "divine ruler" in its original Germanic form. **Otis** might have two origins: one from the Latin, meaning "lazy," and one from the Greek, meaning "keen of hearing." Fans of the late Otis Redding would definitely choose the latter to apply to the great soul singer. **Otto** is a name that belonged to a whole succession of Holy Roman Emperors between the period of 962 and 1215. It is Germanic in origin, meaning "mountain." **Owen** goes back to Celtic roots for "high born."

P   **Pamela** This name actually had its birth in 1590 with the creation of the pastoral poetic work, *Arcadia*. The English poet Sir Phillip Sidney invented the name for a sweet, feminine character in the work. Just as Scarlett might have been the name given to some girls after the debut of *Gone With the Wind*, **Pams** out there owe their name to a fictional character.

Patrick Of all Patricks, the saint whom we celebrate with tokens of green on March 17th is the one most familiar. Yet his life is the stuff of legends and possibly clouded in myth. We think of this man as the ultimate Irishman, but actually, he was probably born in the part of Britain dominated by Rome in the late 300's A.D. His name is Latin and referred to noblemen or senators of Rome. The patrician class was the aristocracy of the earlier empire. Supposedly, Patrick was captured and enslaved by the Irish, but escaped to what is now France. There he studied and gained the kind of faith that took him back to Ireland as a missionary where he converted the rough pagans to Christians in droves. At his death at around the age of seventy-six, all of Ireland had been converted. As far as driving out the snakes from the Emerald Isle, there may be grains of truth mixed with exaggeration in the tale. **Pat**, **Patty**, **Patricia**, and **Tricia** are variants of the the original, as is the Irish **Paddy**.

Paul Another saint whose life is the stuff of legend is the Apostle Paul. The date of his birth is uncertain, but it is known that he was the son of a Roman, which gave him certain rights and privileges, even though he was Jewish and a tentmaker by trade. **Saul** was his given name, from the Hebrew: "asked of the Lord," but after his dramatic conversion on the road to Damascus from Christian-hater to Christian missionary, he changed it to the humble Latin surname, Paul, meaning "little." After his eventful life that truly shaped Christian doctrine, his name became a popular one among the faithful, from the feminine **Paula**, and **Pauline** to the Spanish **Pablo** and Portugese **Paolo**. Six popes have taken the name, including the reformer of the 1960's and 70's, Paul VI.

Peter Continuing with the stories of saints, Peter is another who had a name change due to his religious involvement. Jesus renamed Simon (which is actually a Greek form of the Hebrew **Simeon**, meaning "he heard) when he told him that he would be the rock upon which He would build His church. Peter is Greek for "rock," and from this root we get many "rock" words like **petrified** ("turned to stone") and **petroleum** ("rock oil"). If the Greek language had not been the first to be used in the translation of the Bible, we might have called this Apostle Simeon Kepha, had we employed the Aramaic name that Jesus actually spoke. Having denied knowing Jesus at His betrayal, Peter spent the rest of his life speaking boldly of Christ, so boldly that eventually Emperor Nero crucified him on what is today Vatican Hill. St. Peter's Church is still a place of pilgrimage for those wishing to honor his burial place. Whether or not he actually wrote the two books of the Bible bearing his name has been strongly debated; still, the disciple's name became a popular one. From the Russian czars to the kings of Aragon to the Serbian and Yugoslavian rulers of that name, Peter is scattered throughout history. You **Petes** and **Perrys** will also find the original form of your name popping up in children's literature: "Peter Rabbit," *Peter Pan*, and "Peter and the Wolf." The French version is **Pierre** and the Spanish is **Pedro**. Well, I'm starting to get petered out here. That's mining slang that may have come to mean "exhausted" when the vein of ore turned to just plain rock, though the origin is uncertain.

Philip Though we could stay with the Christian theme and start here with the Apostle Saint Philip, the name is much more ancient and is seen hundreds of years before Christ, worn by men like Philip II, king of Macedon, who conquered Greece in 338 B.C. and cleared the decks for his son, Alexander the Great, to dominate the civilized

Western world. The Greek meaning of the name is "lover of horses" and, historically, was a popular name of French and Spanish kings, including Phillip II (r. 1556-98) who used the Spanish Inquisition to deport the Moors and had his Armada defeated by the English. Paul's letter to the Philippians was written to Christians in Philippi, his first evangelical base in Europe, named for the Macedonian king. **Phil**, **Phillip** and **Phillipa** are offshoots of the original horsey name.

"P" names are widespread, but some are tainted like **Pandora** who was the mythological Greek version of Eve, bringing evil into the world by opening the forbidden box . . . no apples here, but still the penchant for blaming women for our troubles. **Pansy** is another name that has suffered. The French root for "thought" gives us the flower and girl's name. Unfortunately, not many are given that name today because of its negative association with male homosexuals. **Parker** is simple in origin: Germanic for "guard of the park." Especially in Victorian times, it was common to name women for virtues like **Patience** or **Prudence**. **Faith**, **Hope**, and **Charity** are also part of the gallery of encouraging names. **Pearl** has been a popular feminine forename in the necklace of jewel-names like **Ruby**, **Sapphire**, and **Opal**. Its Latin root's meaning is not as attractive as the name seems today: "little ham." The inner body of the sea mussel from which the earliest pearls were extracted reminded sailors of that part of the thighbone. Come to think of it, Ms. Bailey was quite a ham, though Pearl S. Buck wrote some gems. **Penelope** was the faithful wife of Odysseus, and her name has been popular. The Greek root dealt with weaving. **Percival** was "guard of the Grail" in its Celtic origin, while **Percy** meant "keen-eyed" in that same language-base. **Philbert** came from the Germanic for "outstanding" (see **filbert** in Section One). **Phineas** Fogg, from Jules Verne's *Around the World in 80 Days*, stands out as a prominent, though fictional, representative of this Germanic first name, meaning "open-faced." **Phoebe** is a name that has regained popularity. Another name for the Greek goddess, Artemis, who looked over wild things and helped hunters, Phoebe means "shining" since she also had the moon as her domain. During the dark of the moon, she was known as Hecate whom witches look to as a protectress. **Phyllis** is a name honoring spring, coming from the Greek for "leaf." Ms. Diller springs to mind as a popular celebrity bearing the name. **Portia** was once more popular as a feminine name, and its origin deals with providing that harboring protection of the port in its Latin base. **Prentice** is a shortened form of **apprentice**, which is Latin for "learning." The blue-black fruit of the blackthorn shrub is sometimes called "sloe" but is also called prunelle in French because of its resemblance to little prunes, and it gives us the once-common appellation, **Prunella**, also a name for the cloth of those dark robes worn at graduation and by judges and priests.

 Quentin There aren't many "Q" names, but here's one which has had some popularity. Originally, it was a Roman first name and merely meant "fifth." Yes, that may seem like an unimaginative way to name a child – the fifth of the litter – but Roman *last* names were really the important identifying factors. So if you were the fifth Claudius or Antonius, that was all right . . . better than the eighth, Octavius.

Quincy This name was made more popular by the television show about forensic medicine, starring Jack Klugman. There are two possibilities concerning its origin. One is that it is related to Quentin, described above. Certainly, **Quinn** is linked to the name for the fifth of the children. The other origin refers to the plant, the quince, which gets its beginnings in the Latin borrowing of the Greek. The capital of Crete, Canea, used to be known as Cydonia and had a reputation for its aromatic fruit, known in ancient times as the Cydonian apple. As the Latin version got passed into Old French to Middle English, it came to us as "quince."

R **Rachel** The Hebrew that literally means "ewe of God" was the name of Jacob's second wife and first love. I've already talked about how Jacob worked fourteen years to be able to marry her with the blessings of her unscrupulous father, Laban. A little known fact about Rachel is that she seemed to inherit some of her father's greedy nature. When Jacob decided to return to his homeland, she stole Laban's images of his household gods. She hid them in a basket that was part of the riding "saddle" on her camel. When Laban came looking for these pagan idols, probably worth a great deal, he searched throughout Jacob's camp. When he came to his youngest daughter, seated on her camel, she explained that she couldn't rise to greet him because she was experiencing the monthly "custom" of women, and, thus, she kept the treasure hidden. Speaking of hidden treasures, **Raquel** is a variant that Ms. Welsh wears well.

Randolph The Germanic roots that led to this Old English name mean something like "guarded by the wolf." There are many forms of the name, from the Scots' **Randall** to that red-nosed reindeer, **Rudolph**. **Rodolph** and **Rudy** also come from the name. The nickname, **Randy**, doesn't have any relationship with the Scottish root that deals with an ill-mannered or lascivious person. That **randy** comes from "rant," dealing with wildness and violence, as in "rant and rave." **Ralph** is a cousin to Randolph and translates as "counseled by the wolf." Jackie Gleason's "Honeymooners" character, Kramden, made the name very common. **Rolf** is a more Germanic form of this.

Raphael Though the Italian painter and architect made the name prominent during the Renaissance, the original Raphael was an arch-angel whose Hebrew name means "God has healed." **Raphe** or **Rafe** is a common nickname that was especially popular in the South.

Raymond The Frankish name, which came from Germanic roots, originally meant "protector of the counsel (or body of judges)" and probably referred to one who made sure that judgements or laws were carried out. Mr. Burr did well with this as Perry Mason. **Ray** is a popular shortening, seen in actor Milland and golfer Floyd. Related by the same root is **Reginald** which translates as "powerful judge." **Reg** and **Reggie** don't sound like powerful nicknames, but are still somewhat common today. **Reynold** also comes from this name. **Regina** is not kin, owing its origin to the Latin for "queen." However, another common name, **Ronald**, is also related to the aforementioned Ger-manic and means "the power to decree" or "the power to make judgements." This was certainly the case with President Reagan, but not so important for the clown of McDonaldland. **Ronaldo** is another form of the name.

Rebecca You **Beckys** and **Rebas** out there owe your name to the Hebrew, which was also spelled **Rebekah**, apparently meaning "beau-tiful snare." In no way did this generous woman of the Bible entrap Abraham's servant when he sent him to seek out a wife for his son, Isaac. She merely offered water and hospitality. Her brother, Laban (spoken of in the Jacob story, remember), saw all the lavish gifts the servant was entrusted to give and decided that this marriage between cousins would be good for both families. Just as his father, Abraham, did with Sarah, so did Isaac claim her as a sister when he moved onto new land. This was because he was afraid men would kill him to get the beautiful Rebekah if Isaac were known as her husband. Of course, the most familiar story of her life deals with her tricking the elderly Isaac into giving his blessing to Jacob, her favorite son.

Reneé The Latin for "born again" gives us this feminine name which is seen as **René** in its masculine form. The French took the Latin original, **Renato**, and altered it. King René was well-known in France and Italy in the 1400's. I'll always remember the song, "Don't Walk Away Reneé," when I think of the name.

Rex Rex has been a popular masculine name since Roman times when it referred to a king. From Rex Harrison to Rex Reed, the name is a popular one for "kings" of the stage and screen. The Tyrannosaurus Rex, that wicked-looking dinosaur, translates as "ruling king of the lizards." Related to Rex is **Roy**, which comes from the same root, meaning "king." Roy Rogers pops into my head as king of the movie cowboys. **Royce** also originates through this root. Leroy we've mentioned as meaning "the king."

Richard Even though Richard the Lion-Hearted was hardly ever in England, his exploits during the Third Crusade and his fights with his father and brothers made him a dashing figure in English romance. His name has Germanic roots, meaning "powerful and strong," from which we get rich and hardy. Other English kings of that name, Richard II and Richard III, both had violent ends: the former dying a prisoner of Henry IV in 1400 and the latter dying on the battlefield against Henry VII in 1485 at the last engagement of the War of the Roses. The name is still popular in all its forms: **Rick, Ricky, Rich, Dick,** and even **Chard.** The slang for a detective probably has nothing to do with Richard. Calling one a **dick** came from the abbreviation of the word . . . not Dick Tracy. **Rods** and **Roddys** out there should know that their parent name, **Roderick,** is also related to Richard and means "famous power."

Robert This popular name comes from the Old High German and means "bright fame." Kings of Scotland, such as Robert the Bruce whom we've already discussed (see **Bruce**), proudly wore the name as did early kings of France and dukes of Normandy. **Robin** Hood takes his first name from the diminutive form of the name. That same form is given to the bird, Mr. Robin redbreast, from the tradition of giving nicknames to our flying friends like Martin and Jay. Seen in actors like Mitchum, poets like Penn Warren, and authors like Louis Stevenson, this name is one of our most prevalent, with **Roberta, Rob, Robbie, Bert,** and even **Rupert** being variants. Let's Bob along.

Roger Roger Rabbit may make this well-known name less widely used because of its association with the cartoon character, as happened with Elmer (Fudd) and Sylvester (the cat). "Famous spear" is the warlike Germanic root's meaning. The common practice of using names to represent letters in radio communication led to Roger being the code word for the letter "r," meaning "received." Many a baseball fan received a home run ball as a souvenir from Roger Maris.

Rose One of the more popular of feminine names, the origin of the original root, meaning "red," is uncertain. The Greek version is **Rhoda** which Valerie Harper made even more popular with her TV show character. The Latin version, Rosa, has many forms like **Rosalind**, **Roselyn**, **Rosalie**, and **Rosalinda**, all meaning "beautiful as a rose." "Little rose" is the meaning of **Roselle**, **Rosetta**, **Rosita**, and **Rosina**. **Rosemary** and **Rosemarie** combine two names, but also can refer to the "rose of the sea." **Rosabel** speaks of "the beautiful rose." I think of the Kennedy matriarch, the buxom Ms. Russell, and the wife of President Carter when thinking of some of these versions of the name.

Ruth The book of the Bible which tells of this foreign widow's travels with her mother-in-law into the town of Bethlehem in Israel is interesting because it demonstrates one more time the rich mixing of cultures that is part of the Jewish heritage. When this poor Jordanian woman married the wealthy Boaz, she gave birth to the line that will eventually give us King David and Mary, the mother of Jesus. Now, the "ruth" in **ruthless** has no relation to the Hebrew name meaning "companion." The "ruth" here goes back to an Old English root that means "sorrow, pity, or compassion." To be ruthless was to be without any caring feeling. **Rue** comes from the same root. **Ruthenia**, a land given to the former Soviet Union in 1945, shares nothing with either of these "ruths." This area of the Ukraine gets its name from the Russian for "Norsemen." (see **Russia** in Section Four)

Here are some other "R" names. **Rhea** was the wife of Cronus and queen of the universe. She was the mom of Zeus. **Roanna** has Germanic birth, meaning "famed grace." **Rodman** comes from similar roots and referred to a surveyor or guide. **Romeo** isn't used much since Shakespeare's time, but means "good man of Rome" in its original translation. Today, a romancer of women gets this name as a descriptor. **Roscoe** is Germanic for "swift horse." **Ross** speaks only of the horse itself. **Rowena** is Celtic for "white skirt." **Roxanne** or **Roxana** comes from the Persian for "dawn." **Rufus** is of Latin parentage, meaning "red." **Russell** also deals with the same color but comes with more of a French heritage.

S **Samuel** Miraculous births are acknowledged by many religions as signposts marking some great leader or prophet. Such was the case for the great judge of Israel, Samuel. His mother, Hannah, was barren and getting on in years, constantly teased about her lack of children by the other, prolific wife of her husband. After intense and devoted prayer, Hannah was granted her desire for a child and had Samuel whom she dedicated to the priesthood as a tribute to God. His name's meaning has been under debate. Some say the Hebrew root means "heard of the Lord," which certainly reflects Hannah's story. Others argue that Samuel means "his name is mighty." However, most scholars agree that the name is probably derived from a Hebrew base, meaning "the name of God." This wise man was instrumental during the transition from rule by judges to rule by a king, as Israel grew into a nation. An interesting part of Samuel's story tells of a kind of séance in which his spirit appeared at the command of a witch ordered by King Saul who needed advice before a battle with Philistines. The message that the spirit of Samuel delivered wasn't too good. Saul and his sons would join him the next day during battle. When Saul (see Paul for his name's meaning) was wounded during the fight, he took his own life rather than be captured, one of only four suicides recorded in the Bible, including Judas. There are many representatives of the name. I'll speak of Sam Houston later (see Section Four). **Sammy** Davis, Jr. made that nickname well-known. And who will forget that very different "bewitching" witch, **Samantha** (the feminine version), played by Elizabeth Montgomery? Well, the kids probably don't know what I'm talking about . . .

Sarah Biblical names are the most common in the Western world, and Sarah is definitely a popular first name. The wife of Abraham was originally Sarai, but, while God was convincing Abraham to promise circumcision for all His followers, He also changed the wife's name to Sarah, meaning "princess" in Hebrew. Now, Abraham wasn't lying when he called Sarah his sister as he tried to protect himself when settling in a new land. She really was the daughter of his father, but by a different mother. This ploy to save himself from being killed by covetous men almost backfired when the king of the land took Sarah to be his wife. God warned the king in a dream that he was about to bed a married woman, and he returned her . . . not too happily. Sara is another version of the name as are **Sada**, **Sadie**, and **Sally**. From reknown French actress Sarah Bernhardt (originally Rosie Bernard) of the turn of the century to the ungrammatical "nobody doesn't like Sara Lee (foods)," examples of the name have survived thousands of years.

Scott Though this popular name is definitely derived from the old Gaelic tribe that moved to England from Ireland about 1300 years ago, what it means is unclear. It could be "one from the north" or "tatooed" (from the tradition of early warriors marking themselves). It is also a popular last name with the same basic idea behind its origin: "one from Scotland."

Sophia The Greek root for "wisdom" gives us this feminine first name and is seen in other words like **sophomore** ("wise fool"), **philosophy** ("love of wisdom"), and **sophisticated** ("skilled, clever"). Because the intermarriages between German and English royalty had been so common in the 1500's and 1600's, the German princess Sophia's son, George I, was chosen as king of England by the British Parliament in 1714, ending the Stuart (see) dynasty. Of course, this eventually led to George III who let those crazy American colonists get away from the Empire. Ms. Loren is a prominent bearer of this name today. **Sonia** and **Sonya** are Russian diminuatives.

Stephen Also seen as **Steven**, the name goes back to a Greek root, meaning "crowned." This is certainly a fitting name for St. Stephen, who was crowned first king of Hungary. The biblical St. Stephen was probably the saint whose feast "good King Wenceslaus" sat down to in the Christmas carol since the Hungarian king's feast is in August – no snow laying "deep and crisp and even." The only king of England by that name had huge struggles in the 1100's to keep his throne from the granddaughter of William the Conqueror, Matilda. He himself was William's grandson. Maybe another modern-day "king," Stephen King, ruler of the realm of suspense and horror, could fashion a scary tale out of that story. Steve Allen and Steve Martin come to mind when thinking of the nickname. Royal Princess **Stephanie** definitely gets her share of tabloid attention. She bears the feminine version of the name.

Stewart Stewart goes back to an Old English root and translates as "keeper of the hall." The **steward** took care of the running of the castle or estate . . . with the help of stewardesses – er – attendents. **Stuart** comes from this same root and started out as a family name of rulers of Scotland and England. In 1160 they started out as heriditary stewards of Scotland who finally worked their way into the kingship, eventually ruling all of England until 1714 (see Sophia), producing such leaders as James I, who is still known for the King James version of the Bible, and Mary I, who joined with William III to rule jointly. Actor Stewart Granger added romance to the first name, while Jimmy Stewart was born with the more traditional last name. **Stu** and **Stew** are shortenings. The boiled meats and vegetables have no relation to the latter nickname. This **stew** goes back to a Greek root, meaning "to smoke."

Susan **Susanna** was mentioned in Luke 8:3 as one of the women Jesus had healed who felt such gratitude that they helped support his ministry with their gifts. Her name comes from the Hebrew for "lily." All the forms – **Susette, Susie, Suzanne** – have the same floral meaning. Though actress Susan Haywood certainly could be associated with the beauty of the lily, Susan B. Anthony, whose eighty-six years were full of struggle for women's rights, probably didn't worry about being too flowery.

Let's look at other "S" names. **Salome** comes from the Hebrew for "peaceful," from which we also get **Solomon** and the greeting, **Shalom**. The biblical Salome is directly mentioned as the mother of the two disciples, James and John; but historically, she is recognized as the seductive dancer who so pleased her Uncle Herod Antipas that he granted her the wish of her mother, Herodias: to have John the Baptist's head cut off. Whether the dancer and the disciples mother are related is unknown, but unlikely. **Salvatore**, seen shortened in **Sal**, and **Salvadore** (see Section Four) come from the Latin for "savior." **Samson** is a name rarely given – except to luggage – but, in Hebrew, means "like the sun." With a name meaning "majestic" in Greek, Saint **Sebastian** found martyrdom at the hands of the Romans in the 200's. The young, wacky king of Portugal was not so majestic as he tried to battle Muslims in 1578, dying on the battlefield at the age of twenty-four. Remember **Sebastian** Cabot, the sophisticated actor? **Selena** or **Selina** get their names from the Greek word for the moon. **Serafina** and variations of her name probably get their forename from the highest order of angels, the six-winged seraphim. **Seth** was the third son of Adam and Eve, and his name means "appointed" in Hebrew. **Seymour** was originally a French name for St. Maur, the holy Moor. **Sharon** takes her name from the Hebrew for "plain" – not homely, but the plain of Sharon in western Israel. **Sheba** goes back to the queen of the area of today's Yemen who visited Solomon. **Sheldon** comes from Germanic roots, meaning "shield bearer." **Sherry**, as in puppeteer Lewis, might get her name from several sources. The wine we call sherry first came from a town in southern Spain and was known as the wine of Jerez. But there are also feminine names that grew out of the French for someone dear, "cher," like **Cheryl**, **Sheryl**, and the irrepressible **Cher**. **Sherwood**, as in poet Anderson and the famous forest of Robin Hood, is Germanic and refers to "a clearing in the woods." From that some basic root we get **Shirley**. which was a name for a meadow. **Sharlene** is a variant of this. **Sidney**, also spelled **Sydney**, is originally from the French, but it is an English mangling of "St. Denis," the patron saint of France. **Sibyl** goes back to the Greek name for an oracle of prophetess, the most famous being found in the story of Aneas. This woman helps the Trojan on his journey by leading him through Hades as he carries the golden bough across the land of the dead, meeting his departed father who shows him their future descendants, leaders of the Roman Empire. Another spelling of the name is **Sybil**. **Siegfried**, which gives us a few of you Freds, is Germanic for "peace wins." **Sigmund**, as in Freud, has Germanic roots, too, and means "victor." As a name, **Silas** got a bad rap from the misunderstood miser in George Eliot's book, *Silas Marner*, published in 1861. Schoolchildren were regularly forced to meet this reclusive weaver, redeemed by a child's love. The name means "woodsman" in Latin. The biblical Silas was a companion to Paul, both as traveler and prison-mate. Other woodsy names include **Silvester** ("forester"), **Silvia** ("forest maid"), and **Silvanus** ("of the woodland"). A "y" can replace the first "i" for variations of the names. **Sinclair** comes from the French: "St. Clair." I think of Sinclair Lewis, the great American author, as an example. **Spencer** Tracy made this Germanic name popular today. It means "steward" and can also be spelled **Spenser**. It was primarily an English surname seen worn by philosopher Herbert Spencer, who pushed evolutionary theory, claiming the "survival of the fittest"; and Edmund Spenser, great poet of the 1500's. **Stacy** comes from a Latin root, meaning "steady." **Stanley** probably comes from the Greek, **Stanislaus**, "praise of the state." Some heavenly names are **Stella**, from the Latin for "star," and **Sterling**, which goes back to Old English and means "little star." Sterling is also associated with silver because of a tradition of stamping silver pennies with a star. We still see that association when we hear "pound sterling." **Sumner** has Latin roots and referred to an official of the court who put that request for appearance into the hands of those called before the bench. This **summoner** got the name from the root, meaning "to remind secretly." **Sven** comes from the Danish for "youth," but has no relation to **svelte** whose Latin roots mean "stretched" and refer to the willowy, slender figures . . . usually found in youth.

T **Theodore** Teds and Teddys out there get their full name from the Greek, meaning "gift of God." One of the first historical figures seen with the name is Theodoric the Great who beat the German chieftan Odoacer who had ended the Western Roman Empire. **Theodoric** killed him and ruled Italy himself in the early 500's. **Theodora** came along not too long afterward, and though this Byzantine queen was accused of being an actress and prostitute, her long reign with Justinian I made the Eastern Roman Empire strong. Our President Roosevelt was a modern-day leader who made **Theo**s out there proud of the name. Ted Kennedy has definitely been a leader, though the jury is still out as far as the judgement of history. **Theodosia** is another variation of the name.

Theresa Originally Greek, this name means "bearing the harvest." Two very different saints bear the name. One was Theresa of Avila who helped reform the Catholic Church in the 1560's and 70's, founding a reinspired order of Carmelite nuns and spreading her mystical message of life aimed toward perfection along with her friend, St. John of the Cross. The other saint was Theresa of Lisieux whose short, twenty-four-year life as a nun in the 1880's and 90's inspired many with its humility. There will probably be a third Saint Theresa as the one known as "Mother" is examined for the holiness of her long, caring life. **Therese**, **Teresa**, and **Tracy** are other spellings of this name.

Thomas Thomas goes back to an Aramaic root that describes "a twin." Most of you **Toms** and **Tommys** have had to face the negative expression "doubting Thomas" somewhere down the line. The Apostle of this name who had to touch the wounds of Christ before he would believe gave us this phrase, but his later loyalty made the name a popular one. If he had only used his other biblical name, all you **Thoms** would be known as Didymus, Greek for "twin." Can you imagine Didymus Jefferson or Saint Didymus Aquinas or Did Thumb? The feminine versions of Thomas, **Thomasina** or **Thomasine**, aren't as common as they used to be. By the way, the **Tommy-gun** gets its name from its co-inventor, John Thompson, from whom it also gets its more formal name: the Thompson submachine gun.

Timothy The biblical friend of Paul who was a leader of the Christian church in the first century took his name from the Greek, meaning "one who honors God." This Saint Timothy became the first bishop of the Ephesians and was later martyred for his faith. Thinking of modern-day **Tims**, Mr. Conway comes to mind, and **Timmie** and Lassie will always be in my TV memory bank.

Other "T" names are also in need of mentioning. **Tabitha** first appears in the Bible as a good Christian woman who is miraculously brought back to life by Peter in The Acts (9:36-43). Her name means "gazelle" in Aramaic. It later got modern popularity with the witchy daughter on "Bewitched." Her role was so popular on the TV show that she earned a brief spin-off. **Talbot** is not so common, but its Germanic origin refers to a hunter. **Tallulah** has native American Indian origins and probably was imitative of a frog's call in its Cherokee roots. Ms. Bankhead *wouldn't* have liked that. **Terence**, that more formal version of **Terry**, was originally a Roman family name that probably meant "tender." **Thads** out there can trace their name to the Hebrew, meaning "praise." **Thaddeus** was one of the twelve disciples, also known as Lebbaeus *and* Judas the brother of James (not Iscariot). Both Judas and James were also brothers of Jesus. This Judas/Thaddeus/Lebbaeus wrote the book of the Bible known as Jude, his fourth name. **Thatcher** is a first name that obviously refers to a roof-maker in its Old English birth. **Thelma** has uncertain origins but could be Greek for "nurseling." **Theobald** seems to mix Greek and Germanic, and either means "strength of God" or "strong for the people." **Theron** gets his name from the Greek for "beast" or "animal." Remember **Thurston** Howell III, the millionaire of *Gilligan's Island*? That first name comes from "stone of Thor" in its Germanic roots, from which we also get **Thora** ("devoted to Thor, the god of battle and thunder") and **Thyra** ("devoted to Tyr, son of Thor and god of victory"). **Tiffany** probably owes her name to Louis Comfort Tiffany who was a big interior decorator in the first third of this century, known especially for his glass. **Tinas** who aren't nicknames of Christina or Ernestine have pragmatic names that are linked to "tiny." **Toby** is the popular nickname that comes from **Tobias**, Hebrew for "the Lord is good." That name might have been even more popular had it been included in the Bible instead of the Apocrypha (where the book of this name is also known as Tobit). **Trent** seems to come from the Latin for "thirty," but I don't know why. **Trevor** has Celtic roots, meaning "prudent." **Tristram** is also known as **Tristan** and is seen in the romantic tale of *Tristram and Isolde* (*Tristan and*

Iseult), the story of the knight and Irish princess who unwittingly swallow a love potion which gets them in all kinds of trouble. His name first meant "someone who blusters" in Celtic and referred to macho hunters, but it was later associated with the French word meaning "sad." **Tyrone** probably gets his name from the county in Ireland. Its origin is uncertain, though it could come from the Latin for "a young soldier." Mr. Power wore that name well, in and out of uniform.

U **Ulysses** This Latin version of the Greek name, Odysseus, means "wrathful," which the Greek hero of the Odyssey certainly was when he got home after ten years of warring and ten years of wandering to find a wad of men trying to woo his wife. He killed them all in a terrible slaughter. Oddly enough, Ulysses was the first draft-dodger. When Menelaus called upon all the Greek chieftans to aid him in getting back his stolen wife, Helen, Ulysses pretended to be crazy. He had been married to his beautiful wife for a year, had a bouncing baby boy, and certainly didn't want to go off to war. When the call to arms came, he ranted and raved, yoking an oxen and an ass to a plough and roaming through the field like a madman. To test him, the messenger of Menelaus placed the baby in front of the plough, and Ulysses turned it aside, proving his sanity. Later, he had to trick Achilles into going to war with him. Achilles, the great warrior, was trying to get out of this "draft" by dressing as a woman and hanging out with the daughters of a neighboring king. Ulysses pretended to be a merchant and brought a bunch of baubles to the beauties, among which were a few weapons. When Achilles handled these rather than the feminine goodies, he gave himself away. Our 18th president was actually born Hiram Ulysses Grant, but later changed his name to Ulysses Simpson Grant, a name more suited to a man who would lead the Union troops through their own Odyssey during the Civil War. Though his generalship is much admired, his presidential administration gets mixed reviews, especially in the area of the Reconstruction.

We've already talked about Ursula (see **Orson**), but there are a few other "U" names we can mention. **Ulric** is not seen much anymore, but its Germanic roots refer to a "noble lord." **Una** has simple Latin origins, meaning "one" and applied to one who is "unique." **Uriah** might have gone down in history as a great man of Israel had David not fallen in love with his wife, Bathsheba. This led to David sending Uriah into the heat of war and to his death . . . not one of the mighty king's greatest deeds. Uriah's name means "God is my light" in Hebrew.

V **Valerie** The Latin root that gives us words like valor and value is also responsible for this popular name, which means "to be strong." One of the early, great Roman families bore the name in ancient times when strength was valued more than delicacy. A whole province, Valeria, was named for them and gave its name to the medicinal plant that was first found in the area: **valerian**. The **valiant** name has a less-used masculine version, **Valery**, and the root is also seen in **Valentine**, "little strong one" (see Section One). Though Valerie Harper will probably always be known for "Rhoda," I think of her as a popular representative of the name.

A word like **valence** in chemistry comes from that original Latin and refers to the capacity to unite and bond, which seems like a **valid** use of the root. That other valance, spelled with two a's, is that short drapery you might find around a bed canopy originating from a town in France where the cloth was made.

Van This nickname that is seen on actor Van Heflin or singer Van Morrison comes, in most cases, from the Dutch method of describing from where a person was born or the homeland. Someone like Sir Anthony Vandyke, whose popularity in the 1600's brought forth fashion trends such as the Vandyke beard, would have originally translated his name as Anthony "from" or "of" Dyck. This is seen in the German "Von," as in Wernher Von Braun, and the French, Spanish, or Italian "de" or "du," as in Charles De Gaulle, Cecil B. De Mille, or Hernando de Soto.

Veronica Legend goes that as Jesus was trudging to his crucifixion on the road to Calvary, a woman handed him a handkerchief to wipe his brow. When it was returned to her, the image of Christ was impressed upon it. She is known as Saint Veronica, whose Latin name means "image of the truth." Today any representation of the face of Jesus upon fabric is called a veronica. The first part of her name that means "truth" gives us words like **veracity**, **verdict** ("true speaking"), and even the adverb **very** ("truly," "really"). The second part of her name deals with images and gives us words like **icon**, referring to any sacred religious object or image. **Vera** is a name linked to the root, but it comes from Russian, meaning "faith."

Victor Victor has been a popular first name and originally dealt with the warlike nature of man. The Latin for "conqueror" is still used when we proclaim a winner as victorious. Old-timers will remember actor Victor Mature, whereas new-timers might identify the name with **Vic** Morrow or Vickie Vale of *Batman* (the movie). Italians were ruled by a series of kings of the 19th century who shared the name Victor Emmanuel. To call someone **"Victorian"** means they are stuffy or prudish. This originated with the reign of Queen Victoria who encouraged such moral severity. **Vincent** also comes from the same root from which we also get **invincible**, though Van Gogh did not have many victories in the art world until after his death.

Virginia   This name has been around much longer than the colony named for the "Virgin Queen," Elizabeth I (see Section Four about the name of the state). The first recorded Virginia was a member of the Roman family of the name Virginius (from the Latin for "chaste"). Her father was a **centurian** (getting his rank in the Roman army because he commanded a hundred men) who tried to protect her from the lascivious Appius Claudius Crassus. This Crassus (which means "fat" in Latin and gives us the word **crass**, meaning "ignorant" or "coarse") was a decemvir. This group was made up of ten men appointed in 451 B.C. to formulate a code of laws for the Roman people to live by. The imposition was not necessarily welcomed. When this particular judge and lawmaker attempted to rape the sweet Virginia, it led to her father taking the extreme step of killing her to keep her from the lusty Crassus. The tragic tale spread among the people and resulted in a revolt that caused the downfall of the decemvirs.

Vivian   This familiar feminine name applies to those who are "full of life" as it translates from its Latin roots. The **vivacious** Vivian Leigh certainly lived up to her name in a character like Scarlett O'Hara. Vivian Vance, the side-kick of Lucille Ball, will be remembered **vividly** (another of the lively words from the root) for her animated style. We have many words related to the root, from **vivisection** ("to cut while living") to the shout heard in Italian or French: viva or vive, meaning "long life."

Let's look at other "V" names briefly. **Vaughn** goes back to Celtic, meaning "small." The seasonal reference to spring and green things is at the heart of names like **Vernon**, **Vern**, **Verne**, or **Verna** which have Latin beginnings. **Viola** and **Violet** are named for the flower whose Latin roots are tied to the same Greek base that gives us **iodine**, referring to the color. The name of the instrument, the viola, doesn't seem to have any relation. **Virgil** seems to go back to a Latin root for "twig" and was applied to growing and flourishing things. **Vladimir** is a name which has Slavic roots, dealing with "the glory of princes."

 Walter The Germanic origins of this name mean "commander of the army." From that former general of the nightly news, Walter Cronkite, to that leader of cartoonists, **Walt** Disney, the name has proven to be a popular one for males.

Wayne This widely seen name has uncertain origins, but seems to go back to the Old English for a "wagon-driver." It was a common practice for families to use the occupation of the clan as a surname such as Cooper, Carter, Smith, or Mason. Later, these surnames were given as first names, long after their origins were forgotten. Though John Wayne might have driven a wagon or two in some of his Westerns, he was not given his name by his family. A producer gave Marion Michael Morrison his popular film name.

William This name goes back to Old High German and combines two roots to translate as "the will of the helmet." In ancient, tribal northern Europe, it *was* the men in the helmets, the warriors, whose will was dominant. Men like the bastard William the Conqueror, who changed English and Western history with his rule of England, or William I, Emperor of Germany, whose rule (with Bismark's assistance in the late 1800's) led to the growth of his country as a mighty power, are strong examples of those who have borne the name through history. Kings of the Netherlands and a queen, **Wilhemina**, have also made a mark with the name. I think of **Will** Rogers, **Bill** Clinton, **Billie** the Kid, **Willie** Mays, or **Billy** Crystal when I think of variations of the name. "Getting the willies," that uneasy or frightened feeling, doesn't seem to have any link to the first name.

Some other "W" names include **Walcott**, whose Germanic roots deal with "a stone cottage." **Waldemar** is not as familiar as the nickname **Waldo**, which has a Germanic birthplace and means "famed power." **Wallace**, seen in names like that of poet Wallace Stevens, has Celtic roots, meaning "stranger." **Wanda** probably comes from a name of a Slavic people called the Wend, also known as Sorbians. The name means "beloved" and more than likely is responsible for **Wendy, Wendell**, and many other present-day words like **win** or **winsome**. The root is also related to Venus, a Latin connection. **Ward** fits both the actor who led the *Wagon Train* TV series to safety time and again, Ward Bond, and Ward Cleaver, father of the Beaver (played by Hugh Beaumont), on *Leave It to Beaver*. The Old English original meant "to watch over." **Guard**, **warden**, and even **wardrobe** come from the same root. **Warren** also goes back to a similar root, meaning "protector." **Washington** is a first or last name that comes from a place in England and means "town washed by the sea." Washington Irving is one of the most famous of those with the first name. **Webster** has obvious connections to a weaver *and* a spider in its Old English beginnings. **Wesley** is also of Old English, Germanic parentage and means "western meadow." **Whitney**, most widely seen in singer Ms. Houston, has a similar descriptive background, referring to a "white island." The horse, Mr. Ed, made the name **Wilbur** much more humorous than its original Germanic meaning, "wild boar." **Wilfred** is a "lover of peace" as translated from its Germanic beginnings. **Willard** Scott, ubiquitous weatherman, has a first name that means "strong-willed" from the same language base. **Willis**, derived from similar roots, means "shield." **Willoughby** literally translates as "by the willows" from the same Germanic base. **Wilmer** deals with the will again: "famous will." **Winston** was made famous by Churchill during World War II, but the name means "friendly town" and is related to Wanda. On the same language path is **Winifred**, "lover of peace," and **Winthrop**, "friendly village." **Woodrow** and **Woodruff** refer to a forester, though President Wilson wasn't much of a woodsman. **Wright** is a "worker"; **Wyndham** is a "windy village"; and **Wynne** deals with winning or gain – all Teutonic in origin.

X   There aren't many "X" names to talk about. **Xavier**, seen most prominently in the story of St. Francis Xavier, missionary to Japan, goes far back to Arabic roots, meaning "glorious." **Xenia** comes from the Greek for "hospitality." **Xerxes** was a Persian king who invaded Greece in 480 B.C. His name in his language meant "ruling over men."

Y   "Y" names are equally rare. We've already mentioned **Yvonne** (see John). **Yardley** has easy-to-see connections with the Old English for a meadow lawn. **Yarmilla** probably means "loud" in its Germanic beginnings. **Yolanda** alludes to "one who is fair" in the same language base. **Yvette**, made famous by Ms. Mimeaux, means "little vine," with **Yves** referring to the main stem. **Ywain** has Celtic origins: "young warrior."

Z **Zacharias** Zacks out there take their name from one of two sources. The first is the priest who was told by the angel Gabriel that his old wife Elisabeth was going to have a baby. Zacharias didn't believe this was possible and was struck dumb by the angel for his lack of faith. When Elisabeth, who was the cousin of Mary the mother of Jesus, gave birth later that year, her husband wrote down the name the angel had told him to give the child, John (the Baptist). Immediately, his voice returned, and he began praising God. His name means "God is renowned" in Hebrew and gives us **Zachary**, as in President Taylor. The other source for the name comes from **Zechariah**, the Hebrew prophet who lived about six hundred years before Christ. His name means "the Lord remembers." His task was to arouse the Jews to rebuild Jerusalem after they were allowed to return home by the Persian king Cyrus.

Zebulon Zebulon was one of the ten sons of Jacob whose name went on to represent one of the twelve tribes of Israel (two of the tribes were named for Joseph's sons). A thirteenth tribe, Levi, was another of the sons whose tribe became the priesthood and originally had no property. After the country divided itself into Judah and Israel in 931 B.C., the ten "rebel" tribes of Israel were conquered, enslaved, and became the "lost" tribes of Israel. **Zeb**'s name means "he dwelled" in Hebrew. Zebulon Pike of Pike's peak fame is one of our most well-known American examples.

There aren't too many "Z" names, as you can tell. **Zedekiah** was the last king of Judah, the pawn of Nebuchadnezzar. He made a deal with the Egyptians that caused the Babylonians to get mad, destroy his kingdom, and carry **Zed** and all his people into captivity where he met his death. **Ziggy** probably got his name from the last name, Zeigfeld, made popular by Florenz who ran the Follies and produced *Show Boat*. **Zinnia** comes from the flower which got its name from Johann Gottfried Zinn, a German botanist. And we know that **Zorba** was a Greek . . .

SECTION FOUR

Origins of the Names of Places

A | **Acre** Though I'll try to focus on major locations of interest in this section, this city in Israel has an interesting origin. It has no relation to the Old English root from which we get a measurement for a parcel of land, an acre. That word first meant "a place to which cattle are driven" and is related to those words with **agri**cultural leanings. The Old English acre referred to a field or plot of land and wasn't given a standard measurement for a thousand years. Generally, it became the practice to use a long stick as a measuring device, with the number of stick-lengths giving fair and equal ratios to the pieces of land in a village. This stick was eventually given a specific length and called a "rod" with 160 square rods (4840 square yards) equalling an acre. Well, I got off the subject of the city. It got its name during the Crusades when the French named it after St. Jean D'Acre. The Hebrew name is Akko; the Arabic is Accho. The tribe of Asher invaded the area around 1425 B.C. When Paul visited the city in the New Testament book of Acts, it was known as Ptolemais, after one of the kings of Macedonia named Ptolemy whose ancestors ruled the area for centuries. One was a brother of Cleopatra who married her and ruled with her for a time.

Adirondack Mountains That part of the Appalachian mountain chain in New York called the Adirondacks gets its name from the suggestion of a state surveyor in 1838. Whether he knew it or not, the name for the range came from an insulting nickname that the Iroquois gave to the encroaching white man and meant "tree eaters." A type of rough, open cabin is also called an adirondack.

Adriatic Sea This part of the Mediterranean that separates Italy from Yugoslavia and Albania took its name from an ancient port city of Adria which also was related to one of the prominent Roman families, Adria or Hadria. When the Po River clogged the harbor with silt, the port was closed. The most well-known shipping area shifted to the island town of Venice (see page 199), but the name still attached itself to the Adriatic Sea.

Aegean Sea That other branch of the Mediterranean, the Aegean Sea, between Greece and Turkey, probably gets its name from the king of Athens, Aegeus, who was the father of Theseus, the great Greek hero. Aegeus had a problem with his neighbor, Minos, the king of Crete. Once every nine years he had to send Minos seven young men and seven maidens to be eaten by Minos' "son," the Minotaur (actually his wife had fallen in love with a sacred bull and bore the half-man/half-bull . . . It's a long story . . .), in repayment for the accidental death of Mino's true son while the lad was visiting King Aegeus. Theseus volunteered to be one of the seven males meant to be a meal, but with the help of Ariadne, Minos' daughter who had fallen in love with Theseus, he was able to kill the Minotaur and find his way out of the Labyrinth (remember?). Theseus had promised to let his father know of his success by putting a white sail up on the return voyage instead of the black one that usually marked the return of the sacrificial ship. Theseus forgot to do this, either too happy with his success to remember or in grief for the loss of Ariadne who had died (some say he abandoned her) on the return voyage; and King Aegeus, thinking the black sail meant his son was dead, threw himself into the sea, which from that time on bore his name . . . whew!

Afghanistan It was difficult to find exactly what this country's name means except "land of the Afghans." Interestingly, this country was originally called Aryana, land of the Aryans, that northern people who swept through Europe and Asia from around 2000 B.C. to 1500 B.C., conquering, inter-breeding, and settling into an agricultural epoch. The Nazis idealized these people during World War II. Afghanistan has been a pawn of conquerors for so much of its history that the recent Russian occupation is only one minor event in an endless series of invasions. When the Pushtan tribe moved in and dominated the area in the 1700's, a group, the Afghan Gilzais united the country into a state under Ahmed Shah.

The Afghan hound with its long, silky hair actually originated in Egypt, but the breed was honed in Afghanistan, and when the English brought the pooch home after World War I, it was the Afghan breeders who got credit for the pedigree.

Africa This seems to be a time of nationalism and the need for respect of heritage, and we see newly liberated Czechs and Slavs and Serbs and Croats and Ukrainians fighting for a separate land or government. Here in the U.S., one of the many movements dealing with this kind of respect focuses on Afro-centrism and the understanding of the African-American's place in world history. Ironically, the name of that continent, sometimes noted as the cradle of civilization, comes from a Roman name for one of the local tribes of northern Africa. When the Romans conquered Carthage in 146 B.C., they named their new province after this tribe which today are known as the Berbers. The root for this name comes from the Latin from which we get words like "**barbarian**" and meant "outsider." The tribe, it seems, was called the Afer, and Africanus came to be the name of the whole northern section of the continent and eventually, of the continent itself. Originally, the Berbers were a Caucasoid people and were not related to the Arabic people or other, southerly tribal states. History seems to be the story of one people absorbing another, in peaceable or warlike ways, and this has happened to most of the Berbers of today.

Alabama The Yellowhammer State takes its name from that of a tribe of Indians, the Alibamon, which in Choctaw means "clear the thicket" and referred to a tribal "headquarters." Indians played a large role in the history of the state, mainly in opposition to white intruders. It began as early as 1540 when the greedy Hernando de Soto and his band of Spaniards fought Chief **Tuscaloosa** (Choctaw for "black warrior") and killed some 2500 braves in the battle. The home of the Red Elephants at the University of Alabama has nothing then to do with "tusks being looser." The former state capital named for the chief is well-known for the Crimson Tide. The largest city in the state, **Birmingham**, was founded in 1871 and named for the English city that was renowned for its industries. That city across the water was begun in the 600's, but was truly founded in the 1100's. **Mobile**, Alabama, takes its name from a fort christened for Louis de la Mobile, built by the French in 1701. "We Dare to Defend our Rights" is the state's motto. I'll certainly be leaving out many cities as I ramble through the U.S. in this section, but I'll try to hit on those whose origins I've stumbled over or dug into . . . like **Dothan**, Alabama, named for the town in Palestine where the entire Syrian army was struck blind through Elisha's prayer to God so they would not capture him or destroy the area. **Huntsville** was named in 1811 for one of its earliest settlers, John Hunt. Places in Ontario, Canada, and Texas share the name, but not the settler. General Richard **Montgomery** was honored for his death in the Revolutionary War when another Alabama town gave itself his last name in 1819.

Alaska Alaska takes its name from the Russian borrowing of an Aleut word, meaning "great lands." Being the largest state, it certainly contains the greatest amount of land, but not that many people. Its astronomical state flag contains the Big Dipper and the North Star on a field of blue. It's easy to understand how the port city of **Anchorage** got its name as a place to drop anchor. You might think it was another descriptive designation responsible for **Fairbanks**, but, no, that city was named for Charles W. Fairbanks, a Senator from Indiana and Vice-President under Teddy Roosevelt. It was prospector and gold miner, Joe **Juneau**, who gave his name to another of the 49th state's cities. The Aleutian chain of islands in the state comes from that tribe mentioned above whose name means "beyond the shore."

Alexandria The once-mighty Egyptian city was founded by Alexander the Great in 332 B.C. and was a world-renowned center of culture and education. So you would think our American cities were paying tribute to the great port city. Not so. Alexandria, Virginia, was named for the Alexander family that owned land there in 1748. This railroad town was once part of the District of Columbia, but it was given back to Virginia in 1846 as a "free city." Alexandria, Louisiana, was named in 1805 after Alexander Fulton's daughter who bore that name. I'm not certain about Alexandria, Indiana.

Algeria Numidia was the ancient kingdom that is now Algeria. Its king helped the Romans defeat Hannibal in 202 B.C. Of all the conquerors of the area, the Arabs most deeply changed the country, which gets its name from the Arabic, meaning "the islands," referring to a group of these in the harbor of Algiers. Even though St. Augustine was bishop in the area in the early 400's, Christianity eventually fell to Islam. From the 1600's to the 1800's Algeria was one of the Barbary States, known for their pirates and disruption of shipping. Countries had to pay "protection" tributes to those states if they wanted to travel the Barbary Coast. **Barbary** got its name both from the

Berbers (see Africa) and the Turkish corsair, Barbarossa, an admiral known for his barbarous treatment of enemies. It was Thomas Jefferson who, as President, finally got fed up with these rascals when they kept upping the tribute amounts. From 1801 to 1805 he fought against them with the U.S. Navy, bringing forth heroics like those of young Stephen Decatur who led a raid into the Tripoli harbor. A predecessor of Captain Kirk, he commanded the first *Enterprise*. During the Tripolitan War he used this ship to capture the *Intrepid* and then used that vessel to sneak into the harbor of Tripoli and burn the *Philadelphia*, a ship that had once been commanded by Decatur's father but had been captured by the pirates and posed a threat to our naval strategies. In a toast Decatur once said, "Our country, may she always be right; but our country right or wrong." Sound familiar? After brave service in the War of 1812, Decatur had to go back to the Barbary coast to once-and-for-all force the dey of Algiers to renounce the taking of tribute for safe passage and, thus, end piracy in northern Africa. Decatur was killed in a duel by a disgruntled, court-martialed former captain.

Amazon The second longest river in the world got its name because it was reported by 16th century explorers that there were tall women warriors in the interior. Though this was never confirmed, the story was widely told, and the resemblance to the Greek tales of the Amazon nation gave the river and surrounding rain forest this name. The original Greek roots for the word meant "without breasts," from the belief that these fighting women removed their right breasts so they wouldn't get in the way of the bowstring's pull during battle. Another legend about these militant ladies gives us the name of the Amazon ant which takes the young of other species and makes "slaves" of them. The Amazon women were reputed to take children from those they conquered and raise them . . . the girls, naturally.

America This name, applied to both the continents of the Western Hemisphere and to the United States of America, is of Italian descent. The banker and businessman from Florence, Amerigo Vespucci, was living in Spain at the time of Columbus and his voyages. He got the travelling bug in Seville when he heard tales of those journeys. By 1497, he was on a ship and writing about the lands across the Atlantic Ocean. Though there are some doubts about all his reports, he claimed to have been the first to have seen the continent of South America a year before Columbus got away from his island hopping. One thing is for certain: Vespucci replaced the notion that Columbus had fostered that this was part of the East Indies. Vespucci felt they had found a "new world" that was not part of Asia. His own publicity seemed to work when, in 1507, a prominent mapmaker placed the Latinized version of Amerigo's name on the chart of South America, acknowledging him as the discoverer. Though Spain had a very negative response to this, the name stuck and our Italian explorer got more name recognition than any of his counterparts of the era. Chris does get his due, but we'll talk about that later.

Antarctica This southernmost continent of the world has a name that literally translates as "opposite the bear" from the Greek. The constellation, the Great Bear, Ursa Major, also known as the Big Dipper, is well-known for its being the constellation of the north. We think of the word arctic as meaning frigid, but its original reference was to the Greek name for the image they saw in the stars. After Peary located the North Pole in the Arctic in 1909, it became a race between Roald Amundson and R.F. Scott to get to the South Pole. Amundson's trip was grueling but happy, ending in the planting of a flag of discovery on December 14, 1911. Scott made it over a month later but all of his party died on their return.

That close, bright star Arcturus means "guardian of the bear."

Argentina When this country was explored by the Spanish in the 1500's, it was with the hope of finding gold and silver. In fact, the names given to the land related to this desire. Argentina means "silver." First, the area was called the Vice-royalty de la Plata, which also referred to silver. Though no precious metals of any consequence were found, natives today think of the many silvery lakes and rivers in "tierra Argentina." In the 1920's, Argentina was one of the wealthiest nations in the world, and its capitol, **Buenos Aires** ("good air") was the Paris of the New World.

Arizona Most agree that the astronomy capitol of the world got its name from a Spanish adaptation of a Pima Indian name which meant either "place of the little spring" or "place of few springs." It is possible that this state with the Latin motto **Intat Deus**, "God enriches," could have taken its name from an Aztec word meaning "silver." The Grand Canyon State was number forty-eight when it was added early in 1912.

Arkansas When Hernando de Soto came tramping across the land of the 25th state, he was looking for gold. It was probably good that he didn't find any and left the area to a more peaceful growth. The Quapaw Indians, a Sioux people, gave the state its name, which the French passed on. Arkansas means "the people down the stream." The state has had its liberal and conservative moments. When Hattie Carraway became the first woman elected to the Senate in 1932, that was quite a step forward; but when Governor Orval Faubus opposed integration in 1957, he brought negative world-wide attention to the state.

Asia This largest continent extends from the Ural Mountains to Malasia, from Siberia to Saudi Arabia. The Greek root that gives us the name simply mean "place where the sun rises." The Greeks gave it this name obviously because it was east of their land, but were influenced by the Babylonian Akkadians whose name actually referred to setting suns.

Athens The Greeks wanted to name their city, so the story goes, after one of the gods, and it came down to Athena, the goddess of wisdom, or Poseidon, god of the sea. Each gave the humans a gift to be judged for its worthiness. Poseidon gave either a horse or a spring – there's some confusion here – and Athena gave the olive tree. Obviously, the tree was deemed more valuable and thus was Athens named. The goddess, the patron of arts and crafts, was a virgin and was called Pallas (maiden) or Parthenos (virgin) from which we get the **Parthenon**.

Though the Romans called this goddess Minerva, they named a famous school of art the Athénaeum after the Greek temple of learning, the Athenion. It has been a tradition in the U.S. for college towns to take the name, whether it is the home of the University of Georgia or seats of higher education in Ohio and Tennessee.

Australia The most influential astronomer of ancient times, Ptolemy, theorized that there must be some southern continent below the Asian land mass. Around the 2nd century A.D. he was writing about geography and called this probable continent "Terra Australis Incognito," which translates from Latin as "unknown southern land." His work had impact on scholars all the way into the 16th century. When Dutch captain Abel Tasman came across a large island in the 17th century, he was uncertain about how big the land mass was. The island of **Tasmania** was later named for him. The main continent was dubbed New South Wales by Captain James Cook. Later, the lingering influence of Ptolemy led the country/continent to have the down-under name meaning "southern." **Brisbane** was named for Sir Thomas Macdougall Brisbane who was an astronomer, soldier, administrator, and governor of New South Wales. An important influence during the reign of Queen Victoria was Prime Minister **Melbourne**. The city in Australia was named for him in 1837. Because Helen Porter Mitchell was born there, she decided to name herself Nellie Melba when she began her famous career as a soprano. Dame Nellie's popularity was such that when she enjoyed a certain kind of food, it was honored with her name as in **Melba toast** and **Peach Melba**.

Austria Since 1955, when Allied forces finally let this country regain sovereignty, peace and relative prosperity have been enjoyed by the Austrians. The land was known as Noricum before the Roman conquest. By the time of the Holy Roman Emperors of the 10th century, it was called "the eastern kingdom," which is the Germanic meaning of the name of the country. **Vienna** gets its name from the same root that gives us that goddess of love, Venus. It could be said it is the city of love.

Some other places to mention on our tour of the world include **Albania** which was named for a fiesty Illyrian people who were conquered by Rome in 167 B.C., but were very resistant to Roman influence. The Albanii are like many tough tribes which gave their names to the land they occupied. **Alberta**, Canada, takes its name from the hubby of Queen Victoria, Prince Albert. Originally, it was known as "Rupert's land." The **Alps** probably get their name from a Celtic word that meant either "high" or "white," though which one it was seemed to get lost after the Romans incorporated the name into Latin. Both fit. **Alsace**, which is usually tied to Lorraine, was originally Alsatia when it was conquered by Julius Caesar in the first century B.C. It's been passed back and forth between Germany and France since the 1300's. In the 1570's the desire for more slaves led the Portugese to overwhelm the Ngola kingdom in the area of Africa now named for those people, **Angola**. The place mentioned in the Bible as the first to see followers of Jesus called Christians is **Antioch**, which is a Turkish town named for the father of one of Alexander the Great's generals. The **Appalachian** mountain chain takes its name from that of an Indian tribe that lived in a small part of these eastern peaks. **Armenia** is probably most remembered by Americans as the site of a 1988 earthquake that killed 25,000 people. It takes its name from a legendary hero, Aram, who founded the country in the 9th century.

B **Bangladesh** Many children of the 60's remember George Harrison's dramatic fund-raising concert for the starving of this nation. The country has been a pawn of this ruler or that – whether Afghan, Mogul, Muslim, or British – since its existence as a "nation" a thousand years before Christ when it was known as the kingdom of Banga, a name that gradually evolved into Bengal, which we'll look at in India. The country wanted true independence when its last overlord, Pakistan, tried to rule this land from 1000 miles away. By 1971 this movement led to the death of a million people there through civil war. Famine and economic disaster due to the drying up of the jute market led to a world-wide plea for aid in the early 70's.

Barbados This island nation abolished slavery in 1834, but didn't gain independence from Britain until 1966. It was named by the Portugese explorers because of the hanging moss in the trees found there. The name means "bearded" and is related to those **barber**ing words we're familiar with.

Basque Provinces The Basque people are unique in many ways. Fiercely independent, their language, customs, and traditions have origins that remain a mystery. Perhaps the Euskadi people came from ancient Aquitania where they might have been the Ausci, a tribe there, but the lack of relationship between their language and any other in Europe makes these mountain people interesting to sociologists, historians, and linguists alike. St. Ignatius of Loyola and St. Francis Xavier are two of the most well-known Basques, a people whose gene pool doesn't seem to have any links to the rest of the people on their continent.

Bath Yes, Bath, England, was named for the Old English word for washing. The Romans were the first recorded people to take advantage of the hot springs found there and construct huge bathing areas around them near 100 A.D. They called the place Aquae Sulis for its warm water. You'll find towns in Maine and New York with the same name. One of the orders of knighthood in Great Britain is the Order of the Bath.

Belgium Belgium is another of those countries that has been a political football, having been ruled by Dutch, French, Spanish, Austrian, and German governments at one time or another. When the Romans named it the province of Gallia Belgica during Julius Caesar's time it was in honor of the Celtic Belgae tribes who had settled there around 100 B.C. One of its most famous cities, **Brussels**, has Frankish origins and means "village of the marshes." Those famous sprouts are how we Americans have most often seen the name, which can have negative perceptions by some because of this.

Bethlehem The birthplace of Jesus has different meanings in the two languages that are used by its inhabitants today. The Hebrew translation is "the house of bread," but the Arabic rendering means "house of meat." Either way, it's food for thought. The small town south of Jerusalem is also noted as being the burial place of Rachel, Jacob's favorite wife. This was also the home city of Boaz whose direct descendant, David, was part of the line that led to Jesus' parents. The town suffered tragedy when Herod ordered all male infants slain on rumors of the birth of the Messiah.

Bolivia The amazing Venezuelan general Simón Bolívar is the man for whom this country is named. He liberated all of northern South America from Spanish rule in the early 1800's. He would have liked to have formed a huge country like the United States which he wanted to call Greater Columbia, but he couldn't hold the separate nations together and, in fact, was hated as a dictator for a time. Today, Bolívar's liberating achievement is much more highly thought of by the South American people. One of this country's cities was named for another revolutionary of the time, Antonio José de **Sucre**. Another's name means "peace," **La Paz**.

Brazil Pedro Alvares Cabral claimed this land for Portugal in 1500. It was named because the wood of one of the tropical trees looked like burning coals. The popular, red-colored brazilwood is not from the same tree that gives us Brazil nuts. Another interesting note is that slavery wasn't abolished until 1888 in this country. "The river of January" is the translation of **Rio de Janeiro** because it was discovered in that month. St. Paul gets credit for the inspiration behind the naming of **Sáo Paulo** in this fifth largest country in the world.

Bridge of Sighs This place sounds romantic, doesn't it? Knowing its location is Venice, Italy, might make you think of lovers cuddled in a gondola, whispering sweet nothings as they pass under one of the many bridges. Sorry. The Bridge of Sighs connected the prison of Venice to the palace and its interrogation room/torture chamber where many a prisoner would cross on his way to questioning. The sighs were more in anxious anticipation than relaxed romance. New York City had the name applied to a passageway in the Tombs prison.

Brunswick We've already talked about the origins of Brunswick stew (see Section Two) in Brunswick County, Virginia. The original Brunswick was founded in 861 in Germany by Bruno. Translated as "the city of Bruno (brown one)," the large German city inspired those in Georgia, Maine, and Ohio to name towns in those states.

Bunker Hill The first major battle of the Revolutionary War was not fought on this crest in the Boston area known as Bunker's Hill then, but on nearby Breed's Hill. The Americans actually lost the battle, running so short of powder that they were admonished not to waste a shot until they saw the "whites" of the British troops' eyes. Still, their courage and small losses compared to the British boosted the Americans' idea that they could actually beat their English overlords even if it were an uphill battle.

Let's travel to other "B" places. The tiny Arab nation of **Bahrain** was once known as Dilmon, then Tylos, and later Acual. The present Arabic name means "two seas," referring to its island status. The **Balkans** once were states of the mighty Ottoman Empire in the 1600's and included Greece, Turkey, Yugoslavia, Rumania, Bulgaria and Albania. Now the name mainly refers to a mountain range, which is what the word means in Turkish. The **Bastille** is a place that is known across the world as the prison that was beseiged during the French Revolution. Its name means "fortified place," and its root gives us another strong word, **bastion**. The state in Germany known as **Bavaria** gets its name from another of those Germanic tribes of the 5th and 6th century A.D., the Baiovarii. **Borneo** is the third largest island in the world, but actually has more than one nation involved in its land. It was called Burné in 1521, but its true name should be Brunei. If you want to get rained on, go there between November and May. **Bosnia-Hercegovina** has been an unfortunate news headline recently because of Yugoslavian unrest. Before this day and time, it was known as the area that kicked off World War I when archduke Ferdinand of Austria was assasinated in Sarajevo. Bosnia was named for the Bosna river and Hercegovina means "duke," getting its name in the 15th century from a local ruler. **Bulgaria** owes its name to the tribe of Bulgars who conquered the area in the 7th century A.D.

C **Cairo** This capital of Egypt had a slow start as a suburb of Fustat in the 900's A.D. Where is Fustat? Gone. Just as the mighty former Egyptian capital, Memphis, located about 12 miles from Cairo, suffered decline, so did the original city from which Cairo arose. In 1168, Christian crusaders made Fustat a forgotten name. The suburb was left intact and this area grew. Cairo gets its name from the Arabic word for the planet Mars, which means "victorious." It was probably named so because the city's construction started as Mars was in the heavens – according to legend. European colonization of Africa led to a two-sided city. One section, al ˋQuhirah (the original Arabic spelling), was left to the Islamic Arabs, while the wealthy northern invaders lived in another section they called Cairo, a corruption of the Arabic.

Because the area in Illinois where the Ohio and Mississippi Rivers met reminded founders of the city on the Nile, they named the town that grew there Cairo. In fact, during this time in the early 1800's, all of southern Illinois became known as "Little Egypt." During the Civil War's battles in the West, General Grant made his headquarters there. Charles Dickens wasn't impressed when he visited and used his experience there as the model for a less-than-Utopian city of Eden in his book *Martin Chuzzlewit*. Another Cairo exists in Georgia.

Calcutta   When the East India Company of England was granted the right to establish a base on the Bay of Bengal, they consolidated three villages: Govindapur, Sutanati, and Kalikata. The Brits first called their establishment Fort William, but because the temple of the goddess Kali was located in that third village mentioned, the city gradually got to be known by that name. Kali gets her name from the Sanskrit, meaning "black." This strange goddess has a violent history. The ugly, naked, black hag who sports a belt of skulls had to kill a demon whose every drop of blood spilled might form a duplicate demon. Her sickening solution was to drink his blood before it could reach the ground. Her power was so revered that a cult of murderous followers, the **thugs** (a Sanskrit word for a thief from a root meaning "to hide"), ravaged the countryside for six hundred years, ambushing wealthy travellers and strangling them in sacrifice to the demon-slaying goddess. Speaking of black, the expression that refers to some dark, uncomfortable place, "the Black Hole of Calcutta," comes from an incident in which Indian revolutionaries threw captured British soldiers into a tiny, nearly airless prison where many suffocated to death.

California   Though it took the Spaniards a long time to actually colonize this state, they must have originally thought this was a land of magical potential. It was named for an imaginary island of wealth in a tale written in 1510 by Garcia Ordóñez do Montalvo. *Las Sergas de Esplandium* tells of a land of treasure called California. Juan

Cabrillo was the first to land on the coast in 1542. The state might have been named Nova Albion if England had followed up on Sir Francis Drake's claim in 1579. Russians even had claims in the area as late as the 1840's near Santa Rosa. It may well be that the reason for the Monroe Doctrine, barring further colonization of North and South America in 1812, was spurred by fears of Russian Californian intrusions. Most of the major cities of this state show the obvious influence of the Spanish missions that spread through the territory: the angels of **Los Angeles**; the saints named in San Francisco, San Diego, and San José, to touch only a few; the tributes to their homeland in Coronado or **Monterey** ("king's hill"). There are many other influences in the Golden State. A group of German immigrants took the Spanish and incorporated it into their own language when they named **Anaheim** in 1857, meaning "home by the Santa Ana River." **Carlsbad** was so named in 1880 because mineral springs there were considered to be like those in the European Carlsbad, which was named in 1349 "the bath of Charles" in honor of Charles IV (the Fair). Carlsbad, New Mexico, was named nine years later for the same reason. I always thought **Burbank** was named for the great botanist, Luther Burbank, but actually it was a dentist, Dr. David Burbank, who subdivided his land in 1887 to begin the city. The interesting Irish philosopher, George **Berkeley**, contended with John Locke in the 1700's, believing that the material world is rather illusory and only exists in the mind of God. The California town was named for him in 1864, as were cities in Illinois and Missouri. It's ironic that the man-made element **berkelium** was given its name, referring to the the city, not the anti-materialist. We could go on and on . . .

Calvary

The hill where Jesus was crucified with a couple of thieves takes its name from its shape. The Aramaic word, Golgotha, meant "place of the skull." When the Greek translation was completed, the word was "kranion" (from which we get **cranium**). When St. Jerome translated the Bible into Latin in the 4th century, the name of the place still meant "skull" but was now "calvariae." 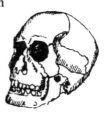 You'll remember the root appearing in the name **Calvin** ("baldheaded") in Section Three.

Cambodia

The recent tragedies of this Asian country are part of a string of conquests by brutal rulers after the fall of the Khmer empire in the 1400's. The European corruption of Kambuja gave us the former name of the country that was founded by the ancient hero,

Kambu. Now known as Kampuchea, the recent revolutions include forced evacuation of the cities, thrusting the population into a rural existence that has seen over a million die through violence or starvation.

Canaan   Christians, Jews, and Moslems are all familiar with the "land of Canaan," the area that is now part of Israel. There are two paths to the naming of this area. When the sons of Noah split up and went out into the depopulated, flood-ravaged land and began settling here and there, according to the Biblical narrative, Ham, one of the boys, had a son named Canaan, which means "to bow down" in Hebrew. That land was certainly forced to do that by the prophecy-driven Israelites. The other version of the name comes from Semitic language roots. By the way, **Semites** get their name from another of Noah's kids, Shem. We're most familiar with anti-Jewish sentiment called **anti-semitism**. Back to Canaan. In the Semitic base the word "Canaan" means "reddish-purple" and referred to dye-makers who dominated the coastal craftspeople. It could be translated from the Phoenician as "land of the crimson wool." The Biblical account probably pre-dates the later association of the land with the rich dye made from the abundant sea life of the area.

Canada   Explorer Jaques Cartier transliterated a Huron Iroquois word, "kanata," which meant "village" and was the name of a tribal community. This huge land has many Indian and French namings, from the "Royal Mount" of **Montreal** to the Algonquian **Quebec**, meaning "the place shut in." Even the popular traveling vehicle, the **Winnebago**, has a name that originated in Canada as an Indian tribal name: "muddy water people." **Manitoba** comes from the Cree Indian and means something like "the God who speaks" or "voice of the Great Spirit." This referred to the sound of water heard splashing on the banks of Lake Manitoba which the Indians heard as divine messages. **Ontario** has an Iroquois origin, meaning either "beautiful lake," "sparkling waters," or "rocks standing by the water." Places in California and Oregon have also used the name. **Ottawa** means "to trade" in its Indian original, but was first called Bytown. Kansas and Illinois also have Ottawas. Of course, the British influence can also be felt as in a place name like **Calgary** whose namesake is the Calgary House in Scotland on the Isle of Mull. Its Gaelic translation means "bay farm" reminding settlers of the water-bound homeland because of the confluence of the Bow and Elbow Rivers on the Canadian site.

Cannes   Cannes was just a tiny fishing village named for its reedy banks (the French for "canes"). But when a wealthy Englishman was barred from vacationing at one of the larger coastal towns because of port quarantine regulations, he sailed down the shoreline to Cannes, stayed there, liked it, and built a huge summer home nearby to snub his nose at the regulators. Others followed, making this a fashionable resort town today and home of the world-famous film festival that we Americans are so familiar with.

Canterbury We've already talked about the horse's gait that comes from this city of cathedrals (see). The ancient town was called Durovernum Cantiacorum by the Roman invaders, describing this as "the fort among the alders." The Old English name from which we get our modern version meant "fort of the Kentish people." **Kent** came from a Celtic word that the Romans Latinized above. It described a bordered area, referring to forts, boundaries, coastlines. Chaucer's tales of pilgrims make this town almost too familiar to students of English literature. You'll find another Canterbury in Australia.

Canton The beauty, mystery, and wealth of the oriental city inspired many settlers and city founders to honor it by naming their cities after the Chinese town, which probably got the European version of its name from the T'ang dynasty. If towns in Connecticut, New York, North Carolina, Massachusetts, Illinois, Mississippi, and South Dakota had used the Chinese name, they might be called Guangzhou. The most famous American Canton is in Ohio. This home of the Football Hall of Fame was named by its founder for an estate in Maryland that was established from profits made through trade with China. Now, some of the Cantons mentioned could have taken their name from the territorial sectioning of a country like Switzerland. The canton is mentioned in the previous description from which Kent is derived. The Romans used the term to deal with divided areas, even something like the corner of a flag.

Casablanca This Moroccan seaport which was made so famous by the Humphrey Bogart movie was named by the Portugese in 1515. "White house" is the translation of the original moniker, Casa Branca. The visitors called the city this because of the whitewash used on the houses there. The Spanish took the name and transcribed it into their language.

Casbah "Come with me to the Casbah" was a movie line that stirred romantic notions. The Arabic word had reference to a "metropolis" or "capital" or "citadel" and was originally the palace of the ruler. Today, casbahs are the native quarters in many cities along the African Mediterranean coast, especially famous in Algiers.

Charlotte The North Carolina town was named before the Revolutionary War after the queen of George III, Charlotte Sophia. Charlottesville, Virginia, was also named for this loyal lady. The Mississippi town was named much later, in 1835. The capital of the Virgin Islands, **Charlotte Amalie**, was named for the woman who was a queen in 1691, wife of the Danish king Christian V.

Chicago The "windy city" or "city of big shoulders" are two of the modern-day nicknames for this famous Illinois metropolis; however, if we translate the name into to the most uncomplimentary form of the Algonquian original, Chicago would be known as "the smelly place." A more euphemistic translation would be "place of the wild onions." It was so named by the Indians for the strong-smelling onions and skunk cabbage that grew on its marshy lakeshore. The Potawatomi would be surprised at the giant Loop and huge industry, though there have been less-than-sweet-smelling problems there during Prohibition and, recently, when water poured into underground passageways in the downtown district.

Chile The Araucanian Indian name for this country doesn't seem to have anything to do with the peppers or beans we Americans associate with the word. Our name for the familiar food comes from a Nahuatl Indian name for the red pepper. The tough mountain Indians of the southern Andes called their home "place where the land ends." The Spaniards could never quite whip these natives into the shape they wanted, though in 1541, when they first started, Pedro de Valdivia fought hard against Chief Lautaro. After about three hundred years of conflict, the country gained independence under Bernardo O'Higgins.

The tale of *Robinson Crusoe* came from the story of Scottish sailor, Alexander Selkirk, being stranded on this country's southernmost Juan Fernandes Islands.

The great mountain range in this country, the **Andes**, gets its name from a Quechuan Indian word for copper.

China Once called **Cathay** by Europeans after a Turkish tribe, the Qitan or Quitay or Khitan, who ruled China in medieval times, China's modern Western name got its beginnings with the Ch'in dynasty of 221 B.C. The Chinese call their land "the middle country," Zhonghua.

These days we're starting to get a bit more sensitive about native names for lands far from our own and have taken to calling Peking by its Chinese name, **Beijing**, which means "northern capital" and was just that to the Ming dynasty of the 1400's.

Manchuria takes its name from the Manchus who ruled China under the Ch'ing ("pure") dynasty from the 1600's to the early 1900's. The Chinese just call the region "the Northeast" today.

Colombia
Yes, Christopher **Columbus** does get some immortality in our look at place names. Originally, this country, known for its coffee and cocaine dealers, was named in honor of a part of Spain and was called New Granada until 1821 when the Spanish were kicked out. It was then part of the huge republic of Gran Colombia (see **Bolivia**), but it broke away in 1863. **Bogatá** was founded in 1538 and probably named for the Indian chief, Bacatá.

In the U.S., the Italian sailor gets honored through the names of cities in Georgia, Indiana, Maryland, Mississippi, Missouri, Nebraska, Ohio, Pennsylvania, South Carolina, and Tennessee. And, of course, we also have the **District of Columbia** set aside as our nation's capital.

Colombo, Sri Lanka's capital, doesn't pay tribute to Chris, but is a European rendering of the native word, Kolamba, that refers both to a "port" and a "leafy mango tree."

Colorado
When the state came into the Union at the hundred year anniversary of America's independence in 1876, it was nicknamed the Centenniel State; but it was the Spanish who claimed the land first, in 1706, initially referring to the river that ran through red rock and, thus, looked crimson. "Colored red" is how it has been translated, though "colored" is the literal meaning. This stopping point on the way to the gold rush has the "mile-high city" as its capital, named for James W. **Denver** who was governor of the territory in 1858 in its heyday. Millionaires became paupers in the silver panic of 1893, but the place is no worse for the wear today.

Congo
The tiny, but fierce hunters, the Pygmies, were probably the first inhabitants of this area of Africa that now contains the **People's Republic of the Congo**. It was not named for the diminuative tribespeople who got their designation from a mythological race of dwarfs. **Pygmy** comes from the Greek for a measurement from the elbow to the knuckles – the Hebrew cubit. The Greeks thought they lived at the source of the Nile and battled migrating cranes each year. The Kongo kingdom was mighty in the area when encountered by

Europeans, and that is where the name, Congo, comes from, once applied to the river, too. **Zaire** is the modern name for the river and the old Democratic Republic of the Congo, and this label comes from a Portugese variation of a Kakono word for "river."

Connecticut As a schoolchild, I always imagined this state was named for some connecting place over a cut. My typical Westernizing mind found out much later that the state's name comes from an Algonquian word that has the geographical meaning "on the long tidal river." This state which honors the robin was a "**New Haven**" for Puritans and strongly utilitarian in its beginnings.

Costa Rica When Columbus landed here in 1502, one of his foraging parties returned with gold and got everyone excited. The Spanish called the country "the rich coast." The name didn't quite pan out because even though the Indians there told of great deposits of gold and silver, none of consequence was found.

Cuba It was hard to find the exact origin of this name, but it probably comes from a native Indian name for "island" taken by Columbus after his visit in October of 1492. The only other cuba's I could find were an African creole word for a child born on Wednesday and a card game that took its name from Latin, "to lay down," alluding to discards, but neither of these seems to have any bearing. Columbus was sure this was Japan or some other great Asian landfall – another mistake.

We may never learn how the U.S. *Maine* blew up in the Havana harbor, but the incident led to Cuba's independence from Spain after the Spanish-American War in 1898. We even ruled the island for a few years after that, but today, we're not on the same side of the political fence . . .

Czechoslovakia This country may never exist again since it has divided itself along ancient tribal lines. The Czechs were a prominent group in the area in the 800's, and when they joined with the Slovaks, the land of Bohemia became fairly powerful – but only briefly. The area was parcelled out hither and yon until a thousand years later when, after World War I, the land was reunited as Czechoslovakia.

One of its more famous times of division was when John Huss (Jan Hus) wanted to reform the Catholic church in the 1400's, and the Hussites created quite a storm of religious controversy when they refused to recognize the notion that the pope was unable to make a mistake. The Reformation got quite a jump start from this Czech priest, even though the Catholics burned him at the stake after he was lured to the Council of Constance in 1414.

Let's touch down briefly at other "C" places. **Capri** is noted in mythology as the island where **sirens** lured sailors to their deaths. All we have left of their musically enchanting voices is the noise of warning on our police and fire vehicles used to help save people from destruction. Capri comes from the Latin for either "goat" ("capra") or "wild boar" ("kapros"), both found on the rocky isle. I haven't been able to trace the translation of the name of the **Caucasus Mountains** that give us the word **caucasian**, which today is synonymous with "white" because it was believed that that is where all of us honkys originated. Mythologically speaking, this is where Prometheus was chained and punished by the gods for teaching mankind about powerful things like fire. The **Chattahoochee River** comes from an Indian name that means "pounded rock" and refers to cornmeal that the natives ground with the strong stone found there. The island of **Corfu** was in the headlines worldwide when a declaration was signed there by the exiled Serbian government during World War I that called for a unified Yugoslav state, joining Serbs, Croats, and Slovenes. The ill-fated union is once again making headlines, this time not so positive. Corfu, by the way, is Italian from the Greek for "crests." **Corsica** was named by the Romans and basically means "small island."

D | **Damascus** Some claim that this is the oldest city in the world that has been continuously occupied. The Syrian capital is very familiar to Christians as the place to which Paul was traveling when he was converted. The Street Called Straight, where he regained his eyesight and was baptized, is still there. Some of you may have tablecloths and napkins you call **damask**. This kind of weaving originated with the Chinese around 1000 B.C., but when Crusaders brought the cloth home to Europe, the city of Damascus got credited. Sword makers in the area were famous for a type of steel so fine that a weapon could be bent from point to hilt without damage. Their superfine formulation was known as **damask steel**.

Delaware Thomas West, the 12th Baron De La Warr, helped found Virginia, rebuilding Jamestown. He was honored by the naming of a river and Indian tribe in the area. When a group of counties that had been melded into Pennsylvania wanted their own government, they called their new amalgamation Delaware, a version of the Baron's name. It's capital, **Dover**, was named for the English city in

1717. That 11th century town on the Dour River is famous for its chalk cliffs and is also responsible for the naming of the New Hampshire village where Quakers were whipped out of town on orders of the Deputy Governor, Captain Richard Waldron, in 1651. Later, this place became over one-third Quaker. There are also Dovers in New Jersey and Ohio.

The "First State" (because it was the first to approve the Constitution in 1787), Delaware had a huge beauty pageant in 1880 with Thomas Edison as one of the judges. The "Miss United States" titleholder was the forerunner of Miss America.

Deseret So, not many of you have heard of this place? You Mormons reading this will definitely tell us that this was almost the name of a state that would have encompassed parts of several present-day western states. "The Land of the Honey Bee," as it translates from the Book of Mormon was to be a Mormon state governed by Brigham Young. Congress didn't quite agree with the request, worried about the lack of separation of church and state and the practice of polygamy. Upright as Mr. Young was, Easterners couldn't accept the notion of twenty-seven wives for one man. In the Compromise of 1850, they made Utah a territory with Young as governor, but this didn't satisfy the Mormons who almost came to blows with the U.S. Army in 1857. The "Beehive State" was only granted allowance into the Union after polygamy was outlawed. The Mormons' newspaper is still called *The Deseret News*.

Dominican Republic The Dominican Republic is part of the island of Hispaniola which was found in 1492 by Señor Columbus. When the Santa Maria shipwrecked there, it became the first Spanish settlement, instantly populated by the crewmen of the ship and called "the birth," La Navidad. Cannibals were probably responsible for making this a short-lived metropolis. The lack of early interest by the Spanish allowed French settlements to take hold on part of the island (see **Haiti**), and a trio of revolutionaries finally helped the place break totally free of Spain in 1844.

Downing Street That place in London where the Prime Minister lives was named for Sir George Downing. This son of a Puritan was one of the first Harvard graduates and later got involved in British politics, provoking two wars with the Dutch when he was envoy. His financial wizardry is what won him the most fame.

Dresden The inane and tragic bombing of the German city on and before Valentine's Day during World War II ruined a wonderful, historic, architectural monument and pointed up some of the stupidity of war. Vonnegut's *Slaughterhouse Five* is just one of the works commemorating the insanity of the destruction. The Slavic name of the city means "forest dwellers on the plain," and it has been a place of importance since the early 1200's. The famous Dresden china actually comes from Meissen, a city a few miles away where the manufacturing moved in 1710.

Some other "D" places include **Dalmatia** which is an area of Croatia that had been tossed about between Italy and Austria. The name of the place is most familiar to us when we apply it to the dog, the **Dalmatian**. These animals were trained to be companions of horses and actually used to run between the wheels of coachs as they rolled through the city. The association with fire engines originated with the earlier breeding. When horses pulled fire wagons, these friendly dogs would help keep the horses calm as they neared the smoke and heat. As a note, they don't get their spots until they are three or four weeks old. **Darjeeling**, which you've heard of if you fancy tea, is a Tibetan name for "place of the thunderbolt." Battle weary British troops used the Indian city as a sanitorium for awhile, starting in 1835. **Dartmouth**, in England, has obvious origins, being at the mouth of the Dart River (which might get its name for the Germanic for "spear"). The city in Nova Scotia was named for the Earl of Dartmouth. The Massachusetts college town was named for the English port. If you like **Dijon mustard**, you might be interested to know this former capital of Burgundy once rivaled Paris in the 13th century. The Roman military camp that started here was named Castrom Divionense. The island of **Dominica** was discovered on Sunday, November 3, 1493 by – you guessed it – Christopher Columbus and so was named "dies Dominica," "day of the Lord." The 13th century saw the founding of the "village on the Dussel," a tributary of the Rhine, giving us today's **Dusseldorf**.

E **Ecuador** When the Spanish arrived here in 1531, they found the kingdom of Quito, an Incan land. Their name for the territory translates geographically as "equator." **Quito**, its capital, still carries the Incan name. The lack of hoped-for riches left the area rather undeveloped during the Spanish conquest of the Americas.

Eden That biblical garden where man and woman got clued in to the idea that they could do good *or* bad things probably had its first mention in Sumerian legends and meant "plain." The notion of an oasis in that plain comes more readily from the Hebrew rendering which means "delight." When the Greek translation of the Bible was complete, the word meant "paradise," and that's how we think of it today. Though both Australia and Nebraska have places named Eden, the original site, oddly enough, was probably in Iraq, say historians – not a paradise for modern Westerners.

Egypt We've already mentioned Cairo (see), but we'll spend another moment in one of the most ancient of lands. The country itself takes its name from an version of the name of the former capital, **Memphis**, whose name originally referred to white walls and then was called Men-nefer. This place known for its **deserts** (from "dehret:" "red land") and **pharoahs** (not the actual name for the king, but meaning "great house," referring to the family and palace) was first called Kemet by its inhabitants, meaning "black land" because of the fertility of the soil around the Nile.

Elba This island became famous as the prison "kingdom" of the exiled Napoleon during his one year stay from 1814-15. The ancient Greeks called it Aethalia, "smokey place," because mining and smelting metal was prominent there. The later Romans called it Ilva, and the name was mangled further as it was passed along.

El Dorado The legend of a land of gold, where the king powdered himself in gold dust every day and washed it off at night, probably had its roots in a true custom of the Chibcha Indians who would honor the gods when naming a new chief by covering him in sweet-smelling resins, powdering him with gold, and throwing gold into the lake where he "baptized" himself on his inauguration day. Of course, this wasn't a daily affair, but the legend got blown out of proportion and prompted many to seek "the golden one," as the Spanish name indicates. The last recorded hunt for the mythic land was made by Sir Walter Raleigh in 1595. Today, you'll find El Dorados in Arkansas and Kansas, but there's not enough gold dust there for a good bath.

Ellis Island Over 20 million newcomers to the U.S. became citizens by passing through the facility on Ellis Island in the New York Bay. From 1892 to 1954, America allowed her population to swell with immigrants who would take her to greatness. The island was owned by a butcher, Samuel Ellis, in the late 1700's. The government got it from his family and kept his name attached.

England
When Julius Caesar came to the land, he named it Brittannia after the tribe of Brythonic Celts who lived there. Brittania it stayed until the invasions of the Angles and Saxons in the 5th century. "Angleland" got spelled a bit differently over the years, but gives recognition to these fierce Germanic people. **Great Britain** is still the designation for the combination of island places that make up the area. I'll talk of Wales, Ireland, and Scotland later.

Liverpool is named for a mythical "liver bird" that you'll find prominently displayed on the tops of some of the buildings there. **London** was known as Londinium when it was founded by Romans in 43 A.D. It probably came from a Celtic word. Canada also has a London.

Ethiopia
Ethiopia got its name from the Greeks who called it "place of the burnt face (or sunburned face) people." Though the inhabitants there may be dark-skinned, tradition has it that a thousand years before Christ, the first son of Solomon and the Queen of Sheba, Menelik I, established his kingdom there. Since the 4th century, this has been a Christian stronghold in Islamic northern Africa. Abyssinia and Aksum are two other historical names for the country.

One of the provinces, **Eritrea**, was christened in 1890 by Italians who took the name from their Roman ancestors' designation of the region, Mare Erythraeum (Red Sea).

Europe
This sixth largest continent was named for the mythological story of the princess of the king of Sidon who was lured onto the back of a beautiful white bull, Zeus in disguise, and taken to Crete to be ravished and to later bear two sons. One was, ironically, Minos whose wife also had dealings with a bull (see **Aegean Sea**). It was probably Herodotus, the Greek historian, who first called the land north and west of Greece "Europe," writing of the constant struggle between those of Asia and Europe. More than likely, the notion came from the same myth. Before Europa's seduction she had a dream in which two continents struggled to possess her, Asia and one without a name – a ha!

Let's travel to other "E" places. **Ephesus** is today in the province of Izmir in Turkey, and its older name is only remembered in Paul's letter to the Ephesians. In 700 B.C. it was conquered by the mighty Croesus who made the temple of Artemis there one of the Seven Wonders of the world. It was later Smyrna and Seljuq. **Lake Erie** was named for the Eriez Indians. The Pennsylvania town by that name started as a fort in 1795. **Estonia** got its name from a Roman version of a tribal title, the Aesti, which probably meant "people of the dawn (or east)." **Mount Etna** (or Aetna) comes from the Greek for "I burn," which suits the volcanic location well. Another famous mountain, **Everest**, highest in the world, was named for Sir George Everest, who didn't climb it, but surveyed Java and India and formulated calculations that allowed the Himalayas to first be measured. Natives call it Chomolungma, "goddess mother of the world."

F | **Falkland Islands** When Brit John Strong landed here in 1690, he decided to honor the treasurer of the navy, Viscount Falkland, by giving the island group his name. In the intervening centuries, Argentina has made its incursions onto the damp, chilly isles off its coast, claiming them for itself. The last invasion ended in violence in 1982. The Falkland War saw the death of almost a thousand men, over two-thirds of them from the South American country. Great Britain flexed her military muscle and reaffirmed her possession.

Finland The Finns are an independent-spirited people who have fought domination for centuries. They call their country Suomi. During World War II, the country supported Germany against Russia, an age-old enemy, but in the end, had to fight the Germans and suffered greatly. Helsinki is the capital, founded in 1550.

Flanders Many English students have read the sad poem by Canadian John McCrae, "In Flanders Fields," about the World War I military cemetery. The once-powerful country has long ago been divided among France, the Netherlands, and Belgium. Its name means "lowland" or "flooded land" in Flemish and fits the sea-washed soil.

Florence The city that bloomed during the Renaissance was named Florentia by Julius Caesar to note the flowers of the area. It was a military base when it started, a hundred years before Christ. It was Cosimo Medici who positioned the city-state for greatness in the 1400's. Two major classes evolved during that time, the "big people" (the wealthy) and "the little people" (the commoners). That's actually what they were called, in translation. Cities in Alabama, Arizona, and Kentucky honor the Italian municipality. The South Carolina Florence was named for the daughter of a prominent railroad man.

Florida Legend has it that Juan Ponce de Leon was looking for Bimini, a fabled location of the Fountain of Youth, when he landed in

Florida in April of 1513. He gave the land the name "Pascua florida" for the "feast of flowers," commemorating the Easter season.

Spanish explorer Menendez called the oldest American settlement **St. Augustine** in 1565 for the saint's feast day. The Sunshine State has been a haven for runaway Tories, escaped slaves, army deserters, and political refugees over its history, though today it mainly harbors retirees from the rat race . . . oh, and one of our favorite rodents, Mickey Mouse. Many visitors know **Daytona Beach**, named for Mathias Day who bought the land in 1870. **Orlando** sounds like it's Spanish in origin, but this city was actually named for Orlando Reeves who was killed in the Indian wars in the 1800's. **Gainesville** honors General Edmund Gaines who was a commander in the War of 1812.

France If you remember the story of the first name, **Frank**, in Section Three, you'll recall how it came to mean "free" because of the Frankish rulers' tradition of granting full freedom to their subjects, very different from the Roman way. One of the cities, **Grenoble**, was named for a Roman emperor, first called Gratianopolis in the 4th century. Arabs actually occupied it in the 9th century. The tragic city of **Dunkirk** that saw the firebombing of 1940 and the rescue of thousands of allied troops has a Flemish name meaning "church among the dunes."

Some other "F" places to visit would be **Fiji**, the island country discovered by Captain Abel Tasman in 1643 and visited by Captain Bligh in 1792 (remember him from the *Mutiny on the Bounty*?). The natives call it Viti. There are hundreds of places that still remember they were forts, like **Fort Benning** which was named for a Confederate general, as was **Fort Bragg**. Now, **Fort Dix** honors a Union general, while **Fort Knox** was named for the first Secretary of War who served in 1918. Major William **Lauderdale** lends his name to the Florida beach town. General **Leavenworth** had his name given to the place most think of as a military prison. Indiana's **Fort Wayne** was named for Revolutionary War general "Mad Anthony" Wayne, beginning in 1794. General William **Worth** was a hero of the Mexican War and had his name given to the Texas fort. Speaking of the military, the town of **Fredricksburg**, Virginia, will probably be most remembered in history as the location where Union general Burnside (see **sideburns**) was humiliated by Robert E. Lee. It was named in 1727 for the father of George III, Prince Frederick Louis. **Mount Fuji** or **Fujiyama** has origins in the Ainu language and either means "fire" or "everlasting life."

G | **Galapágos** It was Charles Darwin who made these islands most famous when he visited on the *Beagle* in 1835. They were first called the Bewitched Islands by the Spanish who found them three hundred years earlier. For a long time they were merely hideaways for pirates. The mapmaker Abraham Ortelius named them Galapágos for the giant turtles found there, the longest living creatures on the planet.

Galilee This area where Jesus did most of His teaching means "ring" or "circle" in its Hebrew translation. It was probably named this not only for the land surrounding the sea, but also for the ring of nations, mentioned in Isaiah, that included Phoenicians, Syrians, and Aramaens.

Ganges River A sacrifice by the daughter of the Hindu mountain god helped save the souls of humanity, according to Hindu legend. When the human, Bhagratha, pleaded with Himalaya to help 60,000 souls of the sons of King Sagara be released after their angry destruction by Vishnu, Ganga was allowed to travel to Earth to become a great, cleansing river. To this day, bodies are washed in the river's waters before being cremated and having the ashes scattered over the surface. This practice actually got a bit health-threatening until the government took steps to prevent disease.

Ganymeade When the German astronomer Simon Marius named the largest moon in our solar system, he was referring to the Greek myth of the cupbearer to the gods. Young Ganymeade was a Trojan prince who was so handsome that he was brought to Mt. Olympus by Zeus to serve the gods their drink. The tale led to the tradition of calling any waiter a Ganymeade. If Marius had focused on the Roman variation of the story, he might have avoided associating the name of the Trojan youth with the satellite "servant" of Jupiter, the largest planet, named for the Roman chief god. The Romans expanded on the story with the notion that there must have been some kind of sexual attraction that caused Jupiter (Zeus) to want this boy. Their translation of the Greek name led to our word, **catamite**, a young boy kept by a pederast. Aquarius, the water bearer, is also correspondent with Ganymeade.

Georgia George II was responsible for letting the philanthropic James Ogelthorpe have a chance to give his utopian ideas a stretch in 1732. Prison conditions in England were so deplorable that Oglethorpe campaigned for reform and succeeded in making the awful plight of prisoners a social issue. It was especially bad on those who owed money. The idea, however, that Georgia was founded by debtors is not exactly accurate. Oh, there *were* those folk amidst the first wave of colonists, but many others were part of the first settlement in **Savannah** (Spanish for "a grassland"). Rum and slaves were forbidden in the early phase of the colony, but human nature and monetary drives led to these rules falling by the wayside. The capital, **Atlanta**, was probably named for the Atlantic and Western railroad company, not the mythological huntress Atalanta who forced all suitors to race her and beat them all, rewarding them with death, until Hippomenes finally distracted her in the race with golden apples, slowing her down enough to win and marry her. **Dalton** was either named for the man who laid it out, John Dalton, or for the maiden name of the wife of Edward White who headed a group that purchased the townsite.

Now, the Georgia of the former Soviet Union didn't get its name from George, but from a Westernization of its ancient name, Gruziya, which was a Russian version of the original place name, a mixture of Arabic and Persian.

George II *was* the namesake of the South Carolina town and the capital of Guyana, both called **Georgetown**. You'll also find Georgetowns in Kentucky, Canada, and the Caymen Islands.

Germany There may be a **germ** of a connection in the idea of something being **germane** and our name for this European country, but they're probably not related. The Latin root for "sprout" or "off-shoot" gives us that name for microbes we associate with disease. Germs do cause German measles, but the country takes its name from one of the fierce Celtic tribes of the area in ancient times, the Germanii. The Romans carried that name to the civilized world. The Frankish people specified another tribe, the Alemanni, when alluding to the land as Alemagne. Actually, Germany really didn't become Germany until 1871 when mighty Prussia organized the many separate principalities into the German empire. If we used the name these people called themselves, we would call this country Deutschland, or "land of the people." **Teutonic** comes from that same root . . . which is germane to this discussion (germane coming from the "offshoot" root, also meaning "of the same parent").

Berlin, also found in Connecticut, New Hampshire, and Wisconsin, would seem to mean "under the linden trees." **Munich**, which was a sort of headquarters for the Nazi movement, was named for the wealthy Abbey of Tegernsee founded in 1471. Munich means "place of the monks."

Gethsemane The garden where Jesus prayed before his crucifixion, where the pressure of the realization of his impending death was so great that his perspiration was made of blood, has a location that is disputed. The idea that it was near the Mount of Olives might seem a most logical choice since Gethsemane is Hebrew for "oil press."

Gettysburg When James Gettys received a land grant in the 1780's for the future Pennsylvania town, little did he realize that it would be the site of the largest battle fought on the North American continent. When Lee retreated from the area on the ironic date of July 4th, 1863, there were well over 40,000 men who had been killed or wounded, fairly equally divided on both sides. By the time Lincoln visited; a little over four months later, there were some 7,000 graves containing Union and Confederate dead. Those reporters who criticized the President's two minute speech may have been reacting to the fact that it followed a highly oratorical two *hour* speech given by Edward Everett; but when the text was printed, people agreed that the eloquence of those few words said reams to the divided country. The southern boys were later disinterred and returned home for proper burial, but the Yankee graves mark, to this day, the place where the wounded country bled deepest, and also began to heal.

Gibraltar The Rock of Gibraltar has a reputation for permanence and steadfastness, but the land has had disputed ownership for almost three hundred years. This "pillar of Hercules," marking the end of the known world in ancient times, was named for a Muslim conqueror who took the penninsula in 711 A.D. Tariq was this Moor's name and the Arabic for "Mount of Tariq" got twisted and slurred from its original "Jabal Tariq."

Gilead The "balm of Gilead" is probably what this location's name is most famous for. Noted several times in the Bible (Genesis 37:25 and Jeremiah 8:22, to name a few), the resin from a tree is the more-than-likely source of the medicinal substance. A substance from the buds of the American poplar tree is the modern "balm of Gilead" and is used in cough syrups. The name of the place means "heap of witness" in Hebrew because this was where Jacob and his father-in-law, Laban, piled up stones to mark the promise they made to each other to stay out of each other's hair.

Gobi This desert in Asia is certainly not a pleasant place for humans, as witnessed by the fact that there are only about three of them per square mile living there. Though it is fairly elevated, from 3,000 to 5,000 feet above sea level, its name comes from the Mongolian for "low desert" because of the salty marshes at its lowest points.

Gotham *Batman* fans recognize this as the name of the city of the Caped Crusader. Washington Irving used this as a nickname for New York City in some of his works. The name originally came from a village in Nottinghamshire, England, where the story is told of a kind of conspiracy of dunces. When the villagers learned that King John wanted to use the area as a hunting lodge, they feared they would be economically strained by having to take care of His Majesty and his entourage, so they acted so moronic for the king's messengers that it was reported that the location was full of idiots. King John went elsewhere to recreate, and the villagers breathed a sigh of financial relief. Ask residents of homes and vacation spots of U.S. presidents and you'll probably hear that it isn't always pleasant to be the center of celebrity. It's certainly debatable whether or not New Yorkers fit the image of "wise fools."

Greece Here's another case of a country's name coming from a non-native source. We should really call this heart of Western civilization Hellas. The Greek flood story tells of Zeus getting angry at the wickedness of men and having his brother, Poseidon, god of the sea, send nine days and nine nights of torrential rain. Luckily, the son and neice of Prometheus, Deucalion and Pyrrha, were forewarned by the Titan and commanded to build a wooden chest to float them to safety. Their child, Hellen, was the progenitor of the Greek peoples. The Romans took the name of one small tribe, the Graeci, and, from them, named the land Graecus.

Greenland With eighty per cent of this huge island covered in ice, it seems odd that it would bear a name suggesting fertility and plant life. It could be said that when Eric the Red named it in the late 900's, he was trying to make it one of the first tourist traps. After being kicked out of Iceland for killing a man, he took off for parts unknown, discovering the icy isle. To make it sound more attractive, he named it Greenland and lured Icelandic settlers to its shores. The isolated colony died out and was "rediscovered" several hundred years later in the 1500's by British sailors. They didn't want it, but Norway and Denmark did.

Eric's son, Leif Erikson, who brought Christianity to the first settlers about 1000 A.D., had the same travel agent's mentality when, blown off course to North America, he gave our continent its first name, Vinland.

We'll travel to a few more "G" places before we move on. **Gabon**, the African home of Albert Schweitzer, was probably named by the Portugese in the 1470's because of its shape which reminded them of a "hooded cloak." **Galatia** is familiar to Christians as the place where Paul addressed one of his letters. Galatians today are Turks, and the area contains Ankara, the capital of Turkey. The Greeks named the land for the Gauls who were in the area. The region of France called **Gascony** was named when the Basque people (see) overran the area. The French called them Vascones in the 500's, and the land was known as Vasconia. How did **Ghana** get its name? Was it from the Gonja tribe, the Ashanti, or the Ga? I'm uncertain. The Portugese called it Gold Coast in the late 1400's, and it really wasn't an actual country until 1957. **Gorki**, one of the largest Russian cities, is one of the few places in the world named for a writer. Maxim Gorky was not even his real name, but the versatile author had his name given to Novgorod when communists were renaming their world after their revolution. The land of **Goshen** was an area of Egypt that Joseph gave to his Israelite kinfolk where they lived until Moses led them out of the changed circumstances. Indiana has another Goshen, named for the Biblical site in 1828. New York has another, famous for its horse racing, named in 1843. Let's look at some "Green" places. Revolutionary War general Nathanael Greene is the source for the naming of **Greensboros** in North Carolina and Georgia, as well as **Greenville**, North Carolina, Mississippi, and Ohio. The South Carolina Greenville was named for an early settler, Isaac Green, while the Texas Greenville got its handle from a general in the Texas revolution. Columbus first called the island, that is today **Grenada**, Concepción in 1498, but it was later renamed in honor of the Spanish namesake. You won't find **Grub Street** in London anymore. It's been renamed Milton Street, but for many many years the place was synonymous with hack writing because the street had been the home to so many scribblers trying to eke out a living by selling their written wares, a practice frowned upon by more literary types. Tobias Smollett was one of the Grub Streeters who told of life there in his book, *Humphrey Clinker*. **Guadalajara** gets its Moorish name from the Arabic for "river (or valley) of stones." Spanish Christians took the place back – with the name intact – in 1085, and Mexico honored it nearly five hundred years later by giving a city there that name. **Guam** was first called "Ladrones" in 1521 because Magellan had some bad encounters with the natives. His name for the place meant "the thieves." The African country of **Guinea** took its name from the Berber appellation, meaning "land of blacks." The South American country of **Guyana** derives its name from an Indian phrase: "land of waters."

H **Haiti** This country's history has been one of constant strife, repression, and revolt. The cycle started when Columbus found peaceful Arawak Indians living there on his visit on December 6, 1492. Their name for the land, from which we get the present name, meant "high ground." The French intruded when the Spanish neglected the colony (see **Dominican Republic**) and founded a plantation community based on slavery and white domination. After the French Revolution abolished slavery, Haiti found itself overturned by a slave revolt that resulted in murder and chaos. One of the slave leaders, Toussaint L'Ouverture, ended up declaring the entire island of Hispaniola free and this provoked Napoleon, who had the rebel slave captured and imprisoned. It didn't stop the revolution on the island that ended in the parcelling out of land to all former slaves. Though the U.S. has tried to help the country over the years, even supplying it a constitution in 1915 written by then Secretary of the Navy Franklin Roosevelt, the predominant story of this impoverished land has been one of corrupt dictatorship and tyrannical domination of the population.

Hawaii The twenty islands of the fiftieth state were probably named for a Polynesian homeland of the original settlers of the place. In fact, "homeland" seems to be the simplest translation of the original Havaiki. Some have argued that the Aloha State could have been named for a chief who led the first travelers to the islands. If Captain Cook had had his way they'd still be known as the Sandwich Islands, not named for any native fast food, but for his patron the Earl of Sandwich.

Hell We get our notions of Hell from a number of sources, blending ideas from various religious beliefs. When the monks were translating the Bible for King James, they tended to consolidate several words into the one place, hell. **Gehenna** was widely used in the Hebrew texts to mean a place of punishment. There was a place outside the walls of the city of Jerusalem noted for its awful practices of child sacrifice in which pagans and even Israelites would burn the bodies of children to the god Moloch. The valley of Hinnom, as the name translates, was a place of evil, suffering, and death. To discourage the heathen rituals, which God had symbolically altered in the story of Abraham's near-sacrifice of Isaac, city officials made the valley into a garbage dump. The reputation clung to the name, which was used throughout the Old Testament to represent a place of torturous pain.

Sheol was another term translated as Hell in the King James Version. This place was associated with both the grave, and thus merely the ending of life, and with a gloomy place where souls were totally out of touch with God and the living, a place of "no exit." This corresponds somewhat with the Greek and Roman idea of **Hades**, the underground dwelling place of the dead who may return to new life only if they let go of their past life memories by drinking of the River Lethe (remember **lethargic** in Section Two?). A deeper part of this subterranean land was **Tartarus** where the wicked faced punishment. From the roots of this word, meaning "twist," we get **torture, torment**, and even **torque**.

It is the Norse myths which give us Hell, or as they called it, Hel. This was the home of one of the wicked children of Loki, a kind of Satan figure in Northern legends. She presided over nine realms for punishing the dead in this cold place.

Our Western depictions of this place of punishment have probably been influenced most by Milton's *Paradise Lost* and Danté's *Divine Comedy*.

Hollywood When Chicago filmmakers wanted to finish *The Count of Monte Cristo* in 1908, they decided to go to a sleepy village in California. They liked it so much they stayed, and the first official studio was established in 1911. It was actually founded in 1887 by a prohibitionist who thought he was beginning an ideal community of sober, moral people . . . little did he know. His wife named the place after the home of friends who lived in Chicago. The Florida city of the same name was developed in the 1920's by a Californian, so the connection is obvious.

Hungary This country that was united by the wise St. Stephen about 1000 A.D. was settled primarily by a Finnish people from the north, the Magyars. The name of this area, which also used to include **Transylvania** (Latin: "out of the woods"), was influenced by the Turks who described the surroundings by its inhabitants, "the ten tribes," the translation of the roots of the country's name.

Lake Huron The second largest lake of the five Great Lakes was named for a tribe of Indians whom the French called "bristly-headed ruffians," a less-than-polite translation of their designation of these people. The Indians gave themselves the name Wendat or Wyandot, which translates as "people of the penninsula." Unfortunately, the Iroquois were their enemy, and this tribe wanted to eliminate the Huron. They escaped the Iroquois to Ohio and fought with the British in the American Revolution. The Lake and a city in South Dakota still bear the name, but the tribe no longer exists, disintegrating in 1959 after spending nearly a hundred years in Oklahoma, moved there by the white man.

The excursion through "H" country continues. There are a number of locations named **Hamilton**. The city in Ontario, Canada, was named for George Hamilton who laid out the town in 1813. The city in Bermuda was named for Governor Henry Hamilton in 1794. Captain John Hamilton was killed fighting Maoris in New Zealand which named a town for him. The Hamilton family in Scotland was given land in 1445 which resulted in another city's name. Our city in Ohio was named for Alexander Hamilton. I'm not sure about the origins of the Australian town. **Harper's Ferry** became well-known after John Brown and his abolitionists captured an arsenal there, hoping to set up a headquarters for freed slaves. Robert Harper bought the place in 1747 to take people back and forth across the Potomac. **Harrisburg** was once the capital of Pennsylvania in 1812 and was named for Joe Harris who established a trading post there in 1718. **Harvard** took its name from John Harvard whose large monetary donation in 1639 caused the university to change its name from Cambridge. If you've seen the musical, *Cats*, you probably remember the **Heaviside Layer** where rewarded felines go. Oliver Heaviside postulated that there must exit a layer of the atmosphere that would reflect radio waves to explain the way they fade. The part of the atmosphere that is now called the ionosphere E layer was once called the Heaviside layer. The home of the Hindu gods are the mountains known as the **Himalayas**, which get their name from the Sanskrit for "house of snow." **Hiroshima** is well-known across the world as the first place the Atomic Bomb was used in war. Since the August 6, 1945, explosion well over a quarter of a million people have died from various effects. The city was founded in the late 1500's, and its name means "broad island." **Honduras** is Spanish for "depths." When explorers came after Columbus' 1502 stopover, they thought its steep shore meant the waters were equally plunging. The bay, river, and other locations named **Hudson** come from Henry Hudson who worked for both the British and Dutch in the early 1600's, searching for a northwest passage to Asia. His explorations ceased when his last mutinous crew set him adrift with his son and seven loyal crewmen, never to be heard from again.

I **Iceland** Iceland was given its unappealing handle by a Norwegian Viking named Floki, and though the northern and eastern sections are certainly frigid, hundreds of volcanoes and hot springs make some parts of the island downright toasty. The capital, **Reykjavik**, translates its name as "smoke bay."

Idaho Where the name of our 43rd state actually originated is not crystal clear. It could well be that Idaho was a made-up name, manufactured from various Indian words. Some say it translates as the "light on the mountain" or "the jewel of the mountains;" others say it came from an Apache name for another Indian tribe. Confederate soldiers and their families leaving the disrupted post-Civil War South made up a large portion of the rush to settle this land after it was announced that gold and silver were there for the taking. The state's capital, **Boise**, got its name from French trappers who gave a river there the name, meaning "wooded river." The town grew up around a fort founded there in 1863 to protect gold miners from local Indians.

Illinois The French explorers of this region took an Indian tribal name and adjusted it to their tongue to come up the the area's early designation. "Superior men" is one translation from the original Indian. Most of us think of Abraham Lincoln as being our great Illinois president, but though his political career certainly started in this state, he was born in Kentucky. There has been only one president born in this state. Though we probably most associate California with this man, Ronald Reagan claims Tampico, Illinois, as his birthplace. **Joliet** was originally named Juliet until 1845, but the name was always meant to honor explorer Louis Joliet.

India Alexander the Great brought the Western world the name for this subcontinent when he pushed his tired troops into the area over three hundred years before Christ. The Sind people of the area were from whom he took the appellation. Indus was his term and the Romans adjusted it to India. The Aryan people who had invaded some twelve hundred years earlier were the dominant force in the area, having brought in their culture and religion (named from the same root: **Hindu**) **Aryan** means "noble" or "high born" or "owners of land." We'll talk more about them in just a bit.

Indiana   Indiana's naming was simple enough. Folks kindly let everyone know that the 19th state was the "place of the Indians." Why Indianans are called **Hoosiers** is quite another story. Could it be that the more countrified, but friendly way of responding to a knock on the door gave us the nickname? Could "Who's yare?" taken from "Who's there?" have been the origin? Or was it a friendly builder named Samuel Hoosier, who so liked Indiana workers that he regularly hired them, who gave us the strange sobriquet? Some theorize that Hoosier came from the name given to those who were peacemakers when parties came to blows, called a "husher." A term for a hill, "hoozer," could have been at the bottom of the byword.

Many of you have enjoyed sending and receiving Christmas cards with the post mark of **Santa Claus**, Indiana, on them. I'm uncertain how the town got the name, but it's there. **Muncie** was named for the Munsee Indians.

When an Indiana cartoonist told his daughter, Marsella, stories about a doll she had found, we got the beginnings of the Raggedy Ann and Andy tales.

Iowa   The Sioux word from which we get the name of this state might have been a mocking or humorous name for a neighboring tribe. Just the way Americans called English **limeys** because of the tradition of carrying limes aboard ship to prevent beri-beri or rickets or the way early American colonists nicknamed Dutchmen "Jan Cheese" (which became **Yankee** over the years) because of the common first name and their penchant for eating and selling cheese; just so, the Sioux name for the Iowa Indians meant "sleepy ones" or "one who puts to sleep." Some have said that, no, the name comes from another root, meaning "this is the place" or "beautiful land," but I kind of like the notion of one tribe razzing another about their laziness or boring qualities. The state is known as the Hawkeye State because of the Black Hawk War of 1832 in which Chief Black Hawk gave up the first land used for white settlement.

Now, a man named Julien **Dubuque** got permission from the Sauk and Fox Indians to mine lead in 1788 in the area where the city bearing his name now exists.

Des Moines has mixed historical background. This name may come from the French, meaning "the middle," referring to the Iowa River that is the largest between the Mississippi and Missouri Rivers. The city's name could mean "the monks," recalling the Catholic missionaries who came through the area. Finally, it may be the

Moingona Indians who give the state capital its name. Their tribal name translates as "river of mounds."

Iran Until 1935, most Europeans called this country **Persia**. This ancient name is attributed to Greek mythology. The hero, Perseus, had many exploits, and one involved saving the beautiful maiden, Andromeda, from a terrible sea monster. After getting her father's promise that he could marry her if he saved her, he promptly whipped out the head of Medusa that he carried around in his handy-dandy bag. The power of the Gorgon's head turned the monster to stone. One of Perseus and Andromeda's children was named Perses, and, supposedly, he settled in the land which was later designated for him and his offspring. The language, Farsi, also comes from this legendary beginning. However, when an army officer became Shah of this land in the 1920's, one of the acts of his government was to officially name the country Iran, meaning "land of the Aryans," reflecting the name the people had been calling themselves for years. We Americans have not been too keen on Iran ever since the son of that Shah was deposed in the late '70's and the Khomeini regime took power.

Iraq Another country recently rather unbeloved by Americans, among many others, was known to the Greeks as **Mesopotamia**, which means "between rivers," the Tigris and Euphrates. The great kingdom of Sumer was one of the most ancient of civilizations in this area where Eden was also said to have been. In 1921 the country became a kingdom legally known as Iraq, which seems to have probably come from the Sumerian city-state of Uruk.

Ireland Ah, sure and the Emerald Isle is precious to many. When the Gaels settled the island around 300 A.D., a society flourished there, disrupted by Vikings in the 800's, until Brian Boru defeated them in 1014. The Irish name for their country is Eire or Eirin, and it is speculated that this may have also come from the Aryans, the "noble" tribe that swept through the world beginning around 1500 B.C., leaving a legacy of conquest and a whole new gene pool for the civilized world's people. Some have noted the country's English name, Ireland, has different origins and may have actually come from the French root for "angry." Well, now, we'll have to watch our Irish tempers concerning that idea.

　　Belfast gets its name from the Gaelic and translates as "ford at the sand bank." It was founded in 1177.

　　Dublin got its name from a "black pool" of water of the River

Liffey that is now filled and part of the land. It was founded by Vikings.

Israel When Jacob got his new name, he probably didn't realize that his legacy would involve one of the more controversial countries of the modern world. Jacob was travelling along with his massive contingent of relatives and animals, worried about meeting his twin brother whom he had tricked so many years earlier. After sending the kin on ahead, he found himself in an all-night wrestling match with someone Jacob could only identify as an angel. Well, apparently, this was no Hulk Hogan among seraphs because when the angel couldn't beat Jacob fairly, he touched him in the hollow of his thigh and threw Jacob's leg out of joint, causing him to limp for the rest of his life. The angel gave him his blessing and renamed him that morning. Israel most likely means "he who strove with God." There have been other translations of the original Hebrew, including "prince of God."

   Jerusalem also has conflicting interpretations. "City of peace" seems the most likely meaning, though "founded by God" could be its origin.

Italy The Greeks actually named the southern part of this country when they colonized it in the 700's B.C. It probably translates as "land of oxen" or "land for grazing." The entire area eventually took on the name.

   Rome got its name from one its founders, the legendary Romulus who, with his brother Remus, was ripped from his mother's arms as a child and thrown into the Tiber River. After the wee ones managed to struggle ashore far from home, a she-wolf took them in and offered a timely meal of her own milk. Later, a shepherd raised them until they were old enough to get revenge on the man who had put them in the drink. It was said that they built a city on the spot where they floated ashore, but this Italian Cain and Abel had later arguments that saw Romulus kill Remus. The childhood outcast lifestyle led Romulus to welcome refugees to his new kingdom. His typically barbaric attitude of the day saw no problem in getting women for his newcomers. He just stole them from a nearby tribe of Sabines. Legend goes on to say that Romulus disappeared one day and was transformed into the god Quirinus. One of the seven hills of Rome is named **Quirinal** which is also the name of the Italian government. The presidential palace is on this hill. One of the other hills in the city was known as the "hill of prophecy" where in ancient times pagan seers spoke and augured. Today, though the name remains the same, it is the headquarters of another religious group and is the location of the **Vatican**. **Naples** was used by the Romans as a kind of Club Med. They kept the Greek settlers name for the place: Neapolis or "new city." At one time **Milan** was one of the largest cities of the Roman Empire and was called Mediolanum when it was founded in 222 B.C. When it fell to the invaders in 476, it suffered quite a setback.

Other "I" lands include **Indonesia** which encompasses thousands of islands, big and tiny. "Indian islands" is the translation, and "the Indies" was a common name for these spicey places. In 1949 they became the United States of Indonesia. The **Ivory Coast** has obvious meaning, though the actual country didn't get its independence until 1960. **Iwo Jima** gets its label from the Japanese and means "sulphur island" since that is what was mined there.

J | **Japan** Here is another case where the Western world knows one name for a place, but people who live there use another. Nippon or Nihon is what the Japanese – er, Nipponese – would tell you is their country's label. "Source of the sun" is its translation, and you will see this embodied in the nation's flag. Marco Polo has been indicated as the one who might have given us the European title. In the 1200's, while travelling through China, he was told of a land of wealth called Zipangu. The country remained a mystery to the West until 1854 when Commodore Perry pried it open and forced a mingling with foreigners.

I've mentioned Hiroshima (see). **Kyoto** was once the capital until Tokyo was given the honor in 1868. Kyoto means "capital city." **Nagasaki** was named for a ruler of the area in the 1100's and was always a fairly friendly port for foreigners after it was opened to trade in 1571. When 1.8 miles of the city was destroyed by an atomic bomb, foreign influences had devastating impact, killing over 35,000.

Jordan The country is known as the Hashemite Kingdom of Jordan because of Muhammed's grandfather, Hashem. It gets its common name from the ancient river Jordan where Jesus was baptized.

Jericho is a name recognized by many when thinking of early biblical history of the area. Its name means "city of palm trees," and it is the location of probably the oldest known settlement in the world, though today it's just a village. Well, it was tough going after the walls came tumbling down, though now it is getting a new place in history with the help of Palestinians.

"J" names do not abound in the world. If President Jackson had not come along, **Jacksonville**, Florida, might still be called Cowford. The name was changed in 1832 to honor Andrew, who had also been the first territorial governor of Florida. Our seventh president is also responsible for the names of **Jackson**, Mississippi, its capital, and Jacksons in Tennessee and Michigan. **Jamaica** takes its name from Arawak Indian roots, meaning "island of springs." Columbus was the first white man to play tourist there in 1494. Horse lovers may recognize the special riding pants called **jodhpurs** which originated in the part of India bearing that name. The former state and present city were named for Rao Jodha, a warrior king of antiquity.

K   **Kansas**   The question of slavery was at the core of this state's organization as a territory. Much as the abortion issue divides the U.S. today, the question of whether or not to own slaves was a subject down which clear lines were drawn. When Lincoln's future presidential opponent, Stephen Douglas, managed to get the anti-slavery clause of the Missouri Compromise repealed, he sparked the fires under this devisive problem. Under his proposal, if a territory wanted statehood, it was up to the majority of its settlers to decide on its status as a slave or free state. This led to drives in all the northern states to get anti-slavery emigrants to move to Kansas to sway the vote. The pro-slavery population was ready for a fight and blood poured across Kansas as a result. By the way, the Sunflower State's name comes from the Kansa or Kansaw Indians whose name meant "people of the south wind."

Kentucky   A state so split during the Civil War that brother literally fought brother, with 75,000 Kentuckians wearing the Union uniform and 35,000 dressed in Confederate gray, its placename has disputed origins. The Cherokee name for the Blue Grass State has been variously translated as "land of tomorrow," "meadowland," "dark and bloody ground," "prairie," and "barrens."

    Louisville was named in 1780 for the French king, Louis XVI who helped the colonists during the American Revolution. A town in Georgia was also named for him.

Kuwait   The Arabic for "little fort" tells the story of this once-unimportant outpost that was settled in 1710. The country's name has now been etched on the consciousness of the world because of the recent invasion and war incurred by Iraq.

    Looking at a few other "K" places, you'll find that **Kenya** comes from the Kikuyu language and and means "mountain of whiteness." Its capital, **Nairobe**, got its name from the Masai for "cold water." It was one of the more pleasant watering holes for the colonial railway in the 1890's. The Russian city of **Kiev** is said to have taken its name from its three founding brothers, Khariv, Kii, and Shtchek. It was there in 988 that Saint Vladimir coerced the people of the city to be baptized for an instant Christianization. Back to mountains, **Kilimanjaro** means "great mountain." From 1392 until the 1940's **Korea** was known as Choson. The modern Westernized appellation probably comes from the Koryo dynasty of ancient times. Choson means "land of the morning sun" and is still used by many natives, especially in North Korea. The once mighty and forbidding **Kremlin** in Moscow is today merely a place where Russian representatives work to build a new, democratic country. Its name comes from the Russian for "citadel" or "fort."

L **Labrador** As the mainland part of the province of New-foundland, this area resisted becoming part of Canada until the 1940's. The story of its naming indicates that the Italian explorer, John Cabot, came in 1500 and with him was a Portugese farmer from the Azores. Labrador means "farmer" or "landowner" in that man's tongue. The **Labrador retriever** got its training *not* from bringing ducks and geese back from the water to their hunting masters. Originally, Labs were used by fisherfolk to help haul fish-nets to shore.

Lebanon This center of strife in internal and external conflicts of the recent past has been both a scene of glorious civilization and ruinous chaos in its long history. It gets its name from the mountain range in the country and means "white" in Aramaic, referring to the capped peaks. Cities in Connecticut, Missouri, and Pennsylvania bear the name.

The capital, **Beirut**, was founded around 1400 B.C. and was known as Berytus. It was there that legend says St. George slew the dragon, accounting for the name of the **Bay of St. George**.

Louisiana The Pelican State got its name from the huge territory dubbed by explorer La Salle in honor of Louis XIV in 1682. The French influence in the area is still widespread. **New Orleans** was named for the French city of Orleans. **Baton Rouge**, which means "red stick" in French, got its name from a red-stained pole that was originally put there to separate two Indian nations. The French founded the town in 1719.

Now, **Louisville**'s in both Kentucky and Georgia were named for the French King Louis XVI who helped the colonists during the American Revolution.

We'll touch down briefly at a few other "L" locations. **Lancaster**, England, was responsible for the naming of Lancaster, Pennsylvania, which in turn was the namesake of cities in California, South Carolina, and Ohio. While the English location was the home of a royal family, the Pennsylvania locale boasts of the residence of President Buchanan. **Latvia** was a province dominated by the Teutonic Knights of the 1200's and was known as part of Livonia. One of the tribal people of the area, the Letts, were the originators of one of the placenames of the region, Latgate, which evolved into the present designation. **Liberia** is well-known as the African country founded by former slaves in the 1820's who gave it the Latin name for "free land." The unsavory reputation of **Libya** – for Westerners – was not part of the earliest history when the Greeks named the land for a tribe living west of the Nile. Cyrenaiia and Tripolitania were also names for the country. The tiny country of **Liechtenstein** took its name from a family of rulers, beginning with Johann Adam Liechtenstein, a prince from Vienna who founded a dynasty. The male-dominated society gave women the right to vote in 1984. **Limoges**, famous for its porcelain and painted enamel, got its name from a Gallic tribe, the Lemovices. Renoir was born there. The Grand Duchy of **Luxembourg** was founded in 963 when Siegfried, Count of Ardennes, got possession of an old Roman fortification. "Small fortress" is the meaning of the name.

M **Maine** The most probable explanation of this state's name comes from the habit of seamen in the 1620's of calling the location "the mainland," though there are those who say there is a connection to Maine, France. Its capital, **Bangor**, was the Kenduskeag Plantation in 1776 and Sunbury in 1787. When Reverend Seth Noble was involved in the official incorporation, legend has it that he was singing a favorite hymn about the Celtic, Welsh city, Bangor, and whether by accident or intention, the name stuck. There's also a Bangor in Pennsylvania.

Augusta, the state capital, was named for the daughter of Revolutionary War general Henry Dearborn, Pamela Augusta Dearborn. It was founded in 1797 and had been previously named Cushnoc then

Harrington. Now, the Augusta in Kansas was named for the wife of its founder, Augusta James, in 1861. Georgia's city was named in 1736 in recognition of Princess Augusta, wife of the British Prince of Wales. Their son became George III.

The town of **Calais**, Maine, was named in recognition of the French support of the American Revolution and honored the French locale.

Madeira That hearty wine, fortified with brandy, originally came from the island of the same name whose translation from the Portugese means "wood," so called because of the heavy forests there. The wine was very popular in colonial America, and Portugese merchants made it a point to stop at the island for the specific purpose of bringing a cask or two to sell in American ports.

Malta Another island with an interesting history is Malta, known as Melita in ancient times, possibly referring to honey. In 60 A.D. St. Paul was shipwrecked there, and a bay still bears his name. From this land the Order of St. John of Jersalem attacked Turks and Barbary pirates in the 1500's. From these knights we get the **Maltese Cross**. The Maltese dog was one of the first breed of lap dogs. They were actually carried in the large sleeves of robes worn by Greek and Roman high born ladies. **Maltese lace** actually originated in Genoa and was brought to the island in the 1830's. And here also comes the first name for the disease contracted by eating meat or untreated milk from infected animals. **Malta fever** is also known as undulant fever. In its animal form it is **Brucelosis**, named for Dr. David Bruce, which can cause abortions in infected stock.

Marseille In 600 B.C. the Greeks named the port Massalia. The people living there called for Roman military aid when troops from Carthage threatened them around 200 B.C. Afterward, the area became a province of Rome, and the surrounding region is still known as **Provence**. The French national anthem is called "**The Marseillaise**" because after it was written, units from that city adopted it as their own, singing it into battle against the Austrians in 1792. Written in one night as a marching song, it was first titled "War Song for (of) the Army of the Rhine."

Maryland No, it wasn't any of the famous queens named Mary for whom this state was named. It was the wife of Charles I of England, Henrietta Maria. That king granted the royal charter to George Calvert who was the first Baron **Baltimore**. Yes, it was this family whose name was given to the city. It was especially the 5th Baron,

Charles Calvert, who was honored by the state. Originally, it was a place that was a sanctuary for persecuted Catholics – even though freedom of religion was very important to the state. **Annapolis** was named for Queen Anne of Great Britain who granted the city its charter in 1708. By the way, the **Baltimore oriole** got its designation because its coloration happened to match that of the Baron's coat of arms.

Massachusetts The Bay State's Indian name comes from the Algonquin for "near the great hill" or "at the big hill." Boston, the Baked Beans State's capital, took its name from Boston, England, which was named for St. Botolph in 654. The **Boston terrier, Boston fern, Boston ivy, Boston lettuce**, and **Boston cream pie** are a few of the city's namesakes. The Puritan State's largest city is also known for the tea party that began the first pollution of the bay. Now, the **Boston Mountains** are in Arkansas.

Cambridge was named by its founders who were graduates of Cambridge, England. Other towns of that name can be found in Maryland and Ohio.

Mexico Our friends from south of the border probably got the name of their country from a great leader of the Aztecs, Mixcoatl. In fact, some of the Aztecs went by the name of Mexica.

Miami Miami, Florida, has been around in some form or another for a couple thousand years, originally a village of the Tequesta Indians where the name for the place meant "big water" or "sweet water," referring either to Lake Okeechobee or possibly a group of Everglades Indians. The Spaniards noted the site in the 1500's, but the white man actually didn't found the city until 1870. The town in Oklahoma and also the Ohio university were both named for a Wisconsin band of Indians whose name meant "peninsula people." Their own name for themselves is translated as "cry of the crane." Due to a mistranslation of their tribal name, they were sometimes called the "naked Indians." The Oklahoma connection came when the tribe was moved to a reservation there.

Michigan Indians were also the originators of the name of this state. "Big lake" has obvious reference to this land of the great lakes and is what the name means. French explorer Antoine de la Mothe **Cadillac** named **Detroit** in 1701, referring to its location: "of the straits." Of course, the car was named for him. The famous falls nearby, which are shared by the U.S. and Canada, **Niagara**, were named by the Neutre Indians as "thundering waters" where Annie Edson Taylor first went over in a barrel in 1901. A Michigan Indian chief, **Pontiac**, is responsible for the nearby city's name, as well as the make of car. The state capital, **Lansing**, was named for a village in New York. The Illinois town of the same name honored John Lansing who built a general store there in the 1800's. In 1620, when Étienne Brulé was sent to explore this territory by Canadian governor Samuel de Champlain, a wild land holding some 10,000 Indians was what was found – not a route to the Pacific as Champlain was hoping for. We think of autos when we think of this state, and Henry Ford's name comes to mind, but it was Ransom Olds who founded the first automobile factory in Detroit in 1901. Ford started his assembly line two years later. John Harvey **Kellogg** has a last name that stands out in breakfast lovers' minds since it was his lab that developed corn flakes as well as peanut butter. Another city in the 20th state was named for him. **Ann Arbor** was named by two founding families from Virginia and New York whose patriarchs both had wives named Ann.

Minnesota Our 32nd state gets its name from a Sioux word for "sky-tinted waters," though some claim the translation for the land of 10,000 lakes means "muddy waters." There in 1832, the source of the Mississippi was found. The state got the nickname "gopher state" from an 1857 cartoon that portrayed shady railroad organizers as striped gophers, critters known to farmers for their destructiveness, which was what some thought the railroads would do to the land.

Mississippi This once rather self-insulated bastion of the traditional South took its name from the river, named by the Ojibwa Indians from a word meaning "big river" or "father of waters." The Magnolia State has produced some of the country's greatest writers such as William Faulkner, Tennessee Williams, and Eudora Welty. The 20th state made it into the Union in 1817, but left not too many years later due to what was felt to be "Northern aggression." **Biloxi** has an Indian name and means "first people."

Missouri When William Duncan Vandiver made a point in 1899 that Missourians were very practical and down to earth, he fostered the nickname for his homeland: the "Show Me" State. The territory had a "give me" beginning when the Spanish rulers offered free land to any settlers in 1795 and brought American pioneers in droves. The slavery issue played a major role in this state's entrance into the Union in 1821. It was one of the last states allowed to be a "slave state" under the Missouri Compromise, which probably delayed the Civil War by several decades. The 24th state's name comes from the Illinois Indians' description of water-going neighbors: "town of the large canoes." From the cynical humorist Mark Twain to the no-frills president Harry S. Truman to the journalistic giant Joseph Pulitzer, the state has produced many who have shown others.

Montana The "M" states abound, and the 41st state, though populated for the past 10,000 years, is one of the newer ones, gaining admission in 1889. The Spanish for "mountain" is the origin of the name for this land that was once called the "land of the shining mountains" because of its many white-capped peaks. When Lewis and Clarke made it there in 1805, they probably wondered if they'd ever find the Pacific Ocean. John Jacob Astor's trading company made a mint on the fur trade through the 1820's and 30's, but it was gold that made Montana once called "the Treasure State." **Billings** got its name in 1882 from its founder, Frederick K. Billings, while the capital, **Helena**, was named for a Minnesota town.

Other "M" locations of interest include the many towns given the name **Madison** in honor of the fourth president. The Indiana city was one of the first in 1808 with Wisconsin, New Jersey, South Dakota, and Georgia all following suit. The **Manhattan** Indians give us the name for the New York island supposedly purchased by Peter Minuit for twenty-four bucks worth of shiny junk. The Kansas town got its same name in 1855. The quest for the atomic bomb was known as the Manhattan Project and was a facet of the U.S. Army Corps of Engineers. The Indian name means "isolated thing in the water," yes, an island. The **Mediterranean Sea** has simple Latin beginnings: "in the middle of the land." **Melanesia** in the South Pacific Ocean includes a number of islands and was given its name for the color of the natives' skin: "the black islands." The **Mojave Desert** was named by the Indians. "Three mountains" is the translation and referred to the pointy peaks of the surrounding landscape. **Mongolia** took its name from the fierce tribe of conquerors who swept up the world in the 1200's. Perhaps its present rulers have hopes of once again finding dominance since they've been on a "population increase" program for many years, doubling their inhabitants between 1952 and 1984. Though some have classified all Orientals as being part of the Mongoloid race, one unusual characteristic of Mongol babies is the presence of the Mongolian spot, a bluish pigmentation of the skin in the region of the lower back, which disappears as the infant ages. **Down's Syndrome** used to be called **Mongolism**, comparing these children born with one extra chromosome to the racial name because of the facial features which give them an Oriental look. Most of us today refer to the disease, which strikes one in every thousand born around the world, by the name of the man who first wrote about it in 1866, John Langdon Down. When the Grimaldi family took over the governing of **Monaco**, the second smallest sovereign state in the world, little did they know that their country would be the subject of so many tabloid articles; but the land, named by Phoenician and Greek sailors, had a Hollywood invasion in 1956 when Grace Kelly married Prince Ranier, and it's never been the same since. **Mozambique** was probably named for an Arab ruler, Musa al-Biqu, and saw its first European when Vasco de Gama noted it in 1498

N | **Nebraska** The old Indian name for "flat water" gives the Cornhusker State its name. After the Louisiana Purchase and this land's settlement, the territory picked up the nickname The Treeplanter's State because of the habit of newcomers to plant trees in the grasslands, almost the reverse of what the Eastern settlers had had to do to the land. The 37th state has given birth to the 38th president, Gerald Ford, once known as Leslie Lynch King, Jr. Willa Cather also grew up there. The city of **Omaha** also comes from an Indian word, meaning "upstream people."

Netherlands This country's name translates as "the Low Countries," and certainly, this area has struggled with its elevation for centuries . . . and also with Romans, Franks, Spaniards, and French. As the greatest seapower in the world in the 1600's, a golden age rewarded the Dutch and their constant thwarting of watery invasions. Many of us think of the country as **Holland**, the Dutch name meaning "woodlands," but this area is only one member of the United Provinces of the Netherlands. **Harlem**, New York, was one of the many places named by the Dutch in the New World, after the capital of North Holland, **Haarlem**, known for its tulips. The New York area is known for its black culture, but was actually a white section of town until 1905. By the 1920's it had become so overcrowded and real estate so undervalued that it turned into only a shadow of its former self. **Amsterdam** was christened for a dam on the Amstel River, and the name was later given to a New York town.

Nevada The Spaniards named the rugged mountains of this area the Sierra Nevadas, the "snow-capped mountains," and miners and other settlers liked the name when, in 1861, the land was made an official U.S. Territory. In 1864, Nevada became the "Battle Born State" because of Lincoln's need to have two more favorable senators to back his war effort. The 36th state has also been known as the Sagebrush State and the Silver State, though that latter nickname became tarnished in the 1890's when silver dropped in value due to more reliance on paper currency by the U.S. government. Though we think of the dry lands of Nevada, **Las Vegas** gets its name from the grasslands that were prominent in the south and means "the meadows" in Spanish. The other major wagering mecca, **Reno**, was named by railroad officials for Union general Jesse Lee Reno, killed in the War Between the States.

New York Had history taken a different turn, this major state might still be known as New Amsterdam, but when England took over its governance in 1664, it was renamed in honor of the proprietor, James, the duke of York and **Albany** (from which the capital city gets its name). At one time this bastion of the Union had a slave population of 10% and surprisingly, some 9000 Indians still live on reservations in the Empire State. The Dutch influence is still seen in many place names such as **Brooklyn**, named for the village in Holland, Breukelen, and Harlem, mentioned above. Albany, mentioned above, was originally Skywater, but the English lord had more influence than the Indians. Still, it was here that Benjamin Franklin met with the Native Americans at the Albany Congress and proposed that a president-general be appointed by the crown and a congress to be chosen by colonial assemblies – later ideas for the Articles of Confederation. Here also was the powerful political group, the Albany Regency whose leader was Martin Van Buren, a later president (see O.K.).

North Carolina The territory encompassing the two Carolinas was named for Charles I of England and called Carolana in his honor in 1629. The 12th state was slow to ratify the constitution due to its rather independent-minded population, and that same quality had residents reluctant to join in the secession, though they finally did side with the Rebs. **Raleigh**, the state's capital, honored Sir Walter Raleigh whose attempt to establish the first British outpost in the New World was unsuccessful. **Durham** was named for Bartlett Durham who was generous with his land and gave it for a railway station that was built there in the 1850's. The Durham in New Hampshire had English roots and went back to 1093 and William the Conqueror's intrusion into that country's place names.

North Dakota The 39th state took the territorial designation that later gave it it's official state name from the Indian word meaning "allies" or "confederation of tribes." This confederation hindered its "Americanization" until the Native Americans were finally over-whelmed by the military in the 1860's. Its capital of **Bismarck** was named in honor of the German chancellor of the time, though secret hopes were that Germans would then invest in the railroad.

Our journey through "N" land takes us to places like **Namibia**, named officially in 1968 after the Namib Desert. This war-torn area saw the deaths of 84,000 blacks when German colonial forces stamped out – temporarily – the fight for freedom in 1908. The Indian sense of humor could be behind the naming of **Nantucket**. Massachusetts was given the place in 1692, which in the Native American tongue means either the romantic "far away land" or the more tongue-in-cheek "sandy, sterile soil tempting no one." The Quakers dominated the area until it became a whaling capital in the 1700's. The jewel of the Bahamas, **Nassau**. was named by the British in the 1600's. This haven for pirates and, later, Confederate blockade runners, was ironically named for royalty, the family name of William III of England. The New World had many "new" places like the 9th state, **New Hamp-shire**, whose town of **Concord** was tagged in a kind of celebration of the settling of numerous boundary disputes in 1765. The Massachu-setts Concord celebrated peace with the Indians, but the California namesake had a similar background as the New Hampshire city. The 3rd state, **New Jersey**, had one of its towns named **Camden** in 1828, well after the Revolutionary War, to honor an English aristocrat. The Earl of Camden had been sympathetic to the colonists, and this earned him a place on the American map. **Hoboken** had a more native name, coming from the Indian for "land of the tobacco pipe." **Newark** was the designation given by Puritans to another New Jersey city in honor of their pastor, Rev. Abe Pierson's, home town in England. **New Mexico** is another of the "new" lands, even though it's our 47th state. There you'll find **Albuquerque**, named by its Spanish governor Valdez after the viceroy of New Spain, the duke of Albuquerque (Spain). From **New Zealand** (the Anglicized version of the Danish location, Sjaelland), to New South Wales, to Newfoundland, "new" places abound in the world.

Nicaragua was more than likely named for a Central American chief, Nicaro. It was there that the Tennesseean William Walker reigned as president for one year in 1856. **Nice** in France was named by the early Greek settlers after their goddess of victory when they defeated a neighboring colony. The Portugese used skin color as the basis for naming the Niger River, giving us **Niger** and **Nigeria**, based on the root word for "black." **Norway**, in the simplicity of the Norse, means "northern way."

O **Ohio** Ohio gets its name from another watery Indian appellation. The Iroquois for "great river" is the origin of the Buckeye State's name. Seven presidents were born in this 17th state where the official beverage is tomato juice. That red drink probably had nothing to do with the naming of the **Cincinnati** Red Stockings (now the Reds) who played the first professional baseball game in Ohio in 1869. The city of their origin got its name when a group of Revolutionary War officers founded the Society of the Cincinnati in 1783 to recognize the ideals of the Roman general Lucius Quinctius Cincinnatus who left his plowshare for the sword in 458, and after winning decisively, was back at his farmwork fifteen days later. George Washington was the first president general of this American group which wanted only to leave the war behind, but reminded the world that they weren't afraid to trade soil for gunpowder in defense of the country. Rival city, **Cleveland**, was not named for a president but for General Moses Cleaveland who surveyed the area in 1796. The spelling change of the name happened when a printer made a practical decision. To save space on a newspaper masthead, he dropped the "a." Georgia and Tennessee also have Clevelands, though theirs are not fodder for stand-up comedians. When the Shawnee signed a treaty with another group of Revolutionary War vets, **Dayton** was created, named for New Jerseyan Jonathan Dayton, who had been the youngest member of the Constitutional Convention. This ambitious fellow never really lived in Ohio very much and eventually found himself embroiled in the Burr Conspiracy, which was attempting to divide the new nation and create a western country. Dayton was indicted in 1807 for high treason but was never prosecuted.

Oklahoma Oklahoma gets its name from the Choctaw Indian for "red people." Famous in history for the great land rush of 1889 in which 50,000 people became landowners in one day, it is called the Sooner State because some of the stealthy settlers snuck out to the land sooner than they were supposed to. The 46th state looks like a cooking pan because of disputes over the strip of territory that forms the handle of that pan. Some unusual notes about the state include the first parking meter in 1935 and the state flower, the mistletoe. Maybe the Boomer State is for lovers.

Oregon The Beaver State was 33rd in admission to the Union, and the common belief is that its name comes from the French word for "hurricane." The Pacific Wonderland claims many natural parks, including the smallest, only 452 inches in total area, created by a pranksterish Irishman as a resort for leprechauns. **Eugene** was the first name of Mr. Skinner, who founded the city in 1846 and where resides the University of Oregon.

Travelling to other "O" locations, you'll find **Odessa** in the Ukraine, which was named for an ancient Greek colony that could have been labeled because of Greek hero, Odysseus. The Texas town of the same name was dubbed by Russian rail workers who thought the western prairie was similar to their Ukrainian homeland. The **Okefenokee** Swamp is rarely a cold place, so where does its Indian meaning, "trembling waters" come from? Many of the plants in the swamp float on its surface and tend to shimmy in the breezes and currents. **Okinawa** is the "rope of the sea" in Japanese because of the way it is "tied" to the chain of Nipponese islands. **Oneida**, New York, started as a religious community for a group called "Perfectionists." They weren't obsessive about getting a job done right; they believed they could become perfect on earth. We might scratch our heads at this notion, especially when we learn that they practiced an omni-marital belief in which all members were considered married to all others and kids were raised communally. A rather imperfect notion when you think about all mothers-in-law being also the wives of their sons-in-law. The Indian name, meaning "people of the standing rock," is today associated with the fine silver-crafting tradition these early settlers began. You'll be in a "great swamp" in **Opelika**, Alabama . . . at least in the translation of the Indian name.

Oranges also give us place names, though the **Orange Free State** wasn't named for a lack of the fruit. It was named for the Orange River, which was dubbed in honor of the Dutch Prince William V of the House of Orange. **Orange**, Connecticut, was also named for him. The fruit *is* responsible for the California county. The **Ozarks** probably got their name from a French trading post that was prominent in the area in the 1700's named Aux Arc.

P **Pacific Ocean** When Balboa first observed this vast ocean from a mountaintop in Darien, Panama, he called it "peaceful," using a Latin version of the word. Knowing today its volcanic ferocity and ability to spawn unruly storms, he might have changed the name.

Pakistan Although this country's name is a kind of made-up amalgamation meant to satisfy its diverse peoples, it turns out to be one that satisfied nearly all the tribal groups. A sort of acronym derived from the P in Punjab, the A in Afghan, the K in Kashmir, and the "stan" in Baluchistan was put together to create a unified nation out of a factional conglomerate. The name was satisfactory also because when translated from Persian "pak" means "pure" or "holy" and "stan" means "land."

Palestine From the Biblical turmoil of early Philistia – named for the Philistines from which Palestine got its name – to the present-day unrest of its refugees, this region has seen constant flux. The Arab conquest in the 600's was certainly only one of the many changes in the ruling class. Crusaders swept through the area in 1099, and Turks ruled for hundreds of years. Today, the country that was recently only a dream in the minds of Arabs scattered throughout the Middle East, is becoming a reality again.

Panama 20,000 workers died of disease and accidents over the course of the building of the most famous edifice of this country, its canal. Its name is probably derived from a Tupi Indian word for "butterfly," though the mosquito is its most famous insect. Its European discovery was in 1501 by Rodrigo de Bastides.

Paraguay This country has never quite recovered from a five year war, beginning in 1865, with Brazil, Argentina, and Uruguay in which half the population was destroyed, leaving one man for every ten women of the remaining 230,000 people. At one point, when José Francia, "El Supremo," ruled from 1814 to 1840, the country seemed on the brink of prominence. He took land from the rich and gave it not to the poor, but to the state to foil an Argentine blockade of the Paraguay's main river. The Guarani Indian name of this country means "a place with a great river."

Paris The City of Lights was once a prominent Roman outpost named Lutetia in 52 B.C. With the onslaught of the barbarian northerners in the 4th century, the town became known by the name of one of the tribes of Frankish fighters, the Parisii. Almost a different country from the rest of France, Paris has been a place of revolt and individualism throughout its history until World War II when it was subdued by the Germans.

Pennsylvania William Penn's father had his ups and downs as an admiral, but finally received some benefit for his exploits when King Charles II granted a large territory to William in 1681 in repayment of debts owed the senior Penn. Charles called it "Penn's woods," but used the more educated Latin formation. The fervently religious William immediately set out to conduct a "holy experiment" in the New World, creating a liberal territory which allowed broad religious and civil freedom. Persecuted Quakers and other pacifist sects flocked to the open-minded land, giving it today's nickname: the Quaker State. Penn rarely got to live among his experiment's subjects and was even briefly deprived of his proprietorship because of his political affiliations. He ended up very depressed when he discovered that his guinea pigs acted rather hoggishly toward one another, constantly bickering over laws and governmental power – not at all behaving as they were supposed to. Many of the Quakers, Mennonites, and Amonnites were banished or jailed during the Revolutionary War for their refusal to fight. Ironically, after the war Washington had to put down an uprising by Pennsylvania citizens due to their resistance to taxation – liquor taxation, that is. The Whiskey Rebellion was a true test of the power of the new federal government, and that government succeeded. **Philadelphia**, founded by Penn, was conceived as a city of "brotherly love" (the meaning of the city's name). This birthplace of American independence was the nation's capitol for ten years, from 1790 to 1800. **Pittsburgh** was named by General John Forbes in 1758 after he threw out the French from Fort Duquesne. He honored another controversial British figure, William Pitt the Elder, who believed in constitutional rights for the commoner. Today's blue collar steel workers might appreciate that.

Peru Betrayal was one of the first acts in the founding of Peru. When Francisco Pizarro, his three brothers, and a small band of Spanish conquistadors turned the Incan Empire on its ear, scaring the natives with their muskets and bravado, Pizarro then pretended friendship with the Incan emperor, Atahualpa. Pizarro received both a room full of gold and one of silver when he held this ruler as his friendly hostage then turned around and killed him. More betrayal proved Pizarro's downfall when he was assassinated by followers of a former partner after Pizarro cheated him. At 65, he could have retired to his "city of kings," **Lima**, in riches had he not been so greedy. This city now is most noted as the namesake for the bean, though its sisters can be found in Ohio and Georgia.

Philipines   Charles V of Spain had his son Philip honored when these islands were designated "Felipinas" by Spanish explorers. Differing sources claim either Ruy Lopéz de Villalobos or Juan de Salcedo as the namee. When the natives got sick of Spanish dominance by 1897, Emilio Aguinaldo felt he was backed by U.S. sympathy. After all, hadn't Admiral George Dewey encouraged his rebellion after the U.S. commander sank the Spanish fleet in Manila Bay? But after the Spanish asked for peace, President William McKinley requested the Philipines as part of the bargain, and Aguinaldo had to fight a new aggressor. 200,000 Filipino deaths later, the U.S. had its island base. Perhaps the United States could be said to have paid the price for these lives during World War II when bold Americans led by the Arkansas general MacArthur liberated the country from a new conqueror, the Japanese. Today, the country still has its political unrest, but no more foreign overlords. We've already talked about Manila, we'll save Quezon City for later . . .

Portugal   Celtic tribes were the original inhabitants of this Iberian coastal country when the Romans made their conquest. One of the Latin settlements was called Portus Cale, but the land itself was called Lusitania, after a federation of these aforementioned tribes. In time, the Roman port gave the country its later name. Legend says that **Lisbon** was founded by Elisha and some of the lost tribes of Israel. The ancient name, Olisipo, is said to have come from the Greek hero, Ulysses. Later, the Romans called it Felicitas Julia for Julius Caesar. Portugal is known for its launching of the great exploration of the non-European world, but part of the motivation for this could also be embroiled in legend. Prince Henry the Navigator, son of King John I, who established a school for navigation and geography, had a desire to contact Prester John, the fabled Christian lord of a kingdom somewhere in the East. This priest/king was purported to have a fabulous realm, and Prince Henry hoped to find him to ally in his fight against the heathen hordes. One of the stories of Prester John (Prester from "Presbtyr" meaning "priest") passed on by Marco Polo was that Ghenghis Khan wanted his daughter to marry the ruler, and when he refused, a tremendous battle ensued, destroying the army of John. Whatever Prince Henry's impetus, he sparked the Age of Discovery in the 1400's. Though he forbade the capturing of slaves, greedier powers overruled his mandate as Portugal became one of the major empires of the world in the 1500's.

Puerto Rico The island whose Spanish name means "rich port" was once called San Juan, with a city of the same name to honor territory's namesake, St. John. When that city moved, a name-swapping occurred. The U.S. victory in the Spanish-American War gave us the island, and it's been a close associate of America ever since. We haven't always treated the place well, exploiting the land for sugar, even though we gave its people citizenship in 1917. After World War II, we were more careful with its economy. Its naming as our 51st state could be in Puerto Rico's future, but there is still a strong movement for independent nation status.

Our trek through "P" places takes us to **Patagonia**, translated as "big feet" in its Spanish beginnings. The European explorers were a bit sarcastic about the southern Argentinian natives' sloppy foot coverings and named the land for the poor shoes of its people. We often hear of the ancient seafarer explorers of **Phoenicia**, but apparently they had no real name for themselves. Some translate the Greek appellation for this band of city states as "merchant," others as "red men," and others as "palm tree." Make up *your* mind. The **Phoenix** is that legendary bird that is reborn in its own ashes, and when "Lord Darrell" Duppa and company rebuilt the Hohokum Indian irrigation canals in this Arizona town, they said the area would rise again, an apt prophesy. Please don't make Polish jokes when learning that the land of this people's origin means "dwellers of the meadow (or plain or field)" in its Slavonic description of the tribe that was the ancestor of the Poles. In the 1400's **Poland**'s culture was of the highest in Europe until neighbors began dividing up the territory. **Polynesia** lumps together numerous island people. The Greek term for the conglomeration means "many islands." The area is another example of the greatest weapon the European explorers brought with them: germs. In some places the population diminshed as much as 96% in a century and a half after the Westerners brought their bugs. No, **Pontiac**, Michigan, was not named for the car that was produced nearby but for the controversial Indian chief who briefly united diverse tribal groups to slow the British engines of conquest. An Illinois town was also named for the Ottawa rebel, as was the vehicle. The **Punjab** was once a central location for the civilization in the Indus Valley, but now the former British province is a state of India and also a province in Pakistan. Its name means "five rivers" from the same Sanskrit root that gives us "**punch**" (a drink with five ingredients). The **Pyrenees** are mountains of legend in the stories of knights and quests, but today they represent a boundary zone between France and Spain. They were named for the daughter of a special friend of Hercules, Bebryx, who was buried there. Her name meant "seed of fruit" in Greek.

Q There aren't that many "Q" locations we can visit in this word journey. **Quincy**, Massachusetts, was not named for John Quincy Adams but for Col. John Quincy, a prominent resident and relative of John Q. It was originally called Merry Mount partly because some of its citizens loved play and more worldly pleasures, though they didn't last long in this Puritan heartland. When the 6th president was born there it was called Braintree. **Queens**, New York, got its name from a queen, of course. She was Catherine of Braganza, the wife of Charles II, who was honored in 1683 by the colonists. The once-capital of the Phillipines, **Quezon City**, was named by and for the first president of the country in 1937, Manuel Quezon. **Quito**, the capital of Ecuador, took its name from an Inca group, the Quitus, who were dominant in the area before 1534 when Spain claimed the volcanic site as its own.

R **Red Sea** Many of us may remember the movie version of the Exodus of the Jewish people from the land of Egypt when Moses raises his staff and, with God's help, parts the Red Sea for their passage. The miraculous occurrence is recorded in Exodus 14: 21-31, but the geographical location is wrong. Due to a mistranslation, the Greek version of the Bible made the Hebrew writer's "Sea of Reeds" or "Reed Sea" the Red Sea, even though scholars have since realized that all other locations mentioned in the Bible place them too far north of the strip of water separating Africa from Arabia. The Israelites would have had to travel three days out of the way to get to the Red Sea. The original Reed Sea was probably a marshy area on Lake Tismah where papyrus reeds grew thickly. Some geologists theorize that volcanic disturbances in the Mediterranean may have caused the sucking away of the water there and then a tsunami-like return. Whatever the explanation for the happening, and whatever mysterious ways may have been taken advantage of for performing wonders, this was the key moment in the final parting of the Israelite slaves from their Egyptian masters. The Red Sea, by the way, gets its name from a reddish algae that forms a kind of scum on the waters during the summer months.

Rhine River This heart's artery of Europe gets its name from a Germanic root that simply meant "to flow" and could be simply translated as "river." In ancient times, the water course acted as a boundary between the fiesty Germanic tribes and the Roman legions. Along this river, in Strasborg, paste gemstones were made that were sort of the first cubic zirconium diamonds of their day. **Rhine stones** are still used in jewelry. **Rhine wine** also got its start along fertile valleys near this river. The Rhône probably has a name origin similar to its sister.

Rhode Island When Giovanni de Verrazano came sailing along the American coast in the New World's early history, he noted that **Block Island** (named for Dutch captain Adraien Block) reminded him of the island of Rhodes. That may have been the source for the naming of our 13th state. Others claim the Dutch "Roodt Eylandt" – "red island" – is the origin of the Ocean State's name, referring to the red clay shores. When dissident religious groups filtered into the area, led by Roger Williams who couldn't stomach the Massachusetts Bay Colony's intolerance (or who couldn't be stomached by it – they banished him), a new colony was founded where religious freedom was the guarantee. Ironic that the Massachusetts Puritans, who sought liberty of worship in the Americas, didn't allow that same freedom among themselves. After Williams made good friends with the local Native Americans, he became president of this new place for escape from religious persecution. He founded **Providence**, naming it for God's providence in finding him this new home. Chicken farmers will note that our American commercial poultry industry got its start here when a breed, the **Rhode Island Red**, was developed. The color red comes pecking its way into the state's beginnings again.

Oh, yes, that original island, **Rhodes**, probably gots its name from the Greek for "rose," so the red connection with the state could still be part of Verrazano's recognition. One of the Wonders of the World, the Colossus, a hundred foot bronze statue, guarded the harbor of the capital city of this Aegean isle until it fell in an earthquake in 224 B.C. The inhabitants let it lie for many years until Arab raiders plundered it, taking the bronze sculpture for their own use. It is said that it took 900 camel loads to remove it all.

Riviera   The Italian for "shore" is at the base of this location's name's meaning, and shore it is, extending many miles from Toulon in France to La Spezla in Italy, encompassing some of the finest beachfront in the world where the wealthy wander its sand in all kinds of dress and undress.

Romania   When Romans entered this land in 107 A.D. they called it Dacia after one of the major tribal groups there. The conquerors' influence was so profound that the very language and customs became so like the rulers that the people began calling their homeland "the land of the Romans." Tossed, twisted, and tattered as these people have been by the fortunes of war and dominance – from Slavic tribes to Soviet rule – they still retain the only Romance language among the Eastern Europeans. Many of us hear the accent of these people in Dracula movies where part of Rumania (as we Westerners call it), Transylvania, plays a prominent role. That location translates as "out of the woods" from its Latin appellation.

Rubicon   Though experts will argue the present-day location of this stream, its name rings through history for the part it played in the beginnings of the Roman Empire. One of the laws of the Roman Senate was that commanders of the various conquered regions could not take their troops across the boundaries of that region without the Senate's permission. When Julius Caesar got the reputation as one of the greatest military commanders of his day, the frightened Senate and a jealous former partner, Pompey, commander-in-chief of the army, who had been married to Caesar's daughter, the peacekeeper Julia, tried to get Caesar to disband his legions. In a momentous decision, Caesar defied the Senate in 49 B.C. and crossed the boundary of Gaul and Rome – that little waterway, the Rubicon – and started a civil war that ended with the death of Pompey in Egypt (where Caesar chased him, also meeting Cleopatra) and the establishment of the Roman Empire. Rubicon means "red," getting its name from rosy mud in its bed.

Runnymeade   Another small location that played a large role in history, Runnymeade was the meadow where a group of rebellious barons, tired of King John's constant need for their money, forced the monarch to sign the Magna Carta in 1215, curtailing his fiscal abuse. This document led many who were not of the feudal class to claim they had rights against an overlord's taxing ways and eventually stimulated the present, more democratic English system of government through Parliament. Runnymeade translates as "meadow on the council island" from its Old English beginnings.

Russia Russia is now Russia again, but scholars are still in disagreement as to the origin of the name which came from a group called the Rus'. Was it a Finnish word for a Swede, or a name for a Norman group, or merely a nonethnic handle for an allied bunch of merchants and traders made up of Slavs, Finns, and Scandinavians? Some say the Rus' got its name from an ancient word for the Volga River, the Rha. Whatever the background, the land gained true status in the world when Ivan the Great refused to pay homage to the conquering Mongol Horde and beat them back from his borders, which he then expanded. He felt he was heir to a new empire to replace the Roman and Byzantine ones, and in some ways he was prophetic. It was Ivan IV, known as "the terrible," who gave us that reputation of the rapacious Russian ruler with the iron hand. This rather paranoid fellow went through seven wives and terrorized the land with an early version of the KGB, even killing one of his sons in one of his rages.

Roaming around other "R" locations takes us to **Rabat**, the capital of Morroco. Founded as a "camp" (the meaning of the word in Arabic) for troops to muster in a holy war against Spain in the 1100's, its formal name was Rabat al-Fath, "camp of victory." The Maltese city of the same name has a different translation as "suburb." Another capital city, **Rangoon**, in Burma got its name in the 1750's as Yangon, "the end of strife," after king Alaungpaya won a victory over rivals, the Mons. **Rangpur**, in Bangladesh, has an attractive translation as "abode of bliss." Continuing with capitals, that of Iceland, **Reykjavik**, means "bay of smoke" because of the hot springs in the area, which set up plumes of steam, giving the waters a foggy quality at times. The Danes ruled here until 1944. Travelling to the stars for a moment, we find **Rigel** gets its name from the Arabic, meaning "left leg of the giant," referring to its location in the constellation of Orion. **Rosario** in Argentina has a religious appellation centered on the rosary.

S **Salem** The Massachusetts town is probably most remembered for its witch trials of 1692, most recently examined in the many-layered play, *The Crucible*, by Arthur Miller, which makes its subtle comparison of the superstitious Puritan villagers to our own psyche during the McCarthy era and its Communist "witch hunts." The town's name means "peace" and was founded after a pact was made by rival settlers Roger Conant and John Endecott. The Oregon Salem resulted in 1851 from a translation of the Indian name for the place, Chemketta, "place of rest." Quakers named the New Jersey Salem, and a group of these settlers honored their home town when they moved to Ohio by giving their new location the same name. Salems in Missouri, Virginia, New Hampshire, and Illinois all remember the "peace" of the Hebrew original, Jeru*sa-lem*, "city of peace." The North Carolina Salem was founded by amicable Moravians in 1766 and merged with nearby Winston in 1913.

Salisbury   The most famous landmark of this area of England is the mysterious group of arranged slabs of rock, Stonehenge. There is another Salisbury in North Carolina that was one of the largest Confederate prisons of the War Between the States. The **Salisbury Steak** comes from a Pritikin of the 1800's. J.H. Salisbury was a physician who pushed for reform in our eating habits, trying to ease the amount of fat in the diet by concocting a patty composed of meat, eggs, milk, bread crumbs, and seasonings.

Samaria   For most Christians, the story of the Good Samaritan is one that stands out as an example of sacrifice and compassion. But there are even more facets to the parable (Luke 10: 33-35) than just an example of kindness to a victim of crime. When the city of Samaria was founded in the 9th century B.C., it was named for a resident, Shemer, whose land was used. Soon, this northern kingdom was overrun by Assyrians and the occupants displaced. However, when a group returned from Babylonian captivity, a factionalism developed between the Samaritans and orthodox Jews. These returned residents of the new Samaria believed they had the true handle on the teachings of Moses and this angered other Jews. When Samaritans were not allowed to help in the rebuilding of the temple, a real hatred grew up between the sects. The Samaritans actually changed the origin of their name, translating a Hebrew term for "observants" to emphasize their "true" understanding of the Old Testament. When Jesus has the Samaritan aid the mugged Jerusalemite, he was also trying to bind some internal wounds among the Jews that went very deep.

Santiago   The Spanish term for Saint James the Apostle is the origin of this place name that starts in Spain in the mists of legend. According to this legend, the saint, who died in 44 A.D., either had his body wash ashore or had it carried by faithful followers to the coast of Spain where it was said he had preached the gospel. There it was buried until it was miraculously rediscovered in the 9th century. This revelation made the location a holy shrine and one of the three top spots for pilgrimages behind Jerusalem and Rome. This shrine was probably a large impetus for the growth of Spain as a Christian nation since prior to that time, the Moors controlled the land. The place became a kindling spot for the reclamation of Spanish soil from the invaders. A group of knights formed the Order of Santiago to protect pilgrims on their journey, and this sense of divine purpose unified the Christian sections of Spain against the rather disjointed Muslims. When Pedro de Valdiva attempted to conquer Chile, he called his capital city "the Santiago of the New Frontier," leaning a bit on the old flame of religious fervor. The Santiago of the Dominican Republic was founded by thirty cabelleros (gentlemen) who were members of the order of knights. Cuba's Santiago is also linked in name to the Spanish shrine.

Sardinia This island off the coast of Italy was founded by Greek fishermen and gives us the name of the fish that was found in abundance there, the **sardine**. An interesting side story dealing with this island, which was given limited autonomy by Italy in 1947, provides us with a word for mocking humor, **sardonic**. One of the early Greek tales about the colony was that a plant grew there that was so bitter that, if eaten, it would cause facial convulsions resembling a horrible smiling grimace – the sardonic smile. Other legends about the plant said a devourer could die of laughter. The Greek root for the island's name means "scornful" or "sneering."

Sargasso Sea This area of the Atlantic has been the stuff of legends where writers have described graveyards of ships entangled in the mat of plant life that lives in the calm "pool" of ocean existing between more swift sea currents – a kind of Bermuda Triangle of olden days. The Sargasso Sea is real, encompassing some two million square miles of the South Atlantic, and was first described by Christopher Columbus. The original Portugese word for "grape" is at the base of its naming because of the grape-like air sacs that keep the seaweed afloat miles from land. Later, the word came to mean seaweed; however, the highly adapted plant and animal life there is not nearly thick enough to ensnarl a ship.

Saskatchewan Canada's Breadbasket gets its name from the Cree Indians who gave a major waterway there a very descriptive rendering which translates: "fast flowing river that turns around when it runs." The winding river of the plains does seem to do this as its path meanders. One of the province's major cities, **Saskatoon**, refers to the Indian name of a tasty berry found in the area. It was founded in 1882 as farmers poured into the land to raise wheat.

Saudi Arabia   The Saud family has been around in this land since the 1400's, but really didn't assert true power until 1902 when ibn Saud used his prowess, starting at age fourteen, to begin a conquest of Arabia. By the age of twenty-four, he was a major figure in the area. By forty-four, he was the ruler of a huge tract that became a place of treasure four years later with the discovery of oil.

Scotland   Scotii tribes from Ireland didn't make it to the northern part of England until the 5th century, but their influence was profound because of their Christianizing impact. The Romans called the land Caledonia and had a great deal of trouble with the locals of the time, who they called Picts or "painted people" because of these barbaric warriors' habit of applying color to their bodies. **Glasgow** gets its name from the Gaelic tongue and means "dear green place." Some say the Celtic for "green glen" is at the heart of this 800-year-old city. Other Glagows can be found in Virginia, Kentucky, and Montana. Why does the London police's Criminal Investigation Division go by the name **Scotland Yard**? The original location for the famous branch of detectives was the site where Scottish royalty stayed on visits to London in the Middle Ages. **Paisley**, Scotland, was where that unusual fabric pattern was first made.

Shanghai   When the Chinese tried to "just say no" to the importation of opium into their country in the mid-1800's, the British didn't like it one bit. After all, there were big bucks in drugs, and Orientals were perfect targets to be a huge market of addicts. Sounds like a pretty evil scenario, doesn't it? But it's basically the situation that started the Opium War that opened Shanghai and many other Chinese ports to foreign trade. In Chinese, the name of this city means "at (or above) the sea," a good description of a port city. Foreign exploitation of China made this and other trade cities fairly dangerous and unattractive places, with anti-foreign sentiment running high among the average Chinese. By the 1870's it was difficult to get men to take the "slow boat to China" and work onboard ship. A common practice for the unscrupulous boat captain was to drug a sailor's drink in, say, San Francisco, carry him unconscious to the ship, and let him wake up miles from shore. He was "**shanghaied**," as the practice came to be known, whether he was going to Canton or Hong Kong or Singapore. By 1898, the Chinese tried to throw out the European and American intruders once more in the Boxer Rebellion, but failed. It's no wonder these people are a bit reluctant to open their arms to those who used them when they could. They've been shanghaied once too often themselves.

Shangri-la This imaginary paradise, created by James Hilton in 1933 in the book *Lost Horizon*, gave us a word for utopia that was especially popular in the 30's and 40's. President Roosevelt so liked it that he used it several times in his career. When his presidential yacht was no longer a safe retreat from the pressures of his office because of the fear of enemy submarines, his hideaway was moved inland to the Maryland mountains to a place he called Shangri-la. It was later renamed Camp David by Eisenhower in honor of his son. Roosevelt's affinity for the name also led to an aircraft carrier being christened Shangri-la in 1944. He had once been asked where an American air attack had originated, and he had replied, "Shangri-la." The naming of the carrier was a tongue-in-cheek tribute to his humorous response.

Sirius Let's get serious about Sirius. From the Greek, meaning "glowing," this star's name is appropriate since it is the brightest of all those twinkling points of light in our sky. Even though it's the same size as the sun, it beams its light at thirty times the intensity of our home star. That and the fact that it is one of the closest neighbors of all celestial gas-burners makes it stand out in the heavens. Its nickname, the Dog Star, comes from the fact that it is part of the constellation Canis Major, one of the "dogs" of Orion. Egyptians noted that Sirius appeared at dawn on the hottest days of the year, and the Romans followed up on this recognition, calling that period the "**dog days**." Actually, Sirius is not alone when it glows in our sky. A white dwarf sister (brother? sibling?), Sirius B, tugs it in its eternal dance, orbiting around it every fifty years. Sirius B must be a much older relative, since it's in its final stages of gravitational collapse, making it about the size of the earth but much, much more dense. In fact, if you took a shovel full of its mass and spread it on your garden, it would weigh about 120,000 tons – a heavy thought.

Sodom and Gomorrah These two ancient cities are always associated with one another since they suffered the same fate in the biblical account. Their residents were noted for being inhospitable to visitors. Not only were they reputed to have exceedingly liberal sexual tastes, legend said that if a guest didn't fit the bed offered, he was either cut to the appropriate size or stretched to the proper mattress length. When Abraham's nephew, Lot, headed that way with his herds after he and his uncle found their herdsmen fighting over grazing land, he found a rich land, but a particularly sorry populace. Though it is certainly an ethnic slur to speak of bargaining as "jewing down," the practice of haggling had already taken place concerning Sodom. Abraham had negotiated with God Himself. When Jehovah appeared to Abraham (along with a couple of angels) to tell him his old wife was going to have a child, He also let him know He was going to destroy Sodom, if rumors about it were true. Abraham said that if there were fifty righteous men in the city would he destroy it? No, God said. Forty-five? No. Forty? No. Thirty? No. Twenty? No. Ten? No. Unfortunately, the haggling over numbers proved a lost cause. When Lot took God's angels under his roof on their visit, the men of the town, "both old and young," surrounded the house and demanded sexual favors of them. Even after Lot offered his virgin daughters for the crowd's pleasure, these lascivious folk weren't satisfied, but tried to break Lot's door down to get at the heavenly guests. The angels had to strike the mob blind, but even then they groped around, trying to find the entrance to the house. The evil influence of the place was so predominant that when Lot told his sons-in-law (and the daughters were still virgins?) he was getting out of the place, they fairly laughed at him and wouldn't leave the X-rated playground. What was the attraction of these frolicking folk that made even Lot's wife turn to look back, turning into a pillar of salt as her reward for her carnal curiosity?

Scholars have argued the location of these cities, but most agree their remains are probably underwater at the south end of the Dead Sea. One prominent theory is that the destruction was caused by the ignition of leaking gas and oil deposits that have recently been located in the area. Since it rained fire and brimstone and the cities burned like a furnace, this theory has some real likelihood. The Mount of Sodom in that same area still sprouts strange salt figures caused by the erosion of masses of NaCl. Sodom itself probably came from a Hittite word for salt, while Gomorrah comes from the Arabic for "to overflow" or "flood."

Apparently, the power of this risqué region left an impression on Lot's two surviving virgin kids. Soon after, while hiding out in mountain caves, they got bored with the lack of men and got dad drunk and had sex with him, both getting pregnant from the incestuous encounter. To this day, **sodomy**, though difficult to pin down in particulars, represents a kind of sexual depravity associated with these biblical bimbos who used and abused rather than focus on the more spiritual side of sexuality.

South Carolina Even though this state was part of a massive area originally called Carolana (see North Carolina), it had an individualism almost from the beginning which led to its being officially separated from its northern sister in 1729. Three years later, a hunk of the new crown colony was amputated to form Georgia. The Palmetto State was the 8th to enter the Union.

South Dakota Our 40th state was a part of the Dakota territory in 1861. The Sunshine State could have been called South Sioux if Congress had gone by the Dakota Indians other name. This wouldn't have been a favorable designation to the natives since the Ojibway translation of Sioux means "enemy." The capital of South Dakota (sometimes known as the Coyote State) is named Pierre not for the man who claimed it for France in 1743, Pierre Gaultier de Varennes, but for a famous fur trader in the area, Pierre Chouteau.

Spain In many ways, Spain's history makes it very different from the rest of Europe. Perhaps the formidable boundary of the Pyrenees mountains was one factor that isolated Spain, but the Arab influence was certainly another. The wide-ranging Phoenicians first traveled to the Spanish shores, calling it Schphannim, meaning "rabbit's coast," from which Spain's name derives. The Romans corrupted the Phoenician original, naming the land Hispaniae. By the 700's, the invading Visigoths were the main rulers, but Muslim incursions from North Africa caused the collapse of the Germanic kingdom. Moors ruled most of southern Spain for several hundred years afterward, giving the country their cultural and architectural influences. Americans are familiar with the Italian Columbus being commissioned in 1492 by King Ferdinand and his wife, Queen Isabella, to seek an Atlantic route to the East and its wealth. That year is of huge significance in world history, but for Spanish Jews that was also the year Isabella forced them all to either convert or leave. When she was not happy with the sincerity of some of the converts, she imposed the Spanish Inquisition, one of the most brutal of all church-sponsored punishments of nonbelievers.

Sri Lanka The "resplendent land" of Sri Lanka (its meaning in Sinhalese) is one of loveliest islands in the world. Ancient navigators sometimes called the place Serendib, which eventually gave us the word "**serendipity**," emphasizing the surprise of finding such beauty where none was expected. Because of British colonial ambitions, the isle was renamed Ceylon in the late 1700's, and that imposed name hung around until 1972. The native Sinhalese take their name from the legend of the father of Vijaya, founder of an early Sri Lankan dynasty, being the son of a lion. The **Sinhalese** are the "lion people."

Sweden This Scandinavian land takes its name from a powerful tribal group, the Svear, who dominated the area in the 700's A.D. In the native tongue of Sweden the country is called Sverige. The northern pagans were some of the hardest for early monks to Christianize, and it took until 1100 to finally say the land had converted, though there still was a smorgasbord of heathen practices. Oh, yes, **smorgasbord** translates as something like "sandwich table" and comes from the harvest feast of the pagans, who gobbled up pickled herring and salted fish in celebration. The sing song rhythm of the Swedish language is actually a way to get double meanings out of many words, depending on the pitch and tone attached to them. The capital, **Stockholm**, got its start because land in the area actually rose in a rebounding effect after glacial pressures were relieved. This caused a once-easily-traversable waterway to become impassable, and in 1252 the island on which the original city rested became an important place for merchants to unload goods on one side and reload on the other for trading to villages to the north. The city's name could be translated as "log island" because inhabitants chained logs together around the island to protect it from thieving invaders.

Switzerland This beautiful country is truly an amalgam of independent peoples. The land has no true language of its own, which is unusual in itself, and its neutrality during major wars has kept its uniqueness intact. Known as **Helvetia** during Roman times, named for one of the tribes in the area, the Helvetii, Switzerland didn't get its present name until 1291 when three **counties** (areas ruled by counts) banded together to form the beginnings of a nation. One of the counties, Schwyz, gave this union its designation. **Bern** comes from the Germanic for "bear," named after Duke Berchtold V survived an attack by bears in 1191 while on a hunting expedition – so the legend goes. Others say settlers from Verona brought the bear symbol with them.

"S" lands abound in the world, so let's look at a few more. **Saratoga Springs**, famous for its Revolutionary War activity, got its name from the Indian for "place of swift water." Another New York location, **Schenectady**, looks Germanic, but also comes from the Native Americans of the area. The Mohawk for "end of the pine plains" was the basis for the city's name. **Scranton**, Pennsylvania, was named for ambitious brothers who expanded the iron industry there, which was first started by another pair of siblings, the Slocums, who gave it its first name, Slocum Hollow. The agony of **Serbia** in recent history makes its name stand out in our minds, but scholars are unsure of the name's exact meaning. Some theorize that the original tribe that gave the region its name had Caucasian origins and meant "man." One of the deadliest battles of the Civil War took place around **Shiloh** church in Tennessee. Though Confederate forces initially won, the Union counterattack was probably the beginning of the end for the South. The name for the battle came from the church, but the church was named for the biblical town in Palestine and is associated with prophecy. The name means something like "he to whom they belong" and was mentioned by Jacob when he told his sons about what would befall them in the "last days." Some students of the Bible say he was referring to the Messiah in a prophetic allusion that indicated that Israel would rule the area until Shiloh came. The vast territory of **Siberia** takes its name from the Tatar for "sleeping land," snoozing under the blanket of cold it is reputed for. Cossacks conquered the area for Russia in 1581. **Sicily** was the home of the Sicani and Siculi tribes, the namesakes for the island. The place has probably one of the most diverse of gene pools, having been controlled by Greeks, Romans, Vandals, Byzantines, Arabs, Normans, and Spaniards. The power of the Mafia, which we Americans think of as being linked to the island, was really enhanced when Allied forces gave many government posts to mafiosi after World War II, replacing Facists with members of these independent "families" who survived Mussolini's attempts to destroy them. **Sierra Leone** translates from the Portugese as "lion mountains" and might have gotten this appellation because of the way thunder sounds in the rocky hills above Freetown. We're more familiar with its neighbor, Liberia, as being a home for ex-slaves, since America was most closely involved with that colony, but Sierra Leone got its start in 1788 – over thirty years earlier than Liberia – from former slaves. Some 400 slaves who had fought for the British in the American Revolution were given the land as a reward and began a colony there with sixty white women, mostly prostitutes. Later, former slaves from Nova Scotia and Jamaica joined them. The **Sinai** peninsula seems to have taken its name from a moon god worshipped by desert people in ancient times. Mistaking tigers for lions gave the island country of **Singapore** its name in the 1100's. The "lion city" (its meaning in Sanskrit) gained independence in 1965.

Soho, a popular district near London, took its name from a hunting cry. The major kind of game that is sought there now are ladies of the evening. The **Solomon Islands** owe their christening to the dreams of wealth that Alvaro de Mendaña de Neira thought would come true here, making the isles rival the wealthy biblical king. Needless to say, the dream bubble popped, but the name stuck. **Somalia**'s name has been in the news lately because of drought, famine, and internal conflict. The country takes its name from nomadic herdsfolk, the Somaal, though biblically, you might know it as the Land of Punt . . . near the land of Touchdown perhaps? **Sonora**, in Mexico, comes from the Spanish for "sound" because of the noise deposits of marble make when struck. If you've ever visited a health **spa**, you might be interested to know that these resort places all take their name from the mineral springs of Spa, Belgium, where royalty bathed in the 18th century. Famous in ancient times, it was rediscovered in 1326 and is known for being the place where Allied forces made peace with the Germans at the end of World War I. **Springfield**, Illinois, is well-known as the residence and burial place of Abraham Lincoln; but did you know there are Springfields in Missouri, New Jersey, Ohio, Oregon, Vermont, and Virginia? Most were named because of some fertile meadow area near a branch of water, though some honored the former residence of its founders. The Springfield in Massachusetts was made famous by the munitions industry that created the **Springfield rifle**. There, also, was the invention of basketball by Dr. James Naismith at the college in the town. **Staten Island** was named by the Dutch in 1661 for their governing body of the time, Staten Generaal (States General). **Stratfords** in Connecticut and Canada honor Shakespeare's home, Stratford-upon-Avon, which started as a Roman ford over the Avon River. The **Sudan** was named by Arab writers "Bilad as-Sudan": "the country of the blacks." It was earlier known as Nubia and the biblical Land of Cush. Though it was once a Christian land, slave trade was a big industry there in the early 1800's. The Mahdi (Arabic for "Messiah"), an Arab leader with a holy zeal, threw out the Egyptian and British forces in the 1880's – but only briefly. Slavery also dominated **Suriname** in South America, which was named for an early Indian tribe, the Surinen. It was known as Dutch Guiana for centuries. **Swaziland** was founded by a tribal offshoot of the Zulu and took its name from a king of their people. **Syria** seems to have gotten its name from a people of the ancient region, the Assur (whose name could be translated "I see" or "I gaze"), but was originally called Aram after the grandson of Noah, son of Shem, who settled in these highlands. The **Aramaic** language spoken by Christ is derived from this name. The **Szchewan** district of China, which we think of for its cooking style, translates as "four streams," referring to tributaries of the Yangtze River.

T **Taiwan** This populous island had a huge immigration situation in 1949 when Chiang Kai-Shek and his nationalist Chinese followers got booted from the mainland. It was named Ilha Formosa by the Portugese when they discovered the "beautiful island" in 1590. The original Chinese designation that the country goes by now means "terraced bay."

Tennessee Cherokee Indian villages on the Little Tennessee River gave the Volunteer State its name. "Tanasi" was what these Indians called their tribal gathering place. It probably translates as "bend in the river," since that was the prominent feature of the river they lived by and also gives the place another nickname, "the Big Bend State." The 16th state might have been called Franklin had three counties in the territory had their way in 1784. At that time, North Carolina controlled the area, and the settlers didn't like it. It took another twelve years, however, for Congress to finally agree to give the location statehood. Until then, it was called The Territory South of the River Ohio. The capital, **Knoxville**, was named for General Henry Knox, an early Secretary of War. **Nashville** was once called French Lick, but North Carolina pioneers wanted to honor General Francis Nash and called it Nashborough. In 1784 the name was altered. The home of country music was probably partly responsible for having one of the two state songs be "Rocky Top." **Chatanooga**, of choo-choo fame, got its name from the Cherokee Indians and means "rock that comes to a point," referring to Lookout Mountain.

Texas A banding together of early Indian tribes in the area gave the Lone Star State its name. The Hasinae Indian word for "friends" or "allies," "tejas," was the term Spaniards used to map this expansive area. The history of Texas is storied in the American saga with phrases like "Remember the Alamo" ringing down the halls of time, but one fact about the 28th state may be new to you. When it was granted statehood in 1845, Congress gave the locals the right to divide into as many as five states, a possibility that still exists today. Let's look at some of the state's cities. **Abilene** was named for Abilene, Kansas, from which cattle herds had been driven. **Dallas** honored George M. Dallas of Pennsylvania who was vice-president under Polk from the year of statehood until 1849. French artists from a failed community were the first settlers in the land of J.R. Ewing. **Galveston** reflects the Spanish influence, having been named for the viceroy of Mexico, Count Bernardo de Gálvez, in 1785. Six thousand people perished in a hurricane there in 1900. Of course, we remember General Sam **Houston** when thinking of the city honoring him. This great leader was against secession from the Union when he was governor in 1861, but opponents forced him out of office, and he died two years later at the age of 70. One of the signers of the Texas Declaration of Independence, Colonel Tom **Lubbock** gave his name to this Texas town. **Pasadena**, in Texas, comes from the Spanish for "land of flowers," but the California Pasadena, for which this translation would be very appropriate considering the Rose Parade, got its name from the Chippewa for "crown of the valley." The **Pecos River** also gives us the name of one of our western mythological characters, Pecos Bill, who was created in 1923 in *Century* magazine by Edwin O'Reilly. Pecos Bill rode mountain lions, used a rattlesnake as a lasso, and died after eating a meal of nitro and barbed wire. When he landed on the ground after riding a cyclone bareback, he created Death Valley . . well, so the storytellers say . . .

Thailand   The first Thai nation was Sukothai, meaning "dawn of happiness," began in 1238. The Chakri dynasty changed the name to Siam in 1782, which was a concession to the Europeans who knew the land by this name, an ancient designation also. The interest in dealing with the West kept the Siamese from having to suffer a colonial takeover by the Europeans. We're most familiar with one of these early kings, Mongkut, known as Rama IV, who was the model for *The King and I*. He was a progressive ruler who brought in Western advisors to teach him their ways. Interestingly, the Thai fought most of their early wars for people, not for land. When Burma or Thailand won a battle in their numerous conflicts, the conquered people were rounded up and moved within the winning country's border. At one point, at each new king's reign, residents were numbered and tattooed in a kind of census. When Siam's name was changed to Thailand in 1939, it wasn't a nationalist move to return to some native name as was the case for many name changes. Land did play a role as Thailand rode the coattails of Japanese expansion. Its rulers saw the renaming as a way to grab more of the surrounding territory in Laos and Burma, including any Thai-speaking people into the new country. After World War II the name was briefly changed back, but in 1948, pre-war political leaders were restored, and Thailand was again made the name. The capital, Bangkok, is known to Thais as Krung Thep, "city of angels" being a loose translation.

Troy The ancient city made famous in classical literature by Homer was named after the son of Dardanous, who was the offspring of Zeus and Electra. This boy, Tros, had a son, Ilus, for whom the city was named Ilium or Ilios. After the city was burned by the Greeks, it was uninhabited for several hundred years. Troy, Alabama, was not named for the Trojans, but for a prominent lawyer; though Troy, New York, did fashion itself after the ancient metropolis of the *Illiad*. **Troy weight** doesn't have anything to do with how Trojans measured goods, but came from Troyes, France, which had its own very efficient weighing system in the 1300's.

Tunisia Tunisia was named for one of its cities, **Tunis**, which was an insignificant village in 814 B.C. when Carthage ruled North Africa. The town gained much more prominence with the Ottoman Turks of the 1300's. Arabs originally called the country Ifrique after the Roman name for the land, which we know as Africa. One theory about the naming of Tunis is that the coastal town had a reputation for gathering one of the prize catches of the Mediterranean, the tunny fish, which we more commonly know as the tunafish.

Turkey The history of this meeting place of the East and West is often neglected in our Social Studies classes, but this land could have been the central focus of our texts had a few events gone differently. Ancient Anatolia (as it was known) saw Troy as a major force until the greed of Paris, desiring the most beautiful woman in the world, Helen, created a war with Greece that ended in Trojan defeat. The land was later known as Phyrgia, and again, greed was part of its legacy as King Midas remains in legend as foolishly wishing that everything he grasped turn to gold – that "**midas touch**." The poor rich man didn't realize that he would almost starve to death since this touch meant he'd have golden grits for breakfast, golden greens for lunch, and golden gravy on his golden potatoes for supper. Next, the area was known as Lydia and its last king, Croesus, was noted for his wealth ("as rich as Croesus" is still a phrase of fable), but lost it all to Persia. His kingdom was said to have invented both coins and dice. Much later a chieftain named Seljuk led his tribe of Turks (meaning "people") across the land, eventually creating the Empire of Rum (their version of the Roman Empire). One of the Turkish states was ruled by Osman, a highly principled man who founded the Ottoman Empire, the most powerful force in the world from the 1300's to the

1500's. **Ottoman** is an Italian version of Osman's name. The capital of Turkey, **Istanbul**, has been through some name changes as well. From the early Greek town of Byzas which became Byzantium which became Constantinople, the place was finally named Istanbul by the conquering Turks of the 1400's, meaning, in a corruption of Greek, "downtown."

Traveling through the "T" territories takes us to places like **Tabasco** where the hot sauce we recognize in the name came from. Its Indian meaning is descriptive of parts of this Mexican state: "damp earth." **Tahiti** could have been called King George Island or New Cythera if original namers had had their way, but the native name, Tahiti, got recorded in a journal and, with a slight change, stuck as the name of this beautiful Polynesian place. Those who vacation at **Lake Tahoe** in California or Nevada may have much fun, but if they translate the Indian name of the place they would find "much water." Love and dedication were part of the building of the

Taj Mahal, named for the favorite wife of Shah Jahan and built between 1630 and 1650. This huge cemetery mausoleum was constructed to house the remains of this woman who bore the Shah fourteen children in eighteen years. "Chosen of the palace" was the nickname the Shah gave this lady, which he also attached to the building itself. **Tallahasee**, the capital of Florida, was also the capital of the Apalachee Indians and means "old town" in their language. **Tanzania** is actually a combination name given in 1964 for the union of Tanganyika and Zanzibar. The original Greek name for the area is Azania, fairly close to the present blend. The famous **Thames River** was known to the Romans as Tamesis and means "dark." **Ticonderoga**, made famous during the battles of the French and Indian War, got its name from the Iroquois, describing a "place between two waters (lakes)." As Magellan made his globe-circling journey in 1520, he named the island group at the southernmost end of South America **Tierra del Fuego**, meaning "land of fire" because the damp, chilly conditions of the place caused natives to keep constant fires burning, carrying their coals from beach blazes to their hearths. It may be a "long, long way to **Tipperary**" from here, but the Irish place was made famous in the above lyric when homesick soldiers sang the song in Europe during

World War I. In Irish the name translates as "house of the well of Ara," which was given to a faithful employee of the King of England who founded the Butler family there. **Togo** was known as the "Coast of Slaves" to sailors of the 1800's, but its name, in the Ewe language, means "behind the sea." The capital of Kansas, **Topeka**, could mean one of two things according to historians: "smoky hill" or "a good place to dig potatoes," two very different translations of the Indian name. The isle of **Tortuga** was the headquarters of buccaneers in the early 1600's and was named by the Spanish for a certain resident, the turtle. The religious Council of **Trent** took place off and on over about ten years in the mid-1500's, trying to "upgrade" the Catholic church to adjust to the protesting reformers like Martin Luther. The Italian town where all this took place was known to Romans a Tridentum, "three-toothed" in Latin. Now, the capital of New Jersey, **Trenton**, was named after a merchant who bought the land from Quakers in 1714. Here is where General Washington launched a surprise Christmas attack on Hessians stationed there in 1776. The town was later the capital of the United States in 1784 and, again, in 1799. Other Trentons can be found in Michigan, Canada, and Nova Scotia. The island of **Trinidad** was named by the Spanish for the "trinity" as were cities in Cuba and Bolivia, but the Trinidad in Colorado was named for an early settler. Both **Tripolis** on the Mediterranean were named for "three cities" in each location. In Lebanon, it was Tyre, Sidon, and Arvad (Aradus), ancient Phoenician city-states, that eventually united into today's city. The Tripoli in the Marines' song is in Libya, named for the three cities of Oea, Sabratha, and Leptis. **Tucson**, Arizona, seems to be a nice short name, but the Indian translation of the city's designation is "village of the dark spring at the foot of the mountains." Whew.

U **Ukraine** Once again free from outside domination, this country, whose name means "borderland" in Old Russian, was the center of Kievan Russia in the 800's. In the 1400's it was the hangout of Cossacks who were caught between Poles and Tartars. Later, Poland ruled until a Cossack uprising in 1648. Thousands of these independent folk were slaughtered by the Nazis during the 1940's. Today, the new Ukraine still exists in a perilous balance on an economic and social tightrope. **Kiev** took its name from three founding brothers in 430 A.D., Kii, Sctchek, and Khariv.

Uranus Our 7th planet was the first discovered with the aid of a telescope when Sir William Hershel noted it in 1781. In honor of that discovery, **uranium** was christened eight years later. The Greek mythological figure, Uranus, has been slightly discussed already (see **aphrodisiac**). When Gaea, the earth mother, produced him along with the Mountains and the Sea, all seemed good. But after she and Uranus became mates and produced a mass of offspring, including the Titans, jealousy and hatred entered the happy universe, ending with one of the Titans, Cronus, gelding his dad. This essentially "cut" Uranus off from the earth and, since Uranus means "sky" or "heavens" in Greek, caused the separation of earth and sky.

Utah We've mentioned some of the history of the 45th state already (see **Deseret**). When it was finally admitted to the Union, Congress decided to honor the Ute Indians. These Navajos actually used the name Utah, which means "upper" or "higher," for a Shoshone tribe. "Do you have to have more than one wife?" was the question the Mormons were finally forced to answer no to before the government would approve admission into our more monogamous society. **Ogden** might have been planned and founded by the Mormons under the direction of Brigham Young, but it was named for a fur trader, Peter Ogden.

Utopia Ironically, this name for an imaginary place of perfection comes from the Greek, meaning "no place." When Sir Thomas More created the perfect state in 1516 and coined the word, he was just following a tradition of mankind's constant search for the ideal, but with a tongue-in-cheek recognition that such flawlessness doesn't exist in this self-oriented world. From Plato to Marx, men have philosophized about what would be the consummate social system, but attempts at implementation have always led "no place."

Our excursion through "U" localities takes us to **Uganda**, which got its name from the Ganda tribe who were ruling the Buganda kingdom when European explorers found them in 1862. **Uruguay** got its official name in 1828 after thirty-three patriots (the Immortals) inspired its people to fight Brazilian control. The name comes from the local Indians and means "river of colored birds." **Utica**, New York, got its name when suggestions were drawn from a hat in 1798. The suggestion that won referred to a North African town that had been the Roman capital of their province of Africa. The Romans gave this city the honor after its people had fought with them against neighboring Carthage.

V

Valhalla This was a kind of heaven for the Norse, and its name means Hall of the Slain. Those brave warriors who fell in glorious battle were chosen by Odin's servants, the Valkyrie (choosers of the slain), to enter one of the 540 doors of this heavenly hall and there eat, drink, and fight (and always be healed each day) until Ragnarok, Doomsday. At that time they would take on giants at the side of Odin.

Venezuela If Columbus had had his way, this country's name today would be the "Land of Grace," Tierra de Gracia, based on his first impression of the place in 1498. Because of the coast's beauty and the innocent, naked natives, he thought he had found the site of the Garden of Eden. A year later, Amerigo Vespucci was along for the ride with Alonso de Ojeda, who named the land "little Venice" (in Spanish, Venezuela) because the natives' stilt-supported huts on Lake Maracaibo reminded him of the Italian city. In the 1530's, Germans were convinced that this was the location of the kingdom of El Dorado, the fabled golden realm, but they came away empty-handed. In the 1600's, Venezuela became the plaything of plundering pirates, and by the 1700's, importation of slaves had raised the population into the hundreds of thousands, though 60% were black. "The Liberator," Simon Bolivar was born here but was eventually disappointed in the results of his battles with Spain for the land's independence, not because he didn't win, but because his own people finally disagreed with his plans for their future.

Venice The romantic canal city of Venice had less than amorous beginnings. Even at the end of the Roman Empire, not much development had taken place among the 118 islands, lagoons, and marshy areas here. Simple fishing folk lived here. But when the barbarian invasions of northern Italy began, refugees from surrounding cities hid out in the area, using the swampy land as a shelter from the violent pagans of Atila the Hun, among others. Even after the raiders had departed, many of these immigrants stayed on, building a beautiful city on the islands that was eventually to become "the Queen of the Adriatic." In fact, Venice grew to be so powerful that her kingdom encompassed a huge area, and she ruled the seas. Crusaders used the watery town as a point to embark on their voyages to the Holy Land. By the 1500's, the Ottoman Empire crushed Venice's power, leaving them crouching in fear behind their **Venetian blinds**. The name of the city comes from a northern Italian tribe, the Veneti, whose name meant "beloved," from the same root from which we get Venus.

Vermont We often think of the Green Mountain State as one of the original colonies, but, in truth, it was number fourteen, having had to fight both New Hampshire and New York for its independent status . . . so independent, in fact, that the land remained a sovereign state after the Revolutionary War until 1791. Its nickname above is the translation of the state's name, given by French explorer, Samuel de Champlain who noted its verdant hills. Vermonters seem to shun the city life since they have the lowest urban population in the nation. The capital, **Montpelier**, also shows the French influence, named for a town in that country (whose name has one more "l").

Vietnam This place name still haunts the American psyche as a land that sucked us into one of the most disruptive events, internally and externally, since the Civil War. Foreign intervention has been part of this country's past since the 600's A.D. when China conquered it and named it Annam or "pacified South." At one time the nation was called Nam Viet, a local translation of another conqueror's term for "the people south of the Yangtze River." In 1802 the name was turned around to its present Vietnam and later became part of French Indochina. Throughout the state's constant turmoil, there remained an ethnic core of a people who managed to eventually stave off and become victorious over Chinese, French, Japanese, and American attempts to shape their destiny.

Virginia Though named for a woman reputed for her virginity, Queen Elizabeth I of England, the "Virgin Queen," this state has several nicknames related to motherhood: "the Mother of States" (eight were created from its land) and the Mother of Presidents (eight of these leaders were born here). In 1584, when Elizabeth was fifty-one, it was Sir Walter Raleigh who suggested honoring his favorite gal, twenty-one years older than he at the time. Virginia earned the nickname "Old Dominion" in the 1650's when the Puritan Cromwells ruled England while the monarchy was tossed out. The nickname was given because the state remained loyal to the crown during this decade of disruption, sheltering nobles form the harsh punishment of the Lord Protector, Oliver Cromwell. The 10th state had a dual personality for many years, with plantations and aristocracy in the agricultural east and loggers and miners in the rugged west, and this schizophrenia led to the birth of a final state from its loins in the 1860's (see **West Virginia**). A favorite tourist spot, **Williamsburg**, was originally named Middle Plantation until 1699 when it was renamed in deference to William III of England.

Voyaging through "V" vicinities, we travel to **Valladolid** in Spain whose name touts the Arab influence in the land and means "city of the governor" in the Muslim conquerors' tongue. **Valetta**, the capital of the island of Malta between Sicily and Tunisia in the Mediterranean may not be familiar to you, but it has an interesting history. It was named for Jean Parisot de la Valette who was the grand master of the Hospitallers. This was a group of knights who formed a religious order dedicated to caring for pilgrims on their travels to holy shrines. They took vows and were basically monks who learned both skills of healing and warfare. Contradictory? Soon after the order was founded it was realized that part of the care and protection of pilgrims might involve fighting off pagan harassers. The Church actually encouraged their efforts in the first centuries of their existence, considering them "soldiers of Christ," and allowing huge donations of wealth and land to go into their coffers for their efforts. Their defensive battles against the Ottoman Turks in the 1500's probably saved Europe from invasion and conquest. They were given Malta in 1530. Still seen today, the Maltese Cross was their symbol. Their hospitals were the finest in all Europe, usually part of inns attached to their monasteries (more like castles) where pilgrims and weary Crusaders could be cared for. Their name, which we now associate with our medical institutions, came from the Latin for "guest" or "stranger" and gives us **host** and **hospitality**. They committed themselves, quite nobly in most cases, to the health of those less fortunate, which eventually led to the creation of public hospitals. **Valparaiso**, Chile, has the Spanish meaning of "vale of paradise" and got its name in 1536 from a conquistador who honored his birthplace across the Atlantic with its christening. Captain George **Vancouver** explored the northwest in 1792 and had cities in Washington and Canada and an island named after him. **Veracruz** was named by Cortes in 1519 as la Villa Rica de la Veracruz, "the Rich Town of the True Cross," though the site was almost abandoned when the conquistadors discovered that the intense rainfall and humidity made the Mexican state unhealthy – rich in mosquitoes and mold. **Verdun** lingers in our history as the French town where one of the bloodiest battles of World War I was waged over a six month period in 1916, leaving over 600,000 casualties, but victory for the Allies whose battle cry against the Germans was "they shall not pass," a "remember the Alamo" of that first worldwide conflict. The town played another important role in history over a thousand years earlier as the site of the Treaty of Verdun which divided the huge empire of Charlemagne among his three feuding sons in 843. The Romans knew it as Verodunum, which was their version of the Celtic, meaning "great fortress." Speaking of wars, World War II saw **Vichy**, France, become the capital of the Nazi-occupied country. The resort town's name became associated with collaboration with the enemy to the free French, though the Romans had a more healthy idea in mind when they named it Vicus Calidus, "warm life-giving waters," because of its prized hot springs and pure waters. When Reverend Vick founded a mission in Mississippi in 1814, he never knew that the town that grew up there, **Vicksburg**, would be the location for a turning point in the Civil War where Grant's siege cut the eastern Confederacy from the West and pushed the Union ever closer to victory. **Queen Victoria** was another monarch who received recognition when travelers named an Australian state, a Canadian city, a metropolis in Hong Kong, a lake and waterfall in Africa, an island in Canada, and an area in the Anarctic after her. To the Romans **Vienna** was known as Vindobona, but its name probably comes from a Hungarian term, Wenia, meaning "victory." The **Virgin Islands** were named by Columbus. When he saw their beautiful, untouched shores in 1493, he was reminded of St. Ursula (see) and her dedicated – and later slaughtered – 11,000 virgin maiden followers. The major Russian naval port of **Vladivostok** on the coast of the Sea of Japan started as a small military outpost, but its importance grew until by 1860 its Russian name became very meaningful: "rule the East."

W **Washington** Hardy, hard-working pioneers founded the Evergreen State, which was first part of what was called Oregon Country, but a sense of humor is part of the laid-back state motto, Alki, an Indian expression meaning "by and by." In 1889, the state named after the first president became number 42 to join the Union. **Walla Walla** also sounds humorous, but this Indian name means "many waters." The state capital, **Olympia**, was named for the nearby Olympic mountains, dubbed as a reminder of the Greek peak. The state's name is one of many that honor George Washington, including cities in Georgia, North Carolina, Pennsylvania, and Texas. Washington D.C. is one of the few national capitals planned to be totally independent of regional influences. It was Thomas Jefferson and Treasury Secretary Alexander Hamilton who convinced rival legislators in the North and South to locate the capital on the federally controlled land where it today exits. Our man on the dollar bill chose the site himself since he grew up there. There is one more location named Washington – in England. George's family had an area named for them before their colonist son gained fame.

West Virginia   As mentioned when talking about Virginia, the people of this our 35th state had always felt separate from the flatlanders to the east. Not only was the geography of what was to become the Mountain State different, but so was the general attitude of its people – concerning slavery (against it), big business (unable to get it because of politics), and heritage (German vs. English). Even in 1776 there were pleas for self-government. The Civil War finally split Virginia, with the western counties adamantly loyal to the Union. They wanted to call their new state Kanawha, Indian for "place of the white stone," referring to salt deposits, but compromise led to the present name in 1863.

Wisconsin   There is some disagreement as to the origin of the name of America's Dairyland. Most believe that the French translation of the Indian, Ouisconsin, means "gathering of the waters," but some argue that the 30th state's name could mean "wild rice country" or "home land." It was first part of the Indiana Territory, then the Illinois Territory, and then the Michigan Territory until Congress finally gave it independent status in 1848. Admittedly, the place has its share of **badgers**, but the nickname, The Badger State, didn't refer to the burrowing beast, named for the badge-like white mark on its forehead; nor did it refer to any harassing, pestering quality of the residents. That slang term for aggressive bothering, badgering, came from the animal's persistent pursuit of its prey into the victim's own home. Some of the first settlers were lead miners, and instead of spending valuable digging time building homes for the cold winter, many of these prospectors merely dug dwellings into the hillsides and got the nickname "badgers" from their burrows. **Milwaukee** is also of Indian origin and means "gathering place by the waters" . . . maybe to brew a little beer?

Wyoming   How did this state in the West get a name from an Indian tribe that lived around the mid-Atlantic coast? The meaning of the name does fit: "great prairie place" or "on the great plain." An Ohio Congressman suggested the name, comparing the flat land to the Wyoming Valley in Pennsylvania made famous by an Indian massacre that took place there. Women played an important role in the history of the Equality State, so named because Wyoming was first to grant women voting rights. Well, females were scarce in this sparsely populated land that was mainly a place where westward traveling pioneers loaded up on supplies as they passed through on the California, Oregon, or Overland trails. In 1870, the nation had its first woman justice of the peace in Wyoming. She was probably needed because the men of the region were in constant warfare over cattle and sheep. The 44th state had the first woman governor in 1924, perhaps influenced by male corruption again as it was revealed that the Secretary of State had secretly leased the huge naval oil reserves under Teapot Dome to another entrepreneur. And, of course, women were able to vote for her. **Laramie** was named for Jaques Laramie who built a cabin on the river, also named for him, in 1820. By 1868, a railroad camp and fort bore his name. **Cheyenne** had such a wild reputation that it was known as Hell on Wheels at one time in the 1860's because of unsavory folk who followed the railroad construction crews that camped in the area. The present name is derived from an uncomplimentary description one tribe gave white men of another, "people who speak unintelligibly," as if we had named the French the "nonsense speakers."

Walking through other "W" domains, we come to the **Wabash River**, made famous for country music fans in the railroad song, "The Wabash Cannonball." The Miami Indian name for the river, later also taken by an Indiana town, means "water over the white stones." **Wake Island** was once known as Halcyon and Helsion, but was later named for British sailor William Wake. **Wales** has always been independent-natured, though it has been part of England since 1282 after resisting Romans, Angles, and Saxons. Even then the king, Edward I, established the tradition of naming the monarch's son as Prince of Wales to honor the feisty Welsh. The name Wales itself reflected the rest of England's feeling for these isolated folk and came from a root meaning "foreigner." The Welsh themselves call their land Cymru, meaning "fellow countrymen." **Wall Street** is today almost the icon for financial dealings, but it got its name from a dirt wall the desperate Dutch erected in 1653 to try and keep out encroaching British. When you've "met your **Waterloo**," it's a sign of final defeat, as it was for Napoleon in 1815 as he was crushed by Allied forces near the village of this name close to Brussels. Mr. Bonaparte lost 40,000 men on that day in June for several reasons. First, the years campaigning hadn't been kind to his health (one word: hemorrhoids) and this affected his concentration. Second, he waited too long to start the battle, wanting the rains of the night before to have a chance to dry from the soggy soil. Waterloo means something like "place of the watery meadow." The Duke of Wellington and his Prussian comrades did lose about 23,000 men, but in the battle of numbers they won a decisive victory. Waterloos exist in Canada and Iowa, also. Speaking of **Wellington**, the duke, who died at 83, helped

New Zealand settlers in 1840 and was honored with the naming of a city there that went on to become the capital of the country. **Wiesbaden**, in Germany, was famous for its mineral springs even in Roman times and got its name for them: "baths on the meadows." **Wilmington**, Delaware, went through a lot of transitions, founded by Swedes who called it Christina (after their queen), then taken over by Dutch, who were supplanted by British who named the place in 1739 after the Earl of Wilmington. **Windsor**, England, was a famous residence of kings since William the Conqueror built a castle there in the 1070's. It's name wasn't officially Windsor until George V changed the royal family name in 1917. The British monarchs were allied with the powerful German line, Wettin, through Victoria's hubby, Prince Albert, but sentiment against the aggressive Germans during World War I made George come up with a more English sounding name. The Canadian Windsor was first called the Ferry because of its importance as a ferrying point from Detroit. Later, the name was changed to Richmond, and then in a compromise among name-feuding residents, the place was named Windsor, which is near Richmond, England. Windsors can also be found in Australia, Nova Scotia, Connecticut, and Vermont. **Winnepeg**, Canada, doesn't have a very attractive translation from the Cree Indian: "muddy water." We're probably most familiar with the sauce that originated in **Worcester**, England, sometimes called Worcestershire. Roman influence was probably involved in its naming, which could mean "camp of men" or "guarded camp." The Massachusetts town changed its name from Quinsigamond to Worcester in 1684 as a slap in the face to Charles II who had revoked the Massachusetts Bay Colony's charter at that time. You see, Charles had lost an important battle against Puritan Oliver Cromwell in that English city which had kept him from being restored to the throne earlier. There's also a Worcester in South Africa. **Wittenberg** was made famous in the early 1500's as the Reformation of the Catholic Church got underway. It was here that Martin Luther protested the greedy and corrupt traditions of the Church by nailing a paper on a church door containing 95 major problems with then present practices. The town was named for the Wettin family mentioned above (see **Windsor**). Several years later in **Worms**, a Church gathering proclaimed Luther an outlaw and heretic, and the protesters gained strengthened resolve that they must break from the uncompromising Church. The meeting was called the Diet of Worms and led to the Catholic powers having to eat a bit of humble pie (not worms: "diet" means "gathering") later and try to draw the reformers back (see **Trent**). Worms was a corruption of the name of an early

Germanic tribe, the Vangiones. That strong fiber, **worsted wool**, takes its name from **Worstead**, England, where the yarn was first spun. "Guarded place" is its name's translation from the Old English.

X There aren't many "X" places to explore. **Xenia**, Ohio, gets its name from the Greek word for hospitality. The longest river in China is known as **Xi Jiang** or "west river." Another river, the **Xingu**, is a tributary of the Amazon and still has parts that have been unexplored.

Y **Yangtze River** The Yangtze River of China is sometimes nicknamed "China's fortune" because of its life-giving fertility, as opposed to the Yellow River, sometimes called "China's sorrow" for its propensity to flood. The Chinese know the Yangtze as Chang Jiang or "long river." The kingdom of Yang, existing about 3000 years ago, is credited with being the source for the river's other name.

Yemen   Yemen was once part of what the Romans called Felix Arabia, "happy Arabia," and the country's present name can be translated as "happiness" or "the right hand" (which brings good) from the Arabic. Its major port city, **Aden**, was known as Eden in Biblical times but wasn't the paradise of Genesis (though the meaning of the name is the same). It was the home of kings of a land known for its gold, Ophir. Today, it is black gold that has brought Yemen riches.

Yugoslavia   The disruption in Yugoslavia has been part and parcel of its history, only seething underground during the over thirty years of rule by Tito after World War II. Even back in the 1840's, the ethnic melting pot was stirring itself when a nationalist movement made up of young Serbs, Croats, Slovenes, and Bosnians boiled over. These idealists wanted a united land where cultural differences would be honored while political solidarity would be the rule. This movement rose and fell throughout the 1800's, culminating when Bosnian youth armed in Serbia shot the Archduke Ferdinand, who would have ascended to the Austrian throne, the country that wanted to absorb a major hunk of what was to become Yugoslavia. This act precipitated World War I. The name Yugoslavia was officially given in 1929 by King Alexander in an attempt to give an identity to the disorganized state. No luck. After he was assassinated, his son tried to keep that identity intact, though he gave Croatia autonomy. World War II and the post-war Communist "empire" put a cap on the inner turmoil of the place, but when the cap was removed with the fall of the Iron Curtain, the civil feuding exploded again with the tragic results we now see. Yugoslavia means "land of the southern Slavs." The warm sirocco winds of the Sahara blow in from the south, giving the country an almost Florida-like feel for several months. The people there call the winds the "yugo" (southern). Watch out for cars called by this name.

Visiting "Y" areas takes us to **Yakima**, Washington, named for the Yakima Indians in 1861. Their tribal designation means "runaway." When Adriaen van der Donck built a mill in the New York area around 1648, the place came to be known by his Dutch title, "jonkheer," "lord" in English. The name of the place derived from this: **Yonkers**. Evidence of how lack of spelling rules and the slurring of former names causes all kinds of changes exists in **York**, England, whose name came from the Roman 6th Legion's ancient headquarters there, Eboracum. Yorks can be found in Maine, Nebraska, and Pennsylvania. **Yosemite** took its name from a Miwok Indian word for "grizzly bear," which was applied to the Uzumati Indian tribe. **Youngstown**, Ohio, was founded by John Young in 1797. The **Yukon** in northwestern North America still reverberates from the gold rush days of the 1890's when over 30,000 people scrambled into the desolate land. Its Indian name means "great river." **Yunnan**, in China, was an almost mythical place in ancient times where a strange people were said to exist "beyond the clouds" (the name's meaning) in misty areas near Tibet, perhaps the basis of Hilton's Shangri La. China finally conquered the area, but it still remains rather non-Chinese.

Z "Z" zones take us to **Zaire**, which for years was the Belgian Congo. The 1971 renaming came from a 15th century Portugese version of the native word for "river." The influence of multi-millionaire, Cecil Rhodes, lingers in southern Africa. In the 1890's he was a powerful figure in finance and politics in the area, controlling the diamond industry and manipulating local governments. Northern Rhodesia broke away from the white man's name by calling itself **Zambia** after the Zambezi River. Cecil's legacy can still be seen in the **Rhodes Scholarship**, funded by his millions after his death. **Zamboanga**, in the Philippines, got its name in 1635 from a Malay word meaning "place of many flowers." **Zanzibar** was called by the Arabs "Zanjubar," "land of the blacks." Another country named for Cecil Rhodes was Rhodesia, but it gave itself a new name in

1980, **Zimbabwe**, from an almost legendary state that existed there in the 11th century. Huge stone ruins testify to its existence and the craft of its people, but little is known about them. Zimbabwe seems to mean "houses of stone," though this is uncertain. **Zion**, a hill in Jerusalem, came to represent the fortunes of Israel when David made it the center of his kingdom and referred to the people of Israel as part of Zion, a "heavenly city of God." Today, Zionism has reached a pinnacle that began in 70 A.D. with the destruction of Jerusalem by the Romans. When Mormons discovered a beautiful canyon in 1861, they named it Zion. Congress wanted to use an Indian name for it, Mukuntuweap, but the ungainly word didn't stick, and Zion National Park in Utah is today's result. Germanic tribesmen changed a Roman name for a mountainous village from Turicum to **Zürich** to suit their own language and heritage. The name came from a Celtic root for "water."

Bibliography

Academic American Encyclopedia. 1992 ed.

American Heritage Dictionary of the English Language, The. Ed. William Morris. Boston: Houghton Mifflin Company, 1973.

American Heritage Illustrated Dictionary. Boston: Houghton Mifflin Company, 1987

Barnhart Dictionary of Etymology, The. Ed. Robert K. Barnhart. The H. W. Wilson Company, 1988.

Bible, The. (King James Version)

Bulfinch, Thomas. Bulfinch's Mythology. Garden City, New York: Doubleday and Company, Inc., 1968.

Colliers Encyclopedia. 1993 ed.

Concise Columbia Encyclopedia, The. Eds. Judith S. Levey, and Agnes Greenhall. New York: Avon Books, 1983.

Encyclopedia Americana. 1989 ed.

Feinsilver, Lillian Mermin. The Taste of Yiddish. South Brunswick, New York: Thomas Yoseloff, 1970.

Hamilton, Edith. Mythology. Boston: Little, Brown and Company, 1942.

Holt, Alfred H. Phrase and Word Origins. New York: Dover Publications, Inc., 1961.

Limburg, Peter R. Stories Behind Words. H.W. Wilson Co., 1986.

Martin, William C. The Layman's Bible Encyclopedia. Nashville: The Southwestern Company, 1964.

—. These Were God's People. Nashville: The Southwestern Company, 1966.

Morris, William and Mary. Morris Dictionary of Word and Phrase Origins. New York: Harper and Row, 1977.

Nave, Orville J. Nave's Topical Bible. Nashville: The Southwestern Company, 1962.

New Encyclopedia Brittanica. 1990 ed.

New York Public Library Desk Reference, The. New York: Stonesong Press, Inc., 1989.

Oxford Companion to the English Language, The. Ed. Tom McArthur. New York: Oxford University Press, 1992.

Oxford Dictionary of English Etymology, The. Ed. C.T. Onions. Oxford: Clarendon Press, 1966.

Oxford English Dictionary, The. 1970 ed.

Partridge, Eric. Origins. New York: Greenwich House, 1983.

Shipley, Joseph T. Origins of English Words. Baltimore: The Johns Hopkins University Press, 1984.

Random House Dictionary of the English Language. Ed. Stuart Berg Flexner. New York: Random House, 1987.

Webber, Elizabeth, and Mike Feinsilbur. Grand Allusions. Washington: Farragut Publications, 1990.

Webster's Word Histories. Springfield, Massachusetts: Merriam-Webster, Inc., 1989.

World Book Dictionary. Eds. Clarence and Robert K. Barnhart. Chicago: World Book, Inc., 1982.

World Book Encyclopedia. 1991 ed.

Wycliffe Bible Commentary. Eds. Charles F. Pfeiffer, and Everett F. Harrison. Nashville: The Southwestern Company, 1968.

Index

Parentheses indicate a related group of words.

INDEX